SH★INE

A Powerful 4-Step Plan for Becoming a Star in Anything You Do

Larry A. Thompson

McGraw-Hill

New York / Chicago / San Francisco
Lisbon / London / Madrid / Mexico City / Milan
New Delhi / San Juan / Seoul / Singapore / Sydney / Toronto

The **McGraw·Hill** Companies

1 2 3 4 5 6 7 8 9 0   DOC/DOC   0 9 8 7 6 5 4

ISBN 0-07-142682-5

Credits
All photographs, including the cover shot taken by Victoria Brynner, are provided courtesy of Larry A. Thompson Organization, Inc., except for the following:

Page 47:   Larry A. Thompson with Muhammad Ali.
            With permission of the photographer, Howard L. Bingham
Page 107: Larry A. Thompson with Drew Barrymore.
            With permission of the photographer, Peter Borsari
Page 209: Larry A. Thompson, Starmaker.
            With permission of the photographer, Mary Ann Halpin, and
            the mural artist, Thomas Suriya.

Credits for song lyrics and other quoted material are contained in the "Notes" on pages 233–234.

McGraw-Hill books are available at special discounts to use as premiums and sales promotions, or for use in corporate training programs. For more information, please write to the Director of Special Sales, Professional Publishing, McGraw-Hill, Two Penn Plaza, New York, NY 10121-2298. Or contact your local bookstore.

This book is printed on recycled, acid-free paper containing a minimum of 50% recycled de-inked paper.

Library of Congress Cataloging-in-Publication Data
Thompson, Larry A., 1944-
   Shine : a powerful 4-step plan for becoming a star in anything you do /
Larry A. Thompson.— 1st ed.
      p. cm.
   Includes index.
   ISBN 0-07-142682-5 (hardcover : alk. paper)
   1. Success—Psychological aspects. 2. Celebrities—Psychology. I. Title.
BF637.S8T48 2004
   158.1—dc22   2004009440

DEDICATION

To my Team of Believers:

My best friend, Fred: May you know my appreciation.
My brother, Marshall: May you know my respect.
My sister, Janice: May you know my admiration.
My daughter, Taylor: May you find your destiny.
My wife, Kelly: May I rest your heart.
My parents, Ann and Angelo: May God rest their souls.

Thanks to the Stars

William Shatner, Cindy Crawford, Drew Barrymore, Sonny Bono, Cher, Jane Seymour, Donna Mills, Charlton Heston, James Brolin, Jim Nabors, Barry White, Don Johnson, Frances Fisher, John Larroquette, Kathleen Turner, Linda Evans, Cheryl Ladd, Iman, Lindsay Wagner, Steve Guttenberg, Mike Douglas, Sally Kellerman, Anthony Perkins, David Foster, Bruce Boxleitner, Jack Scalia, Gloria Loring, Alan Thicke, Michelle Phillips, Donna Dixon, Carroll O'Connor, Steve Garvey, Patti Davis, Tony LoBianco, Ernest Borgnine, Linda Blair, Pamela Bellwood, Charlene Tilton, Kay Starr, Catherine Hicks, Maurice Benard, Jeff Conaway, Melissa Sue Anderson, Tori Spelling, Shannen Doherty, Jamie Farr, Cicely Tyson, Anthony Andrews, Olivia DeHavilland, Julie Harris, Tatum O'Neal, Marisa Berenson, Merle Haggard, Robert Blake, Paul Williams, Jay Underwood, Renee Faia, Mary McDonnell, Tippi Hedren, William Russ, Eric von Detten, Tracey Gold, Perry King, Shawnee Smith, Sharon Gless, Steve Railsback, Polly Draper, Ted Levine, Robert Desiderio, Ann Jillian, Tim Matheson, McLean Stevenson, Richard Moll, Ray Walston, Marc Price, Shelley Fabares, Billy Warlock, Michael DeLuise, Brooke Theiss, Max Gail, Stacy Keach, Don Stroud, Kevin Dobson, Cindy Pickett, Annie Potts, Chuck D, Tommy Davidson, Gary Busey, Adam Carolla, Eric Roberts, Victoria Jackson, Kevin Dillon, Howard Sherman, Jeff Allin, Joan Severance, Scott Valentine, Michelle Little, James Remar, Nick Cassavetes, Jason Bateman, C. Thomas Howell, Deborah Shelton, Jonathan Silverman, David Charvet, Carol Mansell, Warren Wiebe, Livia Squires, Maud

Adams, William Devane, Adrienne Barbeau, Gene Barry, Martha Quinn, Robin Givens, Cathy Lee Crosby, Bobbie Gentry, Shelley Hack, Justine Bateman, Gil Gerard, Tracy Scoggins, Delta Burke, Danielle Brisebois, James Van Patten, Sandy Duncan, Barbi Benton, Jake Steinfeld, Tovah Feldshah, Melanie Chartoff, Emma Samms, Cindy Harrell, Lonnie Shorr, Barbara Parkins, Susan Blakely, Janet Jones, Peter Dobson, Pamela Gidley, Mariska Hargitay, Jeff Altman, Moon Zappa, Ian Buchanan, Edward Albert, Catherine Oxenberg, Jennifer O'Neill, Sybil Danning, Bo Svenson, Joe Cortese, David Birney, Penny Peyser, Debra Sue Maffett, Caryn Richman, Greg Webb, Elya Baskin, Terrence McNally, Lydia Cornell, Ron Perlman, Denise Alexander, Starr Andreeff, Anne Archer, Bill Atherton, Blake Bahner, Karen Baldwin, Jim Barden, Daniel Bardol, Dirk Benedict, Morgan Brittany, Johnny Brown, Rebeccah Bush, Dean Butler, Cathy Carlson, Karen Carlson, Elpidia Carrillo, Andrew Clarke, William Coronel, Cylk Cozart, David Mason Daniels, Reginald T. Dorsey, Sara Douglas, Morgan Fairchild, Sally Flynn, Constance Forslund, Laurie Frank, Robin Ganter, Timothy Gibbs, Karen Grassle, Lynne Griffin, Jim Hager, Jon Hager, Deirdre Hall, Melora Hardin, Clay Hart, Mary Hart, Sam Hennings, Kathryn Holcomb, Brent Huff, Wendy Hughes, Waylon Jennings, Paul Land, Vicki Lawrence, Elissa Leeds, Eb Lottimer, Linda Lovelace, Laurence Luckinbill, Lysette Anthony, Meredith MacRae, Jared Martin, Gina Mastrogiacomo, Cathy McAuley, Everett McGill, Scott McGinnis, Justin Melvey, Jim Metzler, Barry Miller, Karen Mistal, Harry Nilsson, Holly Palance, Richard Pryor, Helen Reddy, Evan Richards, Kyle Richards, Larry Riley, Lisa Rinna, David Rogge, Craig Sheffer, Kimber Sissons, Michael Sottile, Andrew Stevens, Michele Tobin, Terri Treas, Kate Vernon, Heidi Von Palleske, Aarika Wells, Larry Wilcox, Jeff Wincott, Hayley DuMond, Tracy Griffith, Peter Jason, Mark Kiely, Nan Martin, John Enos, David Kimball, Loren Menkin, Bob Jay Mills, Orly Kate Sitowitz, Eddie Daniels, Darlene Mann, Mark Brown, DeeDee Michaels, Eugene Williams, Jim Pirri, Laura Johnson, Christian Leffler, Bruce Nozick, Walter Franks, Marie Wilson, Tom Frykman, Carl Gilliard, Matthew Chaffee, Thomas Tofel, Christine Brent, Maurice Chasse, Perris Knight, Phill Miller, Vinny Argiro, Mahryah Shain, Susan Ilene Johnson, Duke Moosekian, Larry Milburn, Tim Robbins, Sheree J. Wilson, Stephen Geoffreys, Cindy Morgan, Clyde Kusatsu, Tanya Roberts, Millie Perkins, Max Gail, Robin Pearson Rose, John Wheeler, Lou Liberatore, Louis Guss, Veronica Cartwright, David Wohl, Kathleen Wilhoite, Ted Levine, Roger Rose, Tristan Rogers, Sarah Purcell, Melody Anderson, Heather Langenkamp, Candy Clark, Randy Edelman, Jayne Kennedy, Dobie Gray, Victor French, Bud Cort, Stephen Macht, Maren Jensen, Tim Stack, Tanya Tucker, Catherine Bach, Susie Coelho, Carol Connors, Geoff Edwards, Rick James, Leon Isaac Kennedy, Ann Turkel, Ronnie Schell, Sandahl Bergman, Jaime Lyn Bauer, David Groh, Shelly Smith, Ronee Blakley, Penelope Milford, Pamela Hensley, Persis Khambatta, Peter Barton,

Robin Riker, Belinda Montgomery, Adam Baldwin, DeDee Pfeiffer, Lois Chiles, Burt Reynolds, Charo, John Ritter, Bonnie Franklin, Chuck Woolery, Ted Knight, Don Maclean, Redd Foxx, Vikki Carr, Todd English, Jean François Meteigner, Alessandro Stratta, Roy Yamaguchi, Marcus Samuelsson, Kerry Simon, Michael Burger, Sissy Biggers, Anthony Dias Blue, Steven Schirripa, Bruce Vilanch, Elise Neal, Brande Roderick, Mark Famiglietti, Loretta Devine, Coolio, Tony Danza, Michael York, Orlando Jones, Christopher Titus, Kelly Rowland, Paul Sorvino, Mindy Sterling, Chris McDonald, Gene Simmons, Nolan North, Jason Gedrick, Marla Sokoloff, Lisa Edelstein, Sarah Carter, Stefanie von Pfetten, Shane Meier, James Farentino, Alex Mendoza, Blues Traveler, Ron Popeil, Kelly Hu, Carol Burnett, and . . . many more.

Thanks to all the Stars we have represented or who have Starred in our movies for helping to make the Larry A. Thompson Organization a success. And for their enormous contributions to *Shine*, a special thanks to my "Star Agent," Jan Miller; my editors, Nancy Hancock and Judith McCarthy; and my ever-vigilant assistant, Robert G. Endara II.

CONTENTS

PREFACE

Congratulations! The fact that you have picked up this book and started to read it tells me that you want to be more fulfilled in your life—that you want to become a Star. It also tells me that you have taken the first and hardest step to Stardom. You have taken positive action.

You are now standing on the doorsteps of your destiny. You are on your own "Star Search." Feel great about it. Wonderful things are in store for you. Before you continue, you should be warned that the first thing you must learn in order to become a Star is how to be selfish. That's right, selfish!

I don't mean that you should become another Dr. Evil, the *Austin Powers* nemesis. I mean that you must simply stop and think about yourself. If your kids are bothering you to take them to a movie, or your spouse needs a back-rub, or your mother wants you to come for dinner tonight (and not tomorrow night), you must pause, breathe deeply, and say, "No! I have to make the time to read *SHINE: A Powerful 4-Step Plan for Becoming a Star at Anything You Do* to prepare myself for the future I deserve."

Remember, you never *find* time—you *make* time.

If you're so busy attending to the needs of other people that you can't make the time to read this book, I suggest you wait for my next book, *REALLY SHINE: A Powerful 4-Step Plan for Becoming a Saint at Anything You Do.* If, however, you can give me a few hours of your time, I will give you the knowledge to help you fulfill your dreams, and to rise and shine to meet your true destiny.

Let's get started.

The Road to Stardom

The road to Stardom begins at the intersection of Humility and Egomania. It ends at the corner of Hollywood and Vine.

My journey, like most, started in a place that was a far cry from the bright lights of the Hollywood life. It was in the heart of the Mississippi Delta, at the crossroads of Highways 61 and 49 where Robert Johnson sold his soul to the devil to learn to play the guitar.

The "blues wuz born" in Clarksdale, Mississippi, according to legend.

And so was I.

Gaining confidence at the Pyramids.

A Graveyard with Streetlights

When I was a boy, it didn't seem possible that I could grow up to become a lawyer, manage the careers of over 200 celebrities, produce movies and TV shows, write books, lecture, and have a beautiful family in Beverly Hills, California. But I've discovered that anything is possible, even for those born into unlikely circumstances such as mine.

My hometown was rich in culture but otherwise poor. I thought it was a pretty cool place to grow up because of its soulfulness as the birthplace of the blues, but my mother was not so impressed.

"Larry, when you get educated, you've got to get out of this town 'cause there's nothing here for you," she'd say. "This town is nothing but a graveyard with streetlights."

My mother, Annie Thompson, was the first to give me a motivational kick in the butt. I was in my early teens. She felt I needed to start thinking about making something of myself.

"I want you to be somebody ... somebody important.... I don't want you to work all day in that grocery store like your daddy," she said. "See these Movie Stars here in *Photoplay* magazine? Now, they're important. They have respect. I want you to go to Hollywood and be important like them."

Then she told me something that stayed in my mind and kept me motivated for many years to come. She said, "Larry, I've got so much faith in you that I went on up to Memphis and bought a new dress and put it in a box under the bed. I'm saving that dress to wear when you invite me out to Hollywood to meet the Stars and to take me to the Academy Awards—on the night you win one."

I guess that's when I got the appetite to eat Hollywood for lunch. It was like having a chicken bone stuck in my throat, impossible to ignore. Each day thereafter I worked hard at trying to be important and make something special happen so that my mother would get the chance to wear that lonely dress waiting under the bed.

I became driven to build the dream life my mother and I wanted for me. I developed the focus and the ambition and the high-level energy required to get there. But in my rush to get out of town, I forgot to pack a few essential things.

I'd failed to understand, as so many people do, that it's not what you do that counts; it's who you *are*. In Hollywood and New York

City and most other places where power and money are the driving forces, you can easily lose sight of that. In places like Clarksdale, Mississippi, folks tend to look into the core of both an individual and a situation. My mother had that one covered too: "You shouldn't judge a man simply by the height he attains, but also by the width and depth."

The Day My Mother Wore the Dress

Years later, I became "important" enough for the governor to proclaim it Larry Thompson Week in the state of Mississippi and the mayor of Clarksdale to proclaim it Larry Thompson Day in Clarksdale. A large banquet was held to raise money for the Larry Thompson Center for Fine Arts. That evening I brought the Stars back home to my mother. You will meet many of them in this book. With all of the "important" people in attendance, I introduced the two "most important" people I had ever met—my parents, Annie and Angelo Thompson.

It's great to have all of the benefits of a successful career, but you also have to work at being a success as a human being. I can help you in that area too. I learned it the hard way, and hopefully this book will help you learn it in a much easier way.

The Day I Lost My Mind

"Put your hands up in the air, mother*&%#er, or I'll blow your brains out!" It was Quentin Tarantino's cult classic *Pulp Fiction* come to life—my life. Or what I feared was left of it.

Two young thugs screamed at me while waving the barrel of a sawed-off shotgun in my face. It was 7:30 p.m. on November 3, 1983. I was getting out of my car in Beverly Hills when they jumped me.

"Give us your wallet, your cash, your watch and your car keys . . . don't mess with us . . . we'll kill your ass."

Putting my hands up in the air, I thought: "Having my head blown off might be the best way to solve all my problems right now!"

I stood in the middle of the street, reaching for my wallet, tearing at my Rolex, fumbling for the keys to my car, and wondering, "How could this be happening to me? How in the hell did I get to this place in my life?"

My spanked mind started to download a series of events leading up to this fateful holdup. I flashbacked to a few months earlier: *New York. August 27, 1983.* I had just left a meeting with Elizabeth Taylor, Cicely Tyson, and Peter Gallagher. Cicely, my client, and Peter were performing in a play called *The Corn Is Green.* Elizabeth Taylor was the producing partner. There had been a few problems with it, so I had flown to New York to meet with them. It went well, but I had to leave them to rendezvous with another client and close friend, the beautiful actress Donna Mills, who at the time was the queen of prime time television, starring in the CBS hit series *Knots Landing.* We had plans to see the Broadway musical *Cats.* On the way there, my mind was racing down a very unhappy stretch of road.

I was miserable. I was in an unhappy marriage. I was partnered in a successful talent management business with someone who was driving me crazy. I was about to finalize a high-risk deal to buy a motion picture studio, New World Pictures. But the most ironic thing was that here in my life was everything I thought I wanted: a Hollywood studio, a marriage to a beautiful woman, big Stars as clients, wealth, power, fame—all the things I thought would make me happy. However, I realized I had built a house of cards.

I couldn't keep the house standing any longer. I wanted out—out of everything: My marriage. My business partnership. My studio deal. And at that point, I didn't have a clue, or the guts, to walk away from any of it.

I met Donna Mills and we walked arm-in-arm into the theater. Everyone looked up at us and whispered as we were being seated. There I was on Broadway with this famous blonde, about to see one of the most popular musicals in the world, and my thoughts were a thousand miles away.

But then, I heard a song. You know the one. The big number in *Cats,* "Memory," where this cat comes out and goes through her whole life, singing of her memories, regrets, and announcing her rebirth.

Suddenly, it struck me! Yes, I had an Andrew Lloyd Webber epiphany right there in *Cats*! I realized that I had to start my life all over and rebuild everything that I had ever done. So in the middle of watching this play, I began crying. Donna couldn't believe it. "I didn't know you liked this song that much!" she said.

Later my therapist described what I went through as a "psychological implosion." In Mississippi folks would have called it a "nervous breakdown." Whatever it was, I had it during *Cats* on Broadway. Show business had been my life, so it seemed fitting that it should also be the scene of my meltdown. I was deep in the kitty litter at that point.

Before the last *Cat* crept off stage, I'd finally decided after years of anguish and indecision to go home, get my life in order, and figure out what it was that I'd forgotten to pack when I'd left Mississippi for Hollywood.

When I returned to L.A., I began cleaning house. I was determined to get a divorce, split up the celebrity clients with my business partner, and restructure the purchase of New World Pictures.

I called out the lawyers. The next day it looked like the Beverly Hills Bar Association was meeting in my office. I'd brought in a divorce lawyer, a corporate lawyer, a general business lawyer, and a tax lawyer. I'm also a lawyer, but you know the old saying about the lawyer who represents himself has a fool for a client? In my addled state of mind, it would have been the whole truth and nothing but the truth.

I told my small army of attorneys what I wanted to do and they stared at me like I'd lost my mind. "You've either given all this no thought or too much thought," was their general conclusion.

I was on a mission to reconstruct my life and there was no stopping me. I told my wife, Pamela, that I wanted a divorce. I told my business partner I wanted out of our management company. I told my studio partners, Harry Sloan and Larry Kuppin, that I wanted to restructure our studio purchase agreement.

Each one of them reached the same conclusion as my lawyers. "Larry's lost it!" I then decided to speak to no one because I didn't want to hear what they had to say about me, especially since they were probably right.

Stress? That's What I Do for a Living

I distanced myself by turning everything over to the lawyers. I thought I was handling this meltdown pretty well, as meltdowns go.

I stuck with business as usual, so I went to Morton's one night to meet with Nancy Bein, who was a CBS executive. I pitched an idea for a television movie to her. In the middle of my pitch, someone's leg started to jump around violently under the table. Then it hit me, "It's mine!" But when I looked down there, my legs were both perfectly still, so I continued with the conversation. A second later, it felt as though both of my legs were doing a Rockettes routine. Again, when I peered beneath the table, there wasn't a high kick to be seen. "Damn, I am losing it," I thought. Then I got the same flailing sensation in my arms, even though they were perfectly still too. I tried to keep talking to Nancy, but my mind was racing. I couldn't figure out what was happening to me. I wasn't sure I could stand up at that point. Morton's was packed with everybody that was anybody. I didn't want to blow a fuse here. In my mind, my limbs were flailing around like a red snapper yanked from the water. But I got through my pitch and managed to stand up without backhanding any waiters. I headed for the restroom where there was a telephone. I called my doctor and told him to meet me in the emergency room, not far from the restaurant.

I played it cool when I returned to the table. "Do you want any dessert?"

Luckily, Nancy wasn't up for sweets. As soon as the tab was paid, I said goodbye and headed for the hospital. There was something wrong with me. My heart was pounding like I'd just run a marathon inside the restaurant—a 10K with a Morton salad and a lime chicken.

At Cedars-Sinai, the emergency room doctors x-rayed my legs and my arms and took a blood sample. By the time my own doctor showed up, I was sitting in a small room with a white curtain pulled around it. I was wearing one of those rear-ventilated smocks that make you feel like a flasher.

My physician, Dr. Robert Huizenga, who later became known as "O.J.'s doctor" during his trial, said, "Larry, I've looked at these x-rays. I've looked at everything here. There's nothing wrong. Tell me what's going on in your life? Anything different? Any stress?"

I said, "No, not really. You know, I always have some stress in my life. I can handle it well. There's nothing major now. Nothing out of the ordinary. Other than that I am thinking about getting a divorce. I'm talking to my wife and a lawyer about that."

He said, "You know that can be pretty stressful."

"Well yeah, and actually I'm trying to split up a business relationship I've got with this guy, And, also, I am trying to buy a studio with a couple of partners and I'm thinking about restructuring that deal. So, everyone in my life seems to be upset with me, but other than that there's not much going on. You know me; stress is what I do for a living. I can handle it."

The diagnosis was pretty much set at that point.

"Sounds like to me maybe you're under too much stress," he said.

"Maybe you should see somebody."

"What do you mean *see somebody*?"

"You know, a therapist."

"A therapist? What do you mean, a therapist?"

"A psychiatrist or a psychologist."

I told him shrinks were for actors, not lawyers, managers, or producers. I didn't do that kind of thing.

"Well, I think you are under tremendous stress," he repeated. "Everyone needs help now and then. Let me give you this guy's name."

Tired of fighting it, I took the piece of paper with a psychiatrist's name and number. My doctor checked me out of the hospital. Then I headed for the hotel where I'd been living since I'd moved out of the house. Before I fell asleep that night, I thought to myself, "A shrink?"

The next day, I put it out of my mind and went back to business as usual, or so I thought. Normally, I work the phones like a switchboard operator. I plug into one business call after another, switching topics, tones of voice, areas of expertise. I had always prided myself on being able to multitask. But the stress hadn't gone away. As soon as I tried to fire up the frontal lobes, I blew all the circuits. When I took my first couple of calls, I found myself stammering. My mind was not functioning. I couldn't keep one call straight from another. I broke out in a sweat thinking I'd tell the wrong person the wrong thing and blow a deal or two or three. My brain was fried.

Confusion, guilt, hurt, loneliness, uncertainty—all of those emotions were paralyzing me. People often say they feel like they are losing their minds, and for the first time I really understood what that sensation felt like. My brain was literally racing faster than I could keep up with it. My mind was running off without me. I was literally losing my mind. It was terrifying. I'd always thought of my brain as a high-performance super computer. At that point it felt as though there was nothing but cold mush in my cranium.

It was time to make the call my doctor had suggested. I looked in my wallet and I found the name of the psychiatrist, Dr. Paul Hyman. As luck would have it, I got his answering machine. I left a message. An hour later, he called me.

"I can see you in three weeks," he said.

"You don't understand. I need to see you right now!"

He told me he was booked until 7:30 that night.

I said, "I'll be there at seven twenty-nine."

As I drove to his office, my mind felt like it was trying to race my car there. It felt like a boiling teapot ready to blow. I had never experienced that level of pain. My brain ached, my heart ached too.

Scene of the Crime

I parked my car on the street across from Dr. Hyman's office. I turned off the ignition while my mind kept racing toward the finish line. I kept thinking that if I could just make it into this doctor's office, I'd be okay. When I got into his office I knew that he could make this blinding pain in my head go away immediately. I wanted someone to give me a tranquilizer and knock me out.

I got out of the car and took two steps into the street when, *bam!* The two thugs jumped me and threatened to blow my brains out.

While screaming at me one of them pointed the sawed-off shotgun at my head. It occurred to me that if he pulled the trigger at least my pain would be gone. I wasn't the least bit frightened. I felt like the Mel Gibson character in *Lethal Weapon* whose lack of fear came from his belief that since he had already lost everything that was important to him in his life, he had nothing else to lose. With my hands up in the air, I told them they were going about this all wrong. They were calling too much attention to themselves in the middle of the street with a gun.

I had $1,000 in my money clip. I told them they could have that, but they'd be nuts to steal a white Rolls-Royce convertible. Neither of them matched the profile of a Rolls driver. They'd get stopped in three blocks. There I was in the middle of the street with my hands held in the air. They were pointing a gun at my face and I WAS NEGOTIATING WITH THESE GUYS!

While the negotiations with the sawed-off shotgun boys continued, someone walked out of an office, so they motioned me to get behind a tree with them. I couldn't tell if the guy saw us or not. I told them, "Just take my cash, and I won't tell the police anything about this."

They thought about it and ordered me to get on my knees with my hands against the tree. "They're getting ready to blow my brains out," I concluded. My own lack of terror scared me more than anything else. My brain must be totally numb, I thought.

They told me to start counting from 100 backward. I started, "100, 99, 98, 97." Then I thought I heard them running down the street. I slowly turned my head around and looked. They were gone.

After they'd taken off, I slowly got up and FINALLY walked into the psychiatrist's office. I sat down in a chair in his office and started talking as fast as I could. The next thing I knew he was telling me my time was up. "Time's up?" I cried. It seemed that I had just gotten there!

Dr. Hyman told me that trying to figure out what all was going on in my life was like trying to hop a train that was doing 90 miles an hour. He wanted to see me three times a week until he got a handle on my problems. He offered to walk me out but asked me to wait while he checked the messages on his answering machine. He exited and, when he returned, said that a patient who left just before I came in had called from his car phone, saying he thought he saw a mugging or robbery going on in the parking lot. "Had I seen anything?"

"Oh yeah, that was me," I said. "And you didn't mention it?" he asked. "I didn't mention it because they didn't blow my brains out, and they're gone and that's not a problem anymore. That's history. I've got REAL PROBLEMS to deal with!"

He looked at me askance, but I could tell that he understood that my anguish and stress were my priority, and for good reason.

Breakdown, Holdup, and Breakthrough

I went back to my hotel room that evening and sat down with my suit coat in one hand and the room service menu in the other. I had been making decisions about my marriage, decisions about my career, decisions about my life—big decisions. The more I stared at the room service menu, the more I realized I couldn't make a decision about what to eat. The next thing I knew it was 5:30 a.m. and I was still in the chair holding my suit coat and the menu. I hadn't ordered any food, but I did feel a strange sense of relief.

Later I realized that it was in that "blanked out" period that my mind caught up. Much like a computer that locks up while it tries to handle an overload of tasks, I'd gone into the human equivalent of a "blue screen." I locked up externally, but I subconsciously began to evaluate and analyze all the things that led to my breakdown during *Cats* and my emotional and mental meltdown since then.

Life is determined by the decisions you make along the way, and those that I had made were catching up to me. But the primary problem was that in my determination and drive to make it in Hollywood, I'd lost touch with the truly important things in life. And while I was playing the role of a big-time studio mogul, entertainment lawyer, talent manager, and producer, I'd lost track of who I really was. As Dr. Phil would say, I'd become less than my "authentic self." As my mother would say, "You didn't grow in height, depth, and width, you just shot straight up and toppled over."

I guess you could say I had a breakdown, a holdup, and then a breakthrough. I realized one of the truths to be examined in the rest of this book. You have to be careful about pursuing everything you want in life because you just might get it.

That doesn't have to be true. But it is a danger if you become too narrowly focused on success for the sake of success. It's okay to use inner rage for constructive purposes. It can be very helpful to have an inner fire or an "I'll show them" attitude, but in proving yourself, don't lose yourself.

I've seen that happen to supposedly "successful people." It happens to many of us. I know you've read and heard many times before that life is not about the destination, it's about the journey. But what does that clichéd saying really mean? It means that as you pursue your dreams, you can't neglect the rest of your life. Many people achieve their goals only to discover that they don't like who they've become along the way—and neither does anyone else they respect.

In this book I'm going to help you discover ways to become a Star in your own right, but I want you to go about it in a way that will allow you to enjoy success when you find it. I didn't, at first. And a bunch of lawyers are now driving Porsches because of it. I don't want that to happen to you.

How could a person have everything he ever wanted and feel empty? How did I get here? I had been flying at 30,000 feet and suddenly smashed into a mountain I never saw in front of me. I'd escaped the graveyard with nothing but streetlights in Mississippi only to nearly wind up in a shallow grave of my own making, right under the sign that says "HOLLYWOOD."

Fortunately, I dug my way out and rebuilt my life much more carefully this time so that now, I can enjoy the good things that occur. Living by the lessons I discuss in this book, I have a wonderful life now, one that I truly enjoy moment by moment.

As I thought about what I wanted to offer you in this book, there was one thing that stuck out in my mind. You certainly want to look ahead to great times, but you also should recognize and appreciate those that are happening now and have happened in the past. You want to build a great big pile of wonderful memories so that you can reflect on and appreciate the great moments in your life, especially when you might be having a not-so-great moment!

I put together the following list of things I've done in my life—some serious, some silly, some sad, some just plain wonderful—not to dazzle you with my accomplishments or the Star-quality of my life, but to emphasize something that it took me a long time to realize: Life should be lived as a celebration of every minute of every day. It is not a long hard preparation for a party *someday*. The party is this afternoon. So celebrate your life as it happens. Celebrate your talents, your interests, your opportunities, your failures, your loved ones, and your spirit. After you've read through my list, I want you to make a list of the things you've done, and then think a bit about those things that you want to do in the future. I'll go first:

150 Things I've Done

1. Sat on the deck of the Starship Enterprise with Captain Kirk
2. Held Drew Barrymore in my arms
3. Got stoned with Miles Davis
4. Met with the Beatles
5. Have been blessed by three Popes
6. Had a martini with Hugh Grant at the pool at the Hôtel du Cap in Antibes

7. Held Kermit the Frog
8. Went shopping with U2's Bono and his wife in Florence, Italy
9. Watched ringside as Mike Tyson took a bite out of Evander Holyfield's ear
10. Celebrated the World Music Awards aboard the *Shamwari* with Prince Albert of Monaco, Pamela Anderson, and Tommy Lee
11. Did breakfast at Nate 'n Al's with Larry King
12. Set up Cindy Crawford to host her first TV show, MTV's *House of Style*
13. Had a hilarious dinner at Spago's with Don Rickles
14. Rocked with Alex Haley on his porch in Tennessee
15. Purchased Barry Manilow's Rolls-Royce convertible
16. Bought Kirk Douglas's home with his handprint in cement in the driveway
17. Took pictures of David Bowie in my bedroom
18. Strolled along the Great Wall of China
19. Had Barry White explain to me all "380 degrees" of life
20. Lain in the king's burial chamber of Egypt's Great Pyramid
21. Bought a motion picture studio
22. Saw the Rat Pack perform six times at the Sands in Las Vegas
23. Sat with Elvis on the steps of the Clarksdale City Auditorium
24. Dined with Mama Cass in London; my drunken date fell out of the booth
25. Had a day named after me
26. Pissed with Kelsey Grammer at the Carousel Ball
27. Represented Sonny and Cher, and 25 years later made a movie about it
28. Danced with Nancy Reagan
29. Learned strength from Cicely Tyson
30. Almost died on the road to Agra to see the Taj Mahal
31. Signed Donna Dixon to *Bosom Buddies* instead of Tom Hanks
32. Tried to heal my mother when she was sent home after shock treatments
33. Cried with Peter Fonda in Rome about our fathers

34. Wrote two books

35. Produced 17 TV movies

36. Dressed Charlton Heston

37. Rented a limo from a funeral parlor for William Shatner and myself

38. Stayed with Jane Seymour at her castle near Bath, England

39. Made six motion pictures

40. Took a trip around the world

41. Comforted my mother as she lay dying on Halloween night

42. Received eight Emmy, one Golden Globe, and two Prism Award nominations for my productions

43. Managed the careers of over 200 Stars

44. Signed myself as a client

45. Stood on a mountain top at the Cape of Good Hope

46. Made love in a royal balcony box at the La Scala Opera House in Milan

47. Laughed with Monty Python's Eric Idle on a yacht in the south of France

48. Witnessed my father smile and reach up to a "white light" when he died

49. Told Robin Givens in Morton's one night after her interview with Barbara Walters that she was one of the most hated women in the world.

50. Overheard a frustrated Rolls-Royce service guy say to Fred Astaire, "Don't give me that song and dance routine."

51. Drank until the sun came up at the Beverly Hills Hotel with Richard Harris

52. Sat on a dinner dais with President George H. Bush

53. Played golf with Vijay Singh at Shadow Creek

54. Was invited to the Rolls-Royce factory in Crew, England, where I had a Bentley made to my specifications

55. Rode floats in both the Rose Bowl and Mardi Gras Parades

56. Said, "I do" twice

57. Witnessed the visions of the Blessed Virgin Mary at Medjugorie in Bosnia-Herzegovina

58. Produced two TV series

59. Fired by Alan Thicke not once, not twice, but five times as his manager

60. Pitched a project claiming that Jackie Kennedy Onassis would host it only to have her enter the restaurant and be seated in the next booth during the pitch—before I'd talked to her about it

61. Represented Linda Lovelace. After *Deep Throat*, she made *Linda Lovelace for President.* Her campaign slogan was "I may not be the best man for the job, but I'm better than the other c@&k-suckers."

62. Took my family to Rome to see the Vatican

63. Cooked up a deal to have Wolfgang Puck cater my daughter's baptism

64. Watched the Grand Prix in Monte Carlo from a yacht

65. Cruised Alaska with inventor and telemarketer Ron Popeil, as his guest

66. Attended George Harrison's *Concert for Bangladesh*

67. Invited 50 friends to Monte Carlo for my three-day fiftieth birthday party

68. Received a Bible from Charlene Tilton

69. Dined at Chasen's with Ronald Reagan, who sadly told me the same story about his belt buckle three times

70. Got married at Jim Nabor's home in Bel Air

71. Put John Larroquette in his first dramatic television role

72. Celebrated Paul Sorvino's birthday at his daughter Mira's Malibu home

73. Was told by Carroll O'Connor that I was his inspiration for his Southern accent in the popular series *In the Heat of the Night*

74. Helped straighten out Linda Blair's head

75. Managed Drew Barrymore, Tori Spelling, and Shannen Doherty

76. Sipped tea at the Dorchester with *Gone with the Wind* legend Olivia de Havilland

77. Flew to Rome with Tim Matheson and Ann Jillian

78. Received the Entertainment Industry's prestigious Vision Award

79. Partied at the Playboy Mansion and I'm not telling

80. Was on *The Dating Game* twice and never chosen
81. Howled at the moon with Tanya Tucker
82. Ate food prepared by the Iron Chefs
83. Won a bowling trophy with Kiss's Gene Simmons
84. Was given a harmonica by John Popper of Blues Traveler
85. Played Baccarat with Kelly Hu
86. Swam in my pool with CNBC's Maria Bartiromo
87. Raced Angie Harmon down Sunset Boulevard
88. Attended David Bowie and Iman's wedding in Florence, Italy
89. Honored by having a Fine Arts Center named after me
90. Had drinks at the Polo Lounge with Jack Lemon
91. Partied with Goldie Hawn at Caesar's Palace
92. Purchased a Rodin, a Renoir, and a Picasso
93. Listed perennially in *Who's Who in the World*
94. Met Sela Ward on the Spanish Steps in Rome and we went shopping
95. Caught a marlin off Oahu and let it go
96. Awarded the *Show Biz Lawyer of the Year* Record by Capitol in 1971
97. Nominated for the *Looking Good* Style Award along with Warren Beatty, Tom Selleck, and Dan Rather
98. Auditioned over 1,000 Sonny and Cher hopefuls
99. Auditioned over 2,500 would-be redheads for Lucy
100. Proposed marriage to Kelly LeBlanc at the Grand Wailea in Maui
101. Was nicknamed the Man Who Broke Up the Beatles
102. Chatted several times with the awesome Muhammad Ali
103. Sat with Sharon and Ozzy Osbourne at the Four Seasons in Maui
104. Froze my ass off in Red Square
105. Had a week named after me
106. Voted Showman of the Year in 1998 by the US Television Fan Association
107. Watched the Super Bowl with Eric Roberts, Scott Hamilton, and Leonard Nimoy

108. Begged Quincy Jones for the rights to do a movie on his life
109. Played pool with billiards legend, Minnesota Fats
110. Did 10 pushups in my office with Jack LaLanne
111. Stumbled upon Princes Diana and Prince Charles on a deserted beach in Sardinia
112. Lunched Ma Maison with Orson Wells
113. Went to the inaugurations of Presidents Ronald Reagan and George H. Bush
114. Helped President Gerald Ford become a mule
115. Served as an altar boy at St. Elizabeth's Catholic Church
116. Prayed that you would find this book inspirational and helpful
117. Learned to line dance with *Sex and the City*'s Kristin Davis and her friend Melanie Shatner-Gretsch
118. Discovered it was lonely in the middle
119. Watched José Eber cut Farrah Fawcett's hair at Jay Bernstein's home
120. Scored a par on the eighteenth hole of Pebble Beach
121. Played tennis with Rene Russo and Susie Coelho
122. Met the prince of Saudi Arabia at the Hotel Cala di Volpe in Sardinia
123. Celebrated three of my birthdays partying at La Voile Rouge in St. Tropez
124. Had two women walk on my back at the Amanpuri in Phuket, Thailand
125. Fitness trained at home with Pete and Jake Steinfeld
126. Have read the Bible
127. Was a judge on both *Star Search* and *Miss Teen USA*
128. Hid under a table with William Shatner at the MGM Grand Hotel when the shooting started after a Mike Tyson fight
129. Continued to wonder who really roots for you after your parents die
130. Flew on the Concorde from New York to Paris in 3 hours and 11 minutes
131. Heard Paul McCartney and Paul Simon sing a duet at the Adopt-A-Minefield Charity Dinner

132. Have been friends with *ET*'s Mary Hart for many years
133. Experienced four epiphanies in my life so far
134. Told Pete Townshend from The Who to read *The New New Thing*
135. Sat in the Royal Enclosure at the Ascot races in England
136. Set sail on my wife's birthday cruise with 60 guests, including Mira Sorvino
137. Had *The Sopranos*' Steven Schirripa judge Italian food for me on Iron Chef USA
138. Ate caviar with Ruth Gordon in the Russian Tea Room
139. Met fellow southerner Reese Witherspoon at Rape Foundation Luncheon
140. Was ticketed on the way to Palm Springs doing 117 miles per hour in a Corniche
141. Moved into the neighborhood with Hugh Hefner's L.A. Playboy Mansion
142. Went nightclubbing with Sammy Davis, Jr.
143. Sat with B.B. King in his bus while he played his guitar, Lucille
144. Touched by angel Roma Downey, who inscribed her book to my daughter
145. Snow-skied in Aspen with Agent 007, Pierce Brosnan, at Race to Erase MS
146. Wrote in this book "all the things I have learned" from "all the things I have done"
147. Have had one great friend, Fred Alias, all my life
148. Shared a loving life with my sister, Janice, and brother, Marshall
149. Married Kelly LeBlanc at the Good Shepherd Church in Beverly Hills and partied with family and friends for three days at the Bellagio Hotel in Las Vegas
150. Became a multimillionaire along the way

And I would trade any, if not all, of them for the one moment when my little girl, Taylor, was born and my beautiful wife, Kelly, and I cried together with joy.

You should see the list of 150 Things I Plan to Do!

Throughout this book, enjoy applying to your life all the things I have learned from all the things I have done. My list is to get you thinking and dreaming. Thinking about the things you have done, and dreaming about the things you plan to do.

Make your list now of the things you have done. I bet you will surprise yourself at how much you have experienced. When you are finished, make another list of all you dream to do in the next 20 years. Dream big.

Go for it. *Shine* and map out your life to the fullest. I can't wait to meet you one day and learn from your "List of Things You Have Done."

CHAPTER 1
STARDOM

You don't have to be in the movies to be a Star. In every city, small town, school, office, or even family household, there is always at least one person whom everybody thinks is fantastic—a Star.

There is always a "most popular"—"most beautiful"—"center of attention"—"cheerleader"—"president of the class"—"head of the PTA"—"special aunt"—"teacher's pet"—or "boss's favorite."

You know who they are. Even your older brother may have been the Golden Child, perceived in your family as "Mister Do No Wrong." He could wreck the new car, and your parents would say, "Boy, is he a feisty one." But if you made one wrong move, you were banished to Siberia.

What Makes Certain People So Special?

For 30 years I have represented the careers of over 200 Hollywood Stars. I have studied their behavior and discussed with them at length their dreams, fears, and success strategies. I know what makes them different and successful and I know how they think.

I can teach you how to think like them. Their Star-making methods will work for you.

Because I've had so many successful clients, I'm often asked: "What makes a person a Star? What makes them special? How can I excel at what I do just as Julia Roberts or Leonardo DiCaprio have succeeded in their careers?"

Well, despite the hundreds of frustrated Elvis impersonators hound-dogging around the world, you really can't become someone else, but you can become the best "You" you can be.

I know it's easy when you're flipping through a magazine to wish, "Oh, look at her. Look at him. I wish I had this. I wish I had that. I wish I looked like this. I wish I looked like that." Well, be careful. It's okay to be influenced by other people, and maybe to analyze who they are and how they got there, and to model certain things about them, but you don't want to be—nor can you be—anything other than yourself. Developing your own uniqueness will make you a Star, not your ability to imitate another's.

So, trying to be the best of everybody you admire may total up to something that doesn't become you. Therefore, concentrate on who you are and how to make the best of who you are, and be 100 percent you.

You can find fulfillment by using the techniques in this book to help you identify exactly who you are and what unique and positive things you bring to the table. Then, I'll help you find ways to enhance those gifts. That is the secret of "Stars" from every walk of life. They figure out who they are, what they want, and then develop and market their gifts, packaged as that special person.

It is equally important for you to identify and eliminate any negative thinking or self-defeating behaviors that have held you back in the past. Actors are trained to use both good and bad life experiences as resources to draw upon in their performances. In this book, you will learn to do the same, no matter what your chosen field or line of work. I will teach you to transform what has happened to you in the past into a positive force, and to eliminate those past behaviors and thought patterns that may have blocked you from accomplishing your goals and dreams.

The Stars I've worked with, and nearly all of the biggest names in Hollywood, generally share a high degree of self-awareness. In more than a few cases, it may cross the border into self-absorption. Yet, self-awareness is essential to the acting profession and, I think, to success in any field. This is not the same as egomania, although there is plenty of that in Hollywood too.

Self-awareness is simply being alert to not only your moods and emotions, but to the thoughts and actions that accompany them. When the self-aware person feels frustrated, lost, or inadequate, he or she seeks out the source and origins of those feelings through interior dialogue. That leads to greater understanding and, hopefully, greater self-mastery and control over your life. Not everyone who is self-aware manages self-mastery, but once you understand the source of your feelings, you can often learn to control your reactions to them. If feelings of self-doubt, bitterness, victimization, anger, or resentment have prevented you from becoming the Star you want to be, I'll offer you methods for recognizing, stopping, and replacing those self-defeating behaviors with positive patterns and healing inner dialogue.

Reality Check

Everybody is a nobody at some point in life. We all start somewhere. Nobody is born a Star. Even those who might seem to be Stars from birth weren't born in limousines. Most of them went through periods when they worried about making their car payments. They clipped coupons. They dug through the couch cushions to get enough quarters for the laundromat. Just like ordinary mortals.

If you find that hard to believe, take a look at some of the jobs that kicked off the careers of big celebrity Stars you've seen and heard about.

Ashton Kutcher	Dust sweeper in a General Mills plant
Ralph Lauren	Sweater salesman
Maya Angelou	Streetcar conductor
Bill Murray	Chestnut seller
Stephen King	Janitor
Coolio	Fire fighter
Bill Gates	Congressional page
Jack Nicholson	Mail sorter
Mariah Carey	Hat checker

Ronald Reagan wasn't the biggest Star as an actor, but he found his lasting Stardom in politics.

Dennis Rodman	Camp counselor
Garth Brooks	Boot salesman
Ellen DeGeneres	Oyster shucker
Iman	Soldier in Somali military
Brad Pitt	Delivered refrigerators
Jim Carrey	Janitor
Robin Williams	Scooped ice cream
Madonna	Dancer
Jewel	Waitress
Oprah Winfrey	Journalist
Rob Schneider	Dishwasher
Jerry Seinfeld	Lightbulb salesman

So, how do you go from being a lightbulb salesman to becoming one of the highest paid comedians in the history of television? Or from a struggling journalist to one of the most wealthy and powerful women in the world? Everyone arrives in a different way.

When I was a student at the University of Mississippi Law School, I convinced the law librarian to subscribe to a show business newspaper I had heard about called *Weekly Variety*. Of course, I was the only person in Mississippi who read it. Every Friday, I would devour it page by page. I took notes and kept index cards on everybody in Hollywood. I would go down to Leslie's Drug Store in Oxford and buy movie magazines. I would cut out pictures of the people I was studying and staple the pictures to their index cards. I studied a town, a business, and the people in it, all by myself for two years.

I graduated and was sworn into the bar in Jackson on August 20, 1968. They served coffee and doughnuts. I was offered a clerkship with a Mississippi Supreme Court Justice, but decided to pass. Instead, my dad gave me $700. I packed my box of index cards and hung my clothes on a rack in the back seat of a black Oldsmobile with maroon interior and took off for Hollywood. When I left home at age 24 to live in California, *not only had I never been* to California, but I *had never met anyone who had ever been* to California.

I drove three straight days to Hollywood, exited the freeway onto Sunset Boulevard, and eventually reached the corner of Hollywood and Vine—the only street address I had ever heard about. It was

10 o'clock in the evening and it was raining. I got out of my car, stood in the rain, looked around, and cried, cried, and cried. I was where I was supposed to be. I HAD ARRIVED!

A little over a year after I first stood on the corner of Hollywood and Vine, I got a job working on that same corner! I started my career in show business as in-house counsel for Capitol Records. Subsequently, on behalf of Capitol, I negotiated the famed Beatles breakup. Their breakup was a big break for me!

Star Power

Granted, most Stars in Hollywood and many everyday Stars share a certain irresistible quality. Let's call it charisma, magnetism, or just "it." Winners in all walks of life display the same power or self-assurance, whether it's the best carpenters on a construction job or the office worker everyone turns to when there is a problem beyond their grasp. But where does that inner power or confidence come from? What is the source?

While some people, particularly those who succeed in Hollywood, are naturally blessed with physical beauty that draws the eyes of all who encounter them, appearance is only one aspect of self-confidence. Billy Bob Thornton is one of the biggest Stars in the business right now, and he is certainly not handsome in the classic Hollywood leading man mold. The always thankful Renee Zellweger is in great demand as an actress even though her looks are as "un-Hollywood" as her name.

I'm sure you know men and women who have an abundance of self-confidence and exude charisma even though they may not be all that physically attractive. Their self-assurance most likely comes from being comfortable with themselves and confident in their abilities. Note that such Stars rarely believe they will never fail. But they almost always have confidence that failure will not cripple them permanently or prevent them from success down the road. They believe in themselves, and they have learned to overcome negative thoughts and behavior patterns with faith in their ability to persevere.

When you develop an unwavering belief in your own value and worthiness, it becomes infectious. In sometimes amazing ways, other people buy into your image of yourself, and they buy into your dreams too. I can think of no greater example than Clay Aiken, one of the most unlikely "Stars" born on the popular television show *American Idol*. This show is the most recent incarnation of talent contests that date back to the very earliest years of television. It is also a great laboratory for observing people, while following and using the principles, advice, and tips I offer you in this book. If you didn't see Clay Aiken until the last rounds of his *American Idol* competition, you missed an amazing transformation.

When he performed in the early rounds, he was anything but charismatic in appearance. He looked like a street urchin from a Charles Dickens play. Or like one of the Munchkins who wandered in from the *Wizard of Oz* set. A *Rolling Stone* interviewer described him as a "good-natured, Baptist-churchgoing, 24-year-old with a goofy grin, mud flap ears, penguin-size feet, and a pure crooner's voice."

A lot of people felt sorry for him in the early rounds of the competition because he didn't look like he belonged on stage. Yet, when he sang, the power of his voice transformed him and our opinions of him. The joy he expressed was as infectious as it was goofy. Clay Aiken, who'd had a difficult childhood and struggled to find his place in the world, never stopped believing in himself as a singer. I think that is what took him into the final rounds. Even though he lost the competition to the talented and lovable Ruben Studdard, Clay was gracious throughout, and he established himself as the sort of Star that millions of fans wanted to see succeed.

Granted, Aiken has a very marketable gift. His singing voice carried him to success on a very large stage. But we all have unique gifts, skills, and characteristics that we can develop to assure success at some level. You may not become a singing Star recognized around the world, but you might become the Star of your school, of your corporate division, or of your community organization. The important thing is to develop your own unique gifts and to find fulfillment in putting them to a useful purpose.

Our culture focuses on those with performing talents or beauty as defined by very narrow standards, but believe me, while the highs are wonderful in the glamour industries like entertainment and fashion, the lows can be devastating too. It's difficult to find peace and fulfillment when the only measure of success in your business is whether millions of people are willing to pay to see you perform. While the "beautiful people" may be envied, many of them feel that their true values and talents are overlooked. Consider that Charlize Theron wasn't truly appreciated as an actress until she hid her beauty under slabs of makeup to portray a prostitute and serial killer in *Monster*.

I've worked with hundreds of Stars, and I know that beauty can be a burden, as well as a blessing. I call it the "Farrah Factor" because when I think of it, I always flash back to the first time I met a young woman who'd just moved to Hollywood from her home in Texas.

"Hi, happy Thanksgiving. I'm Farrah," she said.

"Sarah?" I asked.

"No, Farrah," she replied.

"Farrah? How do you spell that?"

"F-a-r-r-a-h. Farrah Fawcett."

"Farrah Fawcett. Well, that's a beautiful name. I've never heard that name. So, you're having dinner with us today?"

"Yeah, I'm here with Lee."

That was the first time I ever met Farrah Fawcett, and believe me, I knew she was a Star the moment I got her name right.

It was Thanksgiving 1974, and my wife Pamela and I were having Thanksgiving dinner at Sonny Bono's house. Sonny was a client, a friend, and a great Italian cook. Thanksgiving at Sonny's had become an annual family event. As usual, he was preparing a great meal. What was unusual that particular Thanksgiving was that Sonny and Cher were going through a divorce.

Sonny had invited Lee Majors to dinner. Lee was starring in *The Six Million Dollar Man*, on television, and he was quite popular. He was dating this young girl from Corpus Christi, Texas, whom he'd met when she had a small role on his show. Farrah really hadn't done much careerwise at the time. She had appeared in a few episodes on television series and had done what would become a famous Super Bowl commercial for Noxzema shaving cream with Joe Namath.

Even though Farrah was just starting out as an actress back then, if you had looked up "it" in the Hollywood Star Dictionary, you would have seen her photograph. Her beauty made her a natural-born Star. Such high charisma is difficult to define. The moment you laid your eyes on her, you would have known she was a Star—as I did. I had never in my life seen a prettier face, prettier hair, prettier teeth, prettier eyes, and prettier nose; never had I seen a more bubbly, innocent, infectious personality. She exuded confidence. This girl had everything going for her.

Farrah became a Star and a sex symbol as one of the original *Charlie's Angels,* but when she tried to prove herself as a serious actress, she struggled. Her first three films were bombs, and critics savaged her. To her credit, she never stopped believing in herself. She did a television movie, *Murder in Texas,* in which her performance was widely praised. She then made a daring move to performing on stage on Broadway in *Extremities,* and again her work was so good that people began thinking of her as a serious actress rather than a sex kitten and poster girl. She went on to even greater praise in the television film *The Burning Bed* and the movie version of *Extremities.*

I've known Farrah for many years now, and I've seen how hard she worked to prove herself. Her natural beauty and charisma helped her get started in Hollywood, but she also had to overcome stereotypes and prejudices as well as a sometimes tumultuous personal life. My point is, her life has not been easy in spite of her beauty.

I'm sure your life has had its challenges too. I believe that you can overcome them by developing your unique gifts, learning to overcome habitual negative thoughts and self-defeating behavior patterns, and developing a "sixth sense" for opportunities.

Star Quality

So, if nobody is born a Star, where does the Star quality come from? Is there a store where it can be purchased? Is it for sale on eBay? Can you get it through osmosis just by hanging around others with Star quality?

Well, not exactly. Like wisdom and grace, Star quality is something you acquire—a skill you can learn. People can be trained to be athletes, nurses, musicians, barbers, doctors, mailmen, soldiers, chefs—and Stars. That's the purpose of this book.

In the pages that follow, you'll learn to behave in ways that will provoke a wholehearted, generous, and loving (perhaps even slightly awed) response from those around you. The world is full of people just looking for others to admire. You'll be surprised at how easy it is to become one of the ones they're seeking. Sometimes all it takes is a little secret or two to give you that attitude—or that kick in the pants—you need to get started on your own path to Stardom. And that secret or two or three or four is what I will be imparting to you. In fact, there are four secrets that I'll explain in this book.

The Four Elements of Stardom

All of the Stars I have known or worked with possessed four *essential* and *attainable* elements:

* Talent
* Rage
* Team
* Luck

Of these Four Elements, Talent and Rage come from within. Team and Luck are choices you make. Let's discuss each of them.

TALENT

Each of us is born with the talent to excel at something. The secret is to identify those talents and develop them so we can express them fully. It may be that you don't have the musical talents to star on Broadway but you do have a level of talent that would make you a great "find" for local musical dinner theater or as a music teacher who can enrich the lives of students. Talent comes in many degrees and it is not exclusive to celebrities.

Most people don't think they have a talent because they think of it as simply an artistic ability, but talent encompasses much more than the ability to sing, dance, act, sculpt, or paint. Perhaps it would help to understand "talent" as an easily recognized gift. Not all of us have "artistic talent," but nearly everyone has abilities that can be developed. These abilities range from a knack for cooking great meals to being handy with mechanical things. There are many fulfilled people out there who've developed their abilities and built their lives and careers around them. We all know people who've found fulfillment in sewing, teaching, child care, decorating, marketing, accounting, hairdressing, and a wide range of other abilities that may not always be recognized as "talents" but are important and valuable nonetheless.

I consider "talent" to be all the innate abilities you have that can be developed in order to make your life consistently more fulfilling. Analyze your abilities, your personality, your looks, and your intelligence. These are the talents that make you special and unique.

You may feel that you don't fit in to conventional thoughts of talent or Stardom; that you don't even fit in to your own life! Relax. That sense of uneasiness and restlessness is a good sign. It indicates that you are ready to begin building a more fulfilling life. Most Stars have felt "different," "weird," or "crazy" for much of their lives. It is part of what drives them to develop their talents to a higher level. It is a compelling sense that there is a higher use and greater fulfillment awaiting them. Or, as that noted philosopher, Boy George, once said, "I've always been different. I've always been a show-off. It's just that now, when I shout, 'Look at me,' people actually do look!"

This "outsider" feeling doesn't just apply to performers. A couple years ago a business magazine surveyed a group of successful entrepreneurs to see what, if anything, they had in common. To everyone's surprise, it turned out that the trait they all shared was that every single one of them had hated working for other people. They'd all felt out of place when what they did for a living was just a job. They wondered if something was wrong with them. They thought they'd never fit into the real workaday world. They felt like such outsiders that they decided the only way they'd ever make a living was to work for themselves. So they started their own businesses and thrived by benefiting from their own talents!

"But, I can't think of what my talents are," you say to yourself. Maybe your talent is right in front of you. What if all you can do is make good cookies? I've got not one, but two names for you: Famous Amos and Debbie Fields!

When he was 12 years old, Wally Amos was sent from his parents' home in Tallahassee, Florida, to live with his Aunt Della in New York City. She baked him his first chocolate chip cookie, but he never thought that he'd be famous one day for making his own brand. He dropped out of his senior year at Food Trades Vocational High School to join the Air Force, where he earned his general education diploma, or high school equivalency diploma. He then trained at a New York secretarial school after he was honorably discharged from the Air Force. Eventually, Wally became a theatrical agent at the William Morris Agency, where he worked with Simon and Garfunkel, the Supremes, and other acts.

Wally didn't really become a hot Star until he switched from agent to "oven-preneur" when he created his Famous Amos cookie company. He made a fortune. Then he lost it. Then he started over with the Uncle Noname Cookie Company before once again becoming a spokesman for Famous Amos cookies. He is a great example of someone with a simple talent and a desire and passion. He believes that "life is just a mirror, and what you see out there, you must first see inside of you."

Debbie Fields, as a 20-year-old mother with no business experience, opened her first cookie store in Palo Alto, California, in 1977. She had to give cookies away to get people to eat them. But they did eat those free cookies, and then they were willing to pay for them. Fields now has 700 company-owned and franchised stores in the United States and six more in other countries. She has written two recipe books, hosted a television show, and is a motivational speaker. She has also won a number of prestigious awards for professional achievements. "Once you find something you love to do, be the best at doing it," she says. "Whatever you do in your life, you have to be absolutely passionate about it."

In the chapter on Talent, your assignment will be to list your talents. This self-inventory exercise is necessary because you need to know what you have to work with in order to start turning yourself into a Star. Don't worry, we will find plenty to work with. That's why I've titled this book *Shine: A Powerful 4-Step Plan for Becoming a Star at Anything You Do*. I've seen it happen too often to doubt it. In fact, I've helped make it happen too often to even question it.

By assessing your talents more accurately, you'll be able to answer two important questions:

- Who do people see when they see me?
- Who do I *want* them to see?

RAGE

Success doesn't just happen. It is forced into existence. To be successful, you must be determined to achieve your goal. You can't merely wish, hope, desire, or try real hard to succeed. You can't just have ambition. You must have a RAGE to succeed. You must have tunnel vision—a one-way ticket—do or die. You must have a mad passion for success. You must pay the price. If you don't, your competitors will.

It's common to think of rage as a negative emotion, like "road rage," but the dictionary also defines rage as a form of passion or "something that is desired intensely." For the purpose of this book, I've defined rage as the difference in *saying* you want something and *continually acting* as if you do.

Shortly after the September 11, 2001, attack on the United States, I attended a private get-together in Beverly Hills, hosted by actor Vin Diesel. The purpose of our meeting was to organize The Entertainment Community Ground Zero Relief Fund. I looked around the small gathering, and off to my right stood a very stoic and committed Sylvester Stallone. He looked on and listened with intensity. He exuded then, as he has always, a sense of loyalty, a feeling of focus, and a deep level of involvement. His eagerness comforted me that night.

Recognized as a true, veteran movie Star, Sly, as people in Hollywood know him, would never have attained that status if it weren't for his passion and desire and *Rocky*-like *rage* for success. He has made millions by carefully controlling his career, but he wasn't always in control. He was born into an impoverished, broken family in New York's Hell's Kitchen ghetto and later grew up in a tough Philadelphia neighborhood. He spent several years in foster homes and was kicked out of 14 schools in 11 years. At that point the only recognized talent Sly had was for getting into trouble. But there was something else. He was strong and athletic, and those abilities got him into the American College in Switzerland on an athletic scholarship. He later moved to the University of Miami, where he took theater classes and his instructors told him he didn't have the chops for acting.

So what did Sly do? He worked as an attendant in a zoo, and he cooked pizzas at a restaurant. He still wanted to be an actor but in those days the only work he could find was in small parts, an off-Broadway play, and a couple of adult films.

Four years later Sly did get a lead role in the low-budget movie, *The Lords of Flatbush*, and the next year his career picked up with supporting roles in *Farewell My Lovely*, *Capone*, and *Death Race 2000*. Still, Sly wasn't where he wanted to be. He wanted bigger roles in better movies, and, like everyone, he wanted to have at least enough money to give his family a decent life. When his wife became pregnant, he decided he'd have to make his own breaks.

In 1975, Stallone witnessed a boxing match—the Muhammad Ali–Chuck Wepner fight. Wepner, a little-known club fighter, was predicted to go down within three rounds, but the underdog was still standing in round 15.

That same night, Stallone went home with an idea for a movie story featuring a character named Rocky Balboa, a man with incredible emotion, patriotism, spirituality, and good nature to spare. As Stallone conceived him, Rocky "would be America's child. He would be to the seventies what Chaplin's Little Tramp was to the twenties."

For three and a half days straight, Stallone wrote his first draft of *Rocky*. Studios loved the script, but they weren't so enamored of the strings attached: Stallone, an unknown, wanted to star. James Caan, Ryan O'Neal, and Burt Reynolds were mentioned as more likely candidates. Stallone was initially offered a hefty sum for the screenplay only, but even though he had only $40 in the bank and his wife Sasha was pregnant, he still held out. "I knew if I just took the money, then the whole thing I wrote about in the script was totally false too," he said. "The picture was taking that golden shot in the face of adversity." Eventually, United Artists gave in, putting their faith in Stallone.

In February 1977 the Academy of Motion Picture Arts and Sciences honored *Rocky* with 19 Oscar nominations, later awarding it the 1976 Academy Award for Best Picture. Stallone's triumph was complete. As surely as Rocky Balboa overcame all obstacles to "go the distance" in the ring, Sylvester Stallone himself overcame ferocious odds to put his vision on screen. He delivered a K.O. His rage to succeed paid off in spades.

Now Stallone is hosting the new reality series *The Contender*, wherein he is helping us discover other contenders who exhibit Rage for their success.

As Rocky believed, and as I will repeat over and over throughout the book: If you've got the desire and the passion—the Rage—you can be a Star at whatever you do. Before we go any further, you should know: You are what your Rage is. Remember:

- As your Rage is, so is your will.
- As your will is, so is your action.
- As your action is, so is your destiny.

Every day people arrive by the busloads in Hollywood saying they want to be Stars. But not everyone has the driving Rage for it. Everybody wants to succeed. We all want to be Stars—but do we have the passion and Rage for it? Are you willing to pay the price?

Here's how I've seen the scenario play out in Hollywood time and time again:

LAST PERSON STANDING

There's going to be a big audition for an acting job. Not just an acting job, a career kick-starter opportunity. It's a Star-maker role like the one landed by Julia Roberts in *Pretty Woman*, or Jennifer Garner in *Alias,* or David Schwimmer in *Friends*, or Ashton Kutcher in *That '70s Show,* or even Vivien Leigh in *Gone With the Wind.* It's the Big ... Bigger ... Biggest ... Break of all Breaks Role.

The producers are waiting in a cavernous room at 1 p.m.—the scheduled time for the audition to begin—and in comes a big group of charged-up actors to audition. It's a room with couches and chairs, like the waiting room in a doctor's office. There's a closed door on the opposite wall, and the actors are supposed to be called in, one by one, to read for the part. Two hours go by and the door doesn't open; nothing happens.

After another hour, one of the female actors who came for the audition gets up and says, "I've got another audition across town. I've waited here three hours. I didn't think it would take this long. I've got to go." And she leaves.

About eight o'clock that night, the rest of them are still there, and someone else rises and says, "I've got to leave. I'm supposed to meet someone important for dinner. I can't wait any longer." She leaves too.

Now it's late the next morning and someone says, "I've slept here on the floor all night, I didn't take a shower, I stink. I've had enough—I'm leaving."

Two hours later, another says, "I haven't eaten in a day, and I'm hypoglycemic. I've got to get out of here."

At 1 p.m. the next day, another woman throws her SAG card up in the air and says, "This is ridiculous. I'm insulted. What price do you have to pay? We have waited two days now and they haven't met with one person. Who do these people think they are? How can they treat people this way? I've had enough; I'm outta here."

By the end of the third day there is only one person left in the room, and she is oblivious to the fact that everyone else has given up and left. She did not even know they were there, because she was so focused and passionate about getting this role. She hasn't eaten, slept, or showered. Her boyfriend has left 16 messages on her cell phone. Her parents are worried.

Suddenly, the door to the audition room opens. The producers call out: *"Next?"*

The last and only woman in the room goes in and she gets the role! She was the last person standing.

When push comes to shove, that is what it takes. When the streets are lined with young, beautiful, and talented people all competing for the same job, the difference between those who make it and those who don't is passion and determination and the driving Rage to claim the prize.

Are you prepared to be the last woman or man standing? You must be willing to be the last person standing (LPS) to guarantee your success. You may not have to wait for days to get the role. You may not have to give up your job, your wife, your kids, your health, and your sanity. Hopefully, you won't have to. You may not have to actually be the last person standing. You may even go into the audition, wait a few minutes, and get it. But if you're prepared to be the last person standing, if you're really prepared, if you're really that committed, then when that door opens, you're going to get the part!

It does take that level of commitment, that buying a one-way ticket, that tunnel vision, that maniacal rage to succeed. Remember: If you're not prepared to be the LPS, someone competing against you will be. Never underestimate your competition. That said, once you truly commit to being the LPS, you're not worried about the competition anymore. It's yours to win!

Team

No one becomes a Star without help. All the Stars I've worked with have had supporters, mentors, counselors, spiritual advisers, and fans on which they can rely. Even highly motivated athletes need coaches and competitors to push them to peak performance levels.

No one starts out with a ready-made fan club, of course. But most of us have the next best thing built into our lives already: our families—our parents, a husband, a wife, and the kids—and even our friends. All it takes is someone who believes that you may just be right about yourself. Often, that person is willing to sacrifice along with you to help you realize your dreams. And speaking of dreams: Dream big. Share your dreams. Be proud of them.

In my chapter on Team, you'll read the stories of Stars who are indebted to their early supporters. We'll look at how you can begin to structure your own support team, and formulate a plan to promote yourself or your ideas. You will learn how your Team can help you build and maintain hope.

LUNAR LADIES

I knew this young girl, Lisa, who was a physical trainer and aspiring actress. She loved people and networked well. She supported her friends, especially the five or six girlfriends she had. They were all working very hard in different careers. They all needed support. They wanted to be a Team to help each other. So she put this group of six girlfriends together and they called themselves the "Lunar Ladies."

Once a month, on the night of the full moon, they all got together and went out howling. On those nights, they talked about each other all night long—what they were doing, what they were up to. They asked each other for advice. They gave each other advice. They made phone calls for each other. They made introductions to people. They probably went through one, two, three, four, or five bottles of wine—whatever it took. They drank. They howled at the moon. They talked. They laughed. They played. They helped and supported each other.

The respective careers of the Lunar Ladies have happily flourished, and they still meet on the night of the full moon. By the way, no men were, or are, allowed.

RECRUITING YOUR TEAM

Sometimes, the people from whom you'd most like support are reluctant. If that's the case, I'll teach you how to negotiate support by plotting out specific goals. For example, you might negotiate with your parents that if they'll pay for 18 months of acting lessons, you will, at the end of that time, have landed one part in a show or commercial.

If you fail, you'll get a job and pay them back for the lessons. This gives them a specific measurement by which to judge your success, and it gives you an achievable goal to aim for.

Finally, it helps to know the best way to approach your potential team members. Studies show that people receive information best in one of three ways. Their reception is primarily:

- Visual
- Auditory
- Kinesthetic (feeling)

You will learn how to identify which way people understand you, and how to communicate with them more effectively. You will identify which of these sensory perceptions matches your targeted team member's orientation—and adjust your approach accordingly.

LUCK

A friend of mine watched a TV news report about a fellow who won a huge sum of money in the Illinois State Lottery—$20 million, or some equally astonishing figure.

"Some guys have all the luck," my friend mused. (He's a good friend, even if he's not very original.)

I thought about what he'd said after he left. The fellow who won the lottery was lucky, all right. But so am I—and so are you. If you live in the USA, if you're getting enough to eat and have no chronic diseases, you're already luckier than most of the humans who've ever walked this earth. That's what I call Luck.

Some elements of Luck, I'll admit, you can't control. Rich parents, for example. There's nothing you can do about them. Either you're born rich or you aren't. The trick about random elements of Luck like rich parents or winning lottery tickets is not to waste your effort worrying about them. Or your *lack* of them.

Instead, concentrate your efforts on managing the elements of Luck you *can* control. There's an old saying that Luck is the residue of design. My father had his own version: "The harder you work, the luckier you get." In most cases, working nine-to-five means you aren't working hard enough. Those aren't Stars' hours. Stars work until the work is done. They never watch the clock.

The Hardest Working Men in Show Business

Show Business is two words: "Show" and "Business." All that happens in front of the camera is the "show," and all that transpires behind it is the "business." My buddies have always teased me that James Brown is the hardest working man in "Show" Business, but that I am the hardest working man in Show "Business."

I've accepted that title and ceremonial cape because I can't imagine anyone working any harder than me. Some may work smarter, or may even have more talent or a better team, but it would be impossible to work any harder ... and be alive to talk about it. Working as hard as I have, and do, is probably what has made me so lucky.

As a producer, one is always trying to convince a studio or network that you have the next great idea for a project. Then, you have to convince someone to finance it. In essence, you are always pitching. It really is simply begging. I've accepted it as a way of life. When I go into Giorgio Armani to buy a suit, I just tell them to take out the shoulder pads and put them where my knees are. Then, when I crawl into the buyer's office in my $2,000 Armani suit, I will look good and have no knee bruises.

Working hard is Luck. Being prepared is Luck. Being available is Luck. Remember: You can't get hit by lightning if you're not standing out in the rain.

You can learn to be lucky, which we will examine in the book. Chance occurrences you cannot control. You can pray for them, however.

The Power of the Elements

What's the right mix of these Four Elements? You may have more of one than the other. Strengths in one area may compensate for weaknesses in others. If you have a lot of rage, that's a pretty good start. If you've got the greatest team in the world, maybe you don't have to be a child prodigy. Or, if you have enormous talent, perhaps you don't need as much rage as someone who is less blessed in the talent department. Of course, you may not have all four of these elements in the beginning of your journey to Stardom.

If you do have all of these elements in place—Talent, Rage, Team, and Luck—you're well on your way to being a Superstar.

Tiger Woods is an example of someone who has all four of the elements locked in. Bruce Springsteen is another. Now, Anna Nicole Smith, on the other hand, is someone who's had some rage and luck and has managed to put together a team—but some might argue about the talent. And Pauly Shore—team definitely, luck probably, but talent and rage?

Becoming Your Own First Fan

Now that you know what a Star is, and you even know the four secrets to Stardom, you need to sign up as the president of your own fan club. Above all else, you must believe in yourself. That is the first step toward convincing others to believe in you. You have to believe you are deserving of Stardom and success. You have to believe so hard that you can endure *Adversity* and failure. You must have *Confidence*. You have to have a call to action.

Stars stay on deck even when everyone else is abandoning their ship. They remain steadfast and exude total self-confidence.

There's nothing like it. And it's always been that way. The report on Fred Astaire's first screen test read: "Can't act. Slightly bald. Also dances."[1] Obviously, with a start like that, Astaire had to believe in himself pretty strongly. And, just as obviously, there was a time when he was just about the only one who did.

In 1954, Elvis Presley was kicked out of the Grand Ole Opry with the recommendation that he go back to driving a truck. Well, he eventually did drive other trucks—his own, cash-filled, armored, Brink's trucks!

Jim Carrey became his own first fan performing in Toronto comedy clubs at the age of 15. During this time, things became difficult when his father lost his job and the family found themselves working as night janitors in order to survive. Disillusioned, but determined to retain his sense of humor and filled with a raging desire to succeed, Jim dropped out of school at 16 to pursue a full-time career in entertainment. He believed in himself. He was so convinced that he would be successful, he wrote himself a check, which he dated 1995, for $10 million. He said that one day he was going to get paid $10 million to star in a movie. Two days before his father's death, he signed a $10 million contract to do a film. He placed the old check in his father's coffin as a sign of his belief in himself and his success. That's what I call becoming your own first fan.

BELIEVE IN YOURSELF

Understand, accept, and embrace *who you are*. Do not dwell on who or what *you are not*. Develop who and what *you are* and *be the best YOU*.

There's no one more likely to be a Star than someone who doesn't fit in with the crowd. Remember, "fitting in" isn't a requirement for Stardom. Most Hollywood Stars I've worked with, in fact, talk of feeling awkward and out of it in school. Always remember: *It's hard to stand out while fitting in*. It's true that feeling "different" isn't always comfortable, especially in your teen years. But people don't go to movies to watch "average." They don't buy concert tickets to hear "typical." I'm here to tell you: Different does Hollywood! And Different can, and will, work for you.

Throughout this book, I've included stories about people from all walks of life whose *differences* once seemed like disadvantages but became their claims to Stardom!

ADVERSITY

Just as the pilot on a commercial flight prepares his passengers by telling them there could be turbulence ahead, I'm warning you that your ride to Stardom will be bumpy. So strap yourself in. You will face adversity that can make you bitter or better—there's just a one-letter difference between the two.

Whether you're determined to be a Star in Hollywood, Harlem, or Highland Park, you can expect challenges along the way. That's a given. Your success is determined not by what happens, but by how you handle it.

You must learn to transform your adversities into opportunities. The truly enlightened computer geeks in school who lack social skills don't sit around moping about not being invited to the Friday night beer bust. Instead, they spend their evening perfecting knowledge of new technology in order to eventually create new software and start their own Microsoft Company. Their efforts will inevitably afford them the ability to buy all the beer or beer distributorships they desire. New friends will also show up.

Make the very best of your adversities. If all you have is a lemon, don't make lemonade. Instead, throw away the lemon and spend your energy finding an orange to make orange juice. It tastes better and has a larger commercial appeal.

Dann, a law school classmate of mine, put himself through school by selling cookware door-to-door. If you've ever sold anything door-to-door, you know what a tough job it can be. Many of the most successful business people in the country started out this way, and nearly all of them will tell you that it is great training. You've got to develop real people skills and real selling skills to make it in that business.

Dann's job was made even tougher by the fact that the cookware company had sent him a defective sample skillet. The handle was broken. He continued to request another sample skillet, but the company failed to send him another. That broken frying pan was going to make it pretty hard for him to impress housewives with how durable his line of merchandise was.

So Dann decided to confront the matter head-on. "Do you know how *popular* this cookware is?" he'd ask prospective customers. "We have so many people ordering it that—well, look at this. Look at this sample. Damaged in shipping. I have been trying to get a replacement for this sample for *six weeks,* and they keep telling me that there are just no extras in stock, that every one is being shipped to a customer. Do you think they'd let a salesman walk around with a defective sample if people weren't ordering the stuff so fast that they can't keep it in stock?"

It didn't work *every* time; no sales pitch does. But it worked often enough. With his positive attitude, Dann was able to put himself through school and graduate with a little money in the bank.

Dann made a difference—a *disadvantage*—work for him. Others have done it too, and so can you.

REMEMBER ...

You don't have to be perfect to be a Star—Oprah Winfrey.

Oprah has struggled with her weight over the years and she has often talked of challenges in other aspects of her life. Her intelligence, humanity, and empathy have made her one of the most beloved and inspirational people on the planet.

You don't have to be tall *to be a Star—Danny DeVito.*
Danny became a major Star because his tremendous talent and drive towered over his diminutive size. He may be short, but he's a powerhouse.

You don't have to be beautiful *to be a Star—Howard Stern.*
This guy has a face made for radio. He captured one of radio's largest audiences after his years of struggling and failure. He often refers to his homely looks—which just may be part of his appeal, as most people do not have movie Star looks and can identify with him.

You don't have to be outstanding *to be a Star—Julia Roberts.*
". . . growing up, I didn't excel at anything," Julia told an interviewer. "I wasn't particularly scholarly, I wasn't particularly athletic, I wasn't particularly attractive. I was sort of just very average and mediocre. I didn't have anything to claim for myself, to say: *This is what I am—I am the student, I am the athlete.* I didn't have a claim to stake."[2]

Okay, so if you don't have to be thin, tall, beautiful, or outstanding, what do you need to be? What do you need to have?

Confidence!

Just imagine how different your life could be if

- You could feel good about yourself all of the time.
- You felt comfortable saying no to people.
- You could talk in front of people without feeling silly or nervous.
- You could control that negative voice in your head.
- You could communicate with confidence.
- You had the confidence to change careers.
- You didn't let what other people said to you get you down.
- You could act, walk, and talk with assurance.
- You were never afraid of failure.

When you have an aura of self-confidence, you attract attention. Before long, others start seeing you the way you want them to see you. And increasing your self-confidence doesn't have to be an agonizingly long and painful process.

When Cyndi Lauper was just a conventionally pretty girl (and she is very pretty, by the way), nobody ever heard of her. Then she got the inspired idea to dye her hair and start dressing like a hipster bag lady. Actually, I never thought it would work, but it did. The important thing was that Cyndi *thought* it would work, and it did—because she had confidence in it.

There are as many ways to be a Star as there are Stars in the universe, but with confidence, the basic elements of Talent, Rage, Team, and Luck will allow you to create your own personal map to Stardom.

The first element for us to explore in depth is Talent.

CHAPTER 2

TALENT

Kelly Clarkson wanted to be a marine biologist; instead, this 20-year-old Texan, who had never had a formal singing lesson, captured hearts across the country and was voted American Idol in 2002 in front of 30 million television viewers. Now, she has sold millions of CDs and performed around the world because she tapped into her Talent and the opportunities it provided her.

As a young girl, Kelly's singing voice had been such a natural and normal part of her life that it never occurred to her that she had a special Talent she could build her life around. The enormity and beauty of her voice was recognized quite by accident when a teacher heard the 13-year-old Kelly singing in the hallways at Pauline Hughes Middle School in Burleson, Texas, and encouraged her to join the choir. She then found her niche.

America loves to discover people with Talent. Talent shows have a long history on American television. Before *American Idol* there were many talent shows on television, including the original *Star Search*, on which I appeared as a judge in its first season. Selecting a winner in a talent competition is an awesome task. You have to carefully balance your responsibility to truthfully assess the contestants' abilities with compassion for their feelings. While you need to be totally honest with the hopeful contestant, you also don't want to be a dream-buster.

The three judges on *American Idol*—Randy Jackson, Paula Abdul, and Simon Cowell—each have different styles of expressing their opinions, but they all share equally the wish to discover the next true Star. The brutal honesty of Simon Cowell's opinions infuriates some people, but his final judgments of the actual Talent are very respected, at least among people in the entertainment industry. He constantly raises the bar on what America expects from an Idol. America, so far, has discovered three talented idols in Kelly Clarkson, Ruben Studdard, and the emotional Fantasia Barrino.

Television talent shows generally look for random people with "artistic" Talent like singing or dancing because they believe, as programmers, it makes for better entertainment than searching for the world's most talented scientists and watching them stare down microscopes in search of a cancer cure. Yet, while the talents of accountants, doctors, lawyers, plumbers, marketing executives, secretaries, firemen, or teachers may not draw television audiences, they are no less appreciated by those they serve.

The real world has a much broader and more diverse definition of Talent. In fact, the world has a huge appetite for Talents of all kinds. There are endless opportunities awaiting you once you've identified your Talent. You can find fulfillment and a rewarding career whether you are a good corporate manager, a planning wizard, or a home designer. And while most people don't get to express their Talents to cheering crowds, there is perhaps no greater definition of happiness than the full expression of your Talents on a daily basis. For every Talent, there are limitless possibilities.

There are many Talents that are highly valued and amply compensated even if they are rarely celebrated. Just ask anyone who's ever needed a plumber or an air-conditioning repairman quickly … or a trustworthy babysitter.

America's top corporations look for organizational skills, visionary leadership, creative problem solving, and conflict mediation and resolution abilities that are true Talents but not the sort that win applause and cheers. People with an entrepreneurial Talent for spotting business opportunities, being project managers, having great marketing ideas and acting upon them, are among the most valued human resources in our country and around the world.

Even television has finally come to recognize that Talent isn't only about singing and dancing, as witnessed by NBC's new reality hit *The Apprentice*. Donald "You're Fired" Trump has now broken ground by hosting a Talent show to discover people like you and me, who can't sing and dance, but have Talents in the other areas. If his candidates show an innate ability to be a project manager, they can stay for another week. If one of the hopefuls is a natural-born salesperson and can sell Trump's water or lemonade, they hold on for another week. Each contestant evidences Talent in some areas of the assigned weekly task. In the first season it all got down to 29-year-old New York investment manager Kwame Jackson and 32-year-old Chicago cigar entrepreneur Bill Rancic. In a close race, Bill ultimately evidenced the most Talent and promise. He was awarded the Trump job and the title "The Apprentice."

Some people believe that they don't have Talent. I don't accept that. Everybody has Talent.

Muhammad Ali was loaded with Talent, not only in boxing but also in making people notice him.

What Is Talent?

For the purpose of being truly fulfilled and to attain Stardom, I define Talent as "an innate ability or aptitude for doing anything consistently well that opens your life to opportunities."

Your Talents are gifts from God or a genetic accident at birth, depending on your belief system.

People often confuse an "ability" or a "skill" with a "Talent." They are all different, and it is very important to know the difference. "Ability" is a quality that allows you to perform a task. (I can play golf.) A "skill" is an ability that has been acquired by training. (I can get skilled at golf.) A "Talent" is an "innate" ability. (No matter how skilled I become, I will never be a Tiger Woods.) Likewise, let's evaluate three different lawyers. One has the "ability" to practice law. (She graduated law school and passed the bar.) Another is a "skilled" lawyer. (She has been practicing for a while.) And the third is a "talented" lawyer. (She could eventually become a Supreme Court Justice.)

It is so important that you understand these distinctions if you truly want to attain Stardom. If in your career you have chosen to spend your valuable time working hard at something you only have an ability to do, then no matter how hard you work at it, you will only achieve a certain level of skill. Yet, if you were to spend the same effort, or maybe even less, at something you had a Talent for, you could potentially soar to Stardom. Without underlying Talent, learning a skill is simply surviving, not an opportunity to reach your full potential.

Ask yourself:

- Are you doing things that "please you," or things that "pay you"?
- Are you following "your bliss" or merely "your opportunities"?
- Are you using the Talents you have been given or have you buried them under your fear?
- Are you being "efficient" with your life or "effective"? (Being efficient means doing things right. Being effective means doing the right things.)
- If you let your spirit out, where would it take you?
- Are you still growing? Or are you just growing older?

People who have matched their Talents with their career are often heard saying, "I can't believe I'm actually getting paid to do this. If they only knew how much I enjoyed it, I would have to pay them." I don't mean to get carried away here, but you get my drift. You can only become truly fulfilled and successful when you are doing what you love. In order to put in the long hours, meet the challenges, rebound from the setbacks, and to "keep holdin' on," which success requires, you have to be working in an arena where you are expressing your inner self.

But by the way, I'm not suggesting, as I mentioned earlier, that just because I don't have a Talent to play golf, I should not continue to become skilled at it and enjoy it. Golfers like to joke, "Golf is like sex. You don't have to be good at it to enjoy it." I am saying, however, I will never be a Star golfer. It's my recreation. My Stardom lies in putting my efforts where my Talent is.

Not only are you special, but you are also *gifted*. If you know this and you know exactly what your Talent is, we will put it to use. If you don't know what your Talent is, I will help you find it, even if we have to dig, scrape, and peel away layers of insecurities and denial. It's not always easy to find the Star within.

Four Keys to Unlock Your Talents

What Talents have you taken for granted, failed to develop, undervalued, or overlooked? What personal value lies within you waiting to be unlocked, developed, and offered to the world?

If you're happy with who you are and what you're doing—good. If you want to become a different you or find a new direction—also good! There are many reasons for identifying your personal Star qualities or Talents, but one of the most important is that it focuses your life. It gives you a positive direction, and as far as I can tell, there is nothing that makes for a happier life than expressing and developing your Talents.

Many of you may have already identified and developed your Talents, matched them to opportunities, and are enjoying a certain level of fulfillment. You now wish to understand how to either discover additional Talents you may have or to more fully understand those you already are employing, in order to build on them. Others may either still believe they have no Talent or that they don't know how to find the ones they do have. In either case I want to offer you four keys to unlock the sources of your Talent. They will help you identify, appreciate, and develop all the talents I know you have within you.

I want you to investigate various things about yourself using the four following keys. I've named them simply:

- Learn
- Yearn
- Burn
- Discern

LEARN

Has there ever been a time when you tried to learn something entirely new and it just came naturally to you? Sometimes this happens to people, and they'll joke that they must have done it in a previous life. Or you'll take to a new task so easily that someone will accuse you of lying about your level of experience or of cheating. Several of my writer friends in Hollywood have similar stories of their grade school or junior high English teachers accusing them of copying compositions from books, magazines, or other sources because their writing talents were so superior to their classmates.

If you've ever had the experience of mastering a task or a topic or a concept faster than your peers, it could be that there is a Talent calling out to you, waiting to be unleashed and developed.

If you easily grasp math problems that leave other people cursing their calculators, your Talent is trying to tell you something. Were you the girl in class that everyone looked to when it came time to organizing the homecoming events, the senior prom, or a class trip? Were you the guy who drew funny caricatures of the teachers in art class? Did other kids come to you for help with science questions?

Think about the things that came easier to you than your friends and examine what talents were at play.

YEARN

Think in terms of your yearnings. The things you always gravitate toward often are related to and rooted in a natural ability or Talent. It's usually a consistent pattern in your life, and it's a stronger pull than a simple way to pass the time or leisure activity. If you could do anything you wanted all day long, what would it be? Are you drawn to athletics? Movies? Building things? Fixing cars? Training pets? Collecting stamps? Hunting? Riding horses? Taking care of children or the elderly? Listening to music? Playing an instrument? Solving problems? Putting things in order? What do you naturally seek to do? It doesn't have to be something you were obsessed with or "possessed" by, although that's a strong indicator of a Talent at work.

Are you an avid reader? Your "hidden" Talent may be writing or editing, or your interest in books may lead you to a career in library science, publishing, or retail book sales. Do you find yourself entranced by airplanes, jets, blimps, and helicopters? It could be that your Talent is an "inclination toward aviation," which opens up a sky full of opportunities in careers that include pilots, mechanics, air cargo, air traffic controller, airline administration, and travel industry jobs.

What if you had a number of things that interested you but didn't seem to indicate any particular Talent? Let's say your interests seem to be unrelated and a little "out there," like astronomy, film photography, and science fiction.

Steven Spielberg grew up in Arizona and California with an engineer father who was an amateur astronomer and a science fiction fan. As a boy, Steven shared those interests with his dad but he developed his own special fascination with the family movie camera. Spielberg's father would wake him up in the wee hours of the night and drive him to the desert to watch meteor showers and comets streaking across the night sky.

Spielberg made his first home movies at the age of 10, and he completed his first fictional sci-fi film at the age of 17. He was rejected by the top film schools, but driven by his Talent. Four years later he finished another amateur film, *Amblin*, which earned him a directing contract at Universal Studios. His unique blend of interests fueled a Talent that gave Spielberg the opportunity to become the youngest filmmaker ever contracted by a major studio.

BURN

What gives you a burning sense of fulfillment and makes you just plain happy? Do you remember playing a game as a child and losing track of all time and place? Have you had a similar experience of getting totally lost in an enjoyable task as an adult? When your mind, body, and spirit are all fully engaged at the same time, it's called *flow*, according to psychologist Mihaly Csikszentmihalyi. In his study of creativity, he reports that what most people define as "happiness" is the sense of fulfillment and contentment that occurs when we express our talents in our daily lives. He and others believe that the happiest people are those who enjoy what they do so much that they "get lost" in the flow of it. When people experience flow, they often keep doing it until they are exhausted and beyond. They don't want to stop, and then they can't wait to get back to the task.

For athletic people, getting lost in the flow of an activity often happens while playing a sport. For computer whizzes, it can happen when they are writing software. Painters, writers, actors, carpenters, hairdressers, accountants, lawyers, and nurses even talk about getting into the flow of their work. In this state, you become so focused on the opportunity to use your talents that your brain wave patterns are similar to those during the most restful dreams.

Think about any activity that engages you so completely; examine the possibility that your Talent may lay within it.

DISCERN

Do people compliment you on some ability or behavior? Have your friends always commented on something about you, something at which you excel? (She's really organized. He gets people motivated. She has great taste in clothes. He's funny.) Have family members bragged about your abilities to do certain things? (You should hear her sing! Kids love him. She's the best gymnast in her school.)

Has your boss valued a Talent that you've demonstrated? (Great marketing ideas, unflappable under pressure, wonderful sales skills, a team player.) Can you discern these kinds of comments from serious, objective observations? Maybe these people know something about you that you don't.

Your natural skills manifest themselves in many ways, but sometimes you take them for granted. Just as Kelly Clarkson didn't realize on her own that her singing voice was remarkable, and it took a teacher to point it out, many people don't recognize their own talents until someone else does. Reflect on your life from childhood to the present. What innate abilities did people recognize in you that you took for granted? Did your childhood friends marvel at your ability to do crossword puzzles or word games? Did the other girls in your high school always ask you to help them with their hair and makeup?

What natural attributes attracted people to you, distinguished you, or provided focus for you? Were you the girl that others relied on when they were having troubles with boyfriends? Did they ask you what they should wear to parties? What natural talents and interests were at work there? Think.

What types of people are drawn to you?

What sort of people did you hang out with? You can bet that Jim Carrey, Eddie Murphy, Martin Lawrence, Jay Leno, Ellen DeGeneres, and Margaret Cho were the class clowns who attracted other future comedians and people who enjoyed looking at the funny side of things.

Steve Jobs was an electronics geek before most kids his age knew software from softball, and many of his fellow geeks in suburban Santa Clara Valley, California, including "Woz"—Steve Wozniak—became his business partners as adults. Jobs and Woz, who were members of the Homebrew Computer Club in high school, brewed up the Apple computer and made the world a safe and very comfortable place for generations of geeks who followed.

Your Talent is just one part of the whole package for Stardom, but it is a very important part. By identifying it, developing it, and finding opportunities to apply it, you can reach some of the highest levels of fulfillment. When people feel unsettled, disconnected, stuck, or directionless, it is often because they aren't making good use of their natural abilities. They are like solar panels that aren't getting sunlight. They have all this potential power and energy that they can't unleash. No wonder they feel uneasy.

Pitfalls

Now that we have unlocked ways to let your Talents shine and energize your life, I want to warn you about two pitfalls that can prevent that from happening.

PITFALL 1: WORKING ON WEAKNESS

One of the most common mistakes people make is that instead of identifying their talents and developing them, they focus on their weaknesses instead. Too often people think, "If only I can get better at this I'll have more to offer." That may be true to a small degree, but your greatest opportunities for growth are to build on your natural talents and abilities. If you are lousy in math, studying algebra and geometry and calculus and psychics may help you become competent, but it's doubtful that you will ever rise to the level of a great or even good mathematician. More important, you'll probably never find personal fulfillment and joy in mathematics if it is not something that comes naturally to you.

So once you've learned enough math to balance your checkbook and do other basic calculations, why waste your time on a weakness? Instead, why not look for those natural abilities that give you joy, and then develop them to the highest possible levels? Why dream of being a singer if you can't carry a tune? Why not accept and embrace the talents you have and build your life around them? People who try to make themselves perfect by focusing on their failings live in constant fear. But those who soar on their strengths become fearless.

Mark Twain noted: "We are always more anxious to be distinguished for a Talent which we do not possess than to be praised for the 15 which we do possess."[1]

PITFALL 2: FALSE BEGINNINGS

Be wary of considering things that your parents pushed you into, or any activities that you did simply because somebody else wanted you to do them.

I've seen this situation many times in Hollywood. The first indication is usually when two people show up in my office. The first is the "Talent." The second is a stage mother, stage father, or a "manager" boyfriend or girlfriend. Sometimes, the "talent" person really does have the whole package: a gift, the dream, and the inner drive and desire to be a Star in Hollywood. But far more often it is the parents, or the boyfriend or girlfriend, who have the dream and the drive for them. And when that is the case, I generally tell them that I've got no interest in representing them.

People often have great difficulty facing the truth about themselves. Who we truly are is often different than who we've learned to be in order to survive or to please others. Psychologists call this the difference between the "authentic" and "fictional" selves. Often, we define ourselves according to how others see us or because of the roles that we've accepted (fictional selves), rather than who we really are (authentic selves).

Imagine yourself tagging along to a party given by a friend of your coworker Charlie. The hostess doesn't know you, so when she turns to you and says, "Who are you?" how do you respond?

"I work with Charlie."

That explains to the hostess why you are in her house with Charlie, but it doesn't really define *you* very well, does it? If she questions you further, what would you say to more clearly define yourself?

"I'm Charlie's assistant in the marketing department."

That's a little better, yet it still defines you in the narrow terms of your relationship with Charlie and your job. People often define themselves entirely in terms of their relationship with someone else, or what they do to earn a paycheck, or where they live, or who their parents, brothers, sisters, or grandparents are. In some situations that's fine for establishing context, but it is not acceptable when you are trying to become a Star in your own world.

To be a Star, you must define *yourself* in terms of the potential value you bring to the world and your dreams for doing it. If you define yourself too narrowly or only in the context of your job, your role, or your relationships, then you may never know yourself well enough to identify, develop, and fulfill your talents!

I've known many, many successful people who have built great lives in spite of the limitations of their circumstances, including their birthplaces, their family situations, their financial status, or their physical problems. The only true limits we have are the ones we place upon ourselves when we accept a narrow vision of what is possible for us.

You are more than a job description, or a relationship definition, or a social status. You are a unique package of gifts, talents, skills, knowledge, loves, hates, beauties, fears, flaws, faults, and foibles. To be a Star, you first have to be able to declare who you truly are as defined by that package of characteristics.

Don't let anyone else define you. And don't define yourself according to the expectations, demands, dreams, or limitations forced upon you by someone else.

List Your Talents

By now you should have in mind the Talents you already knew you had, if any, and the Talents you have now unlocked. I want you to list those special qualities. They are the foundation from which we will build your life as a Star.

Take your time. When you're finished, you'll know more about who you are. Don't leave this section until you have listed all the things you and other people like about you and what makes you uniquely "You." Use the keys discussed above: Learn, Yearn, Burn, and Discern.

When I have people in my seminars write down their Talents, some complain that there isn't enough space. Others can't think of a thing to write. I'll tell you what I tell them: "This is no time for modesty! The rest of your life depends on your being honest in assessing your true talents and gifts. Blow your own horn!"

YOUR ASSIGNMENT

List Your Talents

_____

_____

_____

_____

_____

_____

_____

_____

_____

_____

So what did you put down? That you can sew? Sing? Dance? Type? Run fast? Hack computers? Strategize? Invent? That you love to travel? Write? Ski? Bike? Golf? Speak in public? Tell jokes? Help others? These are your special qualities, your Talents. Now, how do you build on them? How do you match those Talents with your opportunities?

Matching Talent to Opportunities

Once a Talent within you is identified and appreciated, it will whisper in your ear every day, "Feed me. Feed me." You need to nourish it with opportunities.

Your Talent will guide you to the opportunities it needs. It has a strong survival sense. You will soon develop an "opportunity habit," and this is exciting and fulfilling. If you have unlocked a Talent for graphic design, you soon will be amazed at how many magazines about design will start to stare you in the face. You never saw them before. Everybody you meet will either be in the graphic design business or know someone in it. As your Talent pushes you, a whole new world will open up for you. If your Talent is not appreciated, no opportunities will appear or be needed.

Too often people have a limited view of where their appreciated talents can push them. Your Talent is never what limits you. It's only a shortsighted *vision* of the possibilities and opportunities you have for your Talent that will be limiting.

You say, "I'm only good at one thing, shopping." Or, "The only thing I can do is cook." Or you say both. So the question is: What can you do with those talents?

So, you can only shop? So, you can only cook? I have two words for you: *Martha Stewart*.

Long before she had enough money to buy or sell ImClone Systems stock, an unknown Martha Stewart was a housewife and home caterer in Westport, Connecticut. While shopping, she noticed a few fancy food products that were selling well in the New England area. She bought a selection of them, placed them in frilly baskets, and sold them from a little shop in a mall called The Market Basket. While running the shop, she had an opportunity to write a book titled *Entertaining*. The book became successful and launched a career. And the woman who could only shop and cook built an empire on her Talents.

Martha Stewart simply had a Talent for appreciating the small, beautiful things in life and the ability to talk and write about them. She made her fortune by creating opportunities and turning a private pastime into a profession. She became the czarina of arts and crafts, whether that meant gilding an Easter egg or assembling a perfect pie.

Martha identified what she was good at and then charted her course. Her life offers many lessons, both good and bad. We'll look at the bad a little later. But say what you want about her, it cannot be denied that Martha Stewart made the most of her talents and opportunities. She became a Star of the shopping and cooking circuit. She matched her talents to her opportunities.

Here's another example: This fellow, who became famous for his ability to see opportunities and act on them, grew up in a high-rise apartment building in Flushing, New York. He lived in a one-bedroom apartment with his parents, who ran a dry cleaning shop.

The most exciting thing in Flushing was the airport across the street, where the Goodyear blimp was kept in a hangar. This boy hung out in the hangar and became a "blimp rat." He helped the Goodyear blimp pilot and crew every day. At first they didn't pay him, but they did answer all of his questions, and this young boy had a very good mind so he asked a lot of questions.

Eventually they did pay him, and then, after he'd gone to college and earned a business degree, he began paying them. He hired the Goodyear pilot and several crew members to work for him in an aviation business that he started as part of a class project in college.

"Little Lou," as they first called him, had learned so much about the aviation business that he launched the world's biggest helicopter taxi service in New York City at the age of 22. Later, he became one of the country's largest leasers of commercial blimps to companies all over the world, including Budweiser and MetLife. He also started a business that sold partnerships in commercial jets that were then leased to airlines around the world.

Lou Pearlman had so much success using his Talent for aviation that he had time to "dabble" in another interest—pop music. He'd had a band when he was a teenager and always wanted to get back into music, so he helped recruit, train, and finance a couple more bands with the money he made in aviation. Those bands were the Backstreet Boys and *NSYNC.

He made millions, and some say billions, just taking his natural talents and interests and turning them into highly profitable business opportunities.

There is no doubt that Lou Pearlman is a very smart guy, and his timing was perfect when it came to launching his boy bands. But who is to say that you can't do just as well by exploring the opportunities and possibilities that your talents and interests open up for you?

Keep an open mind because there are bound to be more applications and possibilities for expressing your talents than you might first imagine.

TALENT	OPPORTUNITIES
Sewing	Fashion design/Upholsterer/Tailor
Chemistry	Brewer/Medical research/Anesthesiologist
Artistic	Illustrator/Collage artist/Graphic designer
Mechanical	Engineer/Machine shop owner/NASA
Athletic	Coach/Trainer/Sports marketing
Math whiz	Accountant/Casino manager/Actuary
Writer	Journalist/Author/Editor
People person	Salesman/Retailer/Real estate agent
Debate	Lawyer/Politician/Judge
Storyteller	Director/Screenwriter/TV commercials
Computer whiz	Software designer/Programmer/Technician
Musician	Studio musician/Songwriter/Instructor
Care giver	Hospice worker/Nurse/Day care operator
Finances	Banker/Investment adviser/Stock trader
Animals	Veterinarian/Pet importer/Dog trainer
Organizer	Convention or wedding planner/Closet maker
Building	Architect/Carpenter/Cabinet maker
Woodsman	Hunting guide/Park ranger/Camp owner
Pilot	Airline pilot/Military pilot/Aircraft test pilot
Nautical	Fisherman/Tour boat operator/Cruise pilot
Natural leader	CEO/Managing editor/Army general

You Are the Star

Now that you have unlocked your Talents and they are officially ready for development and opportunities, how do you build a fun, fulfilling, and rewarding life around them?

To determine where to start with your talents, it might help to know where you want to go. To determine where you want to go with your talents, it might help to begin at the end: I want you to write your obituary. My obituary? That's right—your obituary!

I can hear you squirming: "Gosh, he just got me excited and now he wants me dead!" Not dead ... *focused*.

Focused on your future as a Star. If you don't like to think of this as writing your obituary, think of it as doing a search on Mapquest.com. That's the wonderful Web site where you can get directions for anywhere you want to go. You start by typing in your destination. Then you're asked to type where you want to start. That's what this exercise does. In life, as on Mapquest, to figure out how to get to a place, you first have to know where it is you want to go. What's your life destination and what part did your Talents play in it?

In your obituary, I want you to list five or more special qualities and five or more accomplishments for which you'd like to be remembered. You were generous? You climbed a mountain? You won awards in your profession? You married a heart specialist? You became a millionaire at 26? You were the CEO of a public company? You had three daughters? You raised money for children's charities? You graduated from the Culinary Institute of America? Your paintings were known for their beautiful sunsets? You won the American League batting title in 2010?

As an inspiration, here's a look at Frank Sinatra's remarkable life:

Francis Albert Sinatra, the legendary entertainer and premier romantic balladeer of American popular music who dominated the spotlight of musical Superstardom longer than any performer before him, died of a heart attack on Thursday, May 14, 1998, in Los Angeles California. He was 82.

Adored by millions, "Ol' Blue Eyes" was a self-styled saloon singer whose masterful interpretation and flawless execution of some of America's most beloved songs earned him a reputation as the most influential popular singer of the twentieth century. He refused to compromise in life. He lived it on his own terms. His trademark song was "My Way."

Born in Hoboken, New Jersey, on December 12, 1915, the son of Italian immigrants, Natalie ("Dolly") and Martin Sinatra, he was a 13-pound baby. The birth was difficult. His left earlobe was torn off and forceps scarred his throat; the doctor thought him stillborn. His grandmother, Rosa Garavanti, picked up the newborn and shoved him under cold running water until he began to choke and cry—and eventually breathe.

Sinatra's father, Martin, was a boxer and member of the fire department. His mother, Dolly, was a nurse who became a power in local Democratic politics. Raised in a rough neighborhood, Frank soon learned the art of street survival. What he learned and with whom he learned it stayed with him throughout his life and earned him a bad boy reputation.

In 1933, Sinatra went to hear America's crooner, Bing Crosby, and left the theater, determined to be a singer but not a Crosby copy-cat, rather a bel canto Italian singer. He picked up what jobs he could, including a short stint as a singing waiter. In 1935, as a member of a vocal quartet, he won the Major Bowes Amateur Hour competition.

By 1939 he was singing with bandleader Harry James for $65 a week, but soon joined trombonist Tommy Dorsey. Observing Dorsey, he realized that Dorsey played snatching quick breaths through the side of his mouth, and he vowed to learn to play his voice like an instrument. He began swimming and running to improve his lungs, and learned to breathe in the middle of a note without breaking it. He was the first popular singer to use breathing for dramatic effect, and he learned to use a microphone to enhance his voice.

By the end of 1941, Sinatra had replaced the legendary Crosby at the top of the Downbeat poll. He broke from the Dorsey band in 1942 and, with a series of concerts at New York's Paramount Theater, burst into the nation's awareness in a way that was not matched until the arrival of Elvis Presley in the fifties, the Beatles in the sixties, and later Michael Jackson.

His popularity had waned by the early fifties, and he had to fight hard to be cast in the soon-to-be classic film, From Here to Eternity (1953), *as Maggio, a cocky, streetwise Italian-American soldier who is beaten to death by the villainous Ernest Borgnine. In a dramatic career comeback, his performance won him an Oscar for best supporting actor.*

In the 1950s, he formed the "Rat Pack" with Dean Martin, Sammy Davis, Jr., Joey Bishop, and Peter Lawford and spent his time jetting between Las Vegas, Los Angeles, and New York's Copacabana club. As the proclaimed "Chairman Of the Board," he made almost as much news offstage as on. Through his Rat Pack and alleged organized crime associations, he was a cultural phenomenon who endured setbacks and scandals to eventually become a White House intimate.

In more than 200 albums, his music led the evolution from Big Band to vocal American music. His hairline receded and his waist thickened over the years, but Sinatra's light baritone only grew deeper and richer. His signature songs included "I'll Never Smile Again," "Night and Day," "Young at Heart," "One for My Baby," "How About You?" "Day by Day," "I've Got You Under My Skin," "Old Man River," "New York, New York," "Come Fly with Me," "Strangers in the Night," "That's Life," and, with daughter Nancy, "Somethin' Stupid," a number-one smash during the rock era.

His movie credits include musicals, such as Anchors Aweigh, On the Town, Guys and Dolls, The Tender Trap, High Society, *and* Pal Joey*—and more serious fare, such as* The Manchurian Candidate, Von Ryan's Express, *and* The Man with the Golden Arm, *which brought him another Oscar nomination.*

Always charitable in a quiet way, he received the Kennedy Center honor in 1983 and was awarded the Medal of Freedom by his friend President Ronald Reagan in 1985.

Sinatra married four times. His first wife, Nancy Barbato, his teenage sweetheart, bore him three children. After 13 years of marriage, he left her and, in 1951, he married Ava Gardner, one of Hollywood's biggest stars. The tumultuous marriage did not last, and in 1966 he married a young actress named Mia Farrow—

another relationship that ended quickly. She was 21 at the time, and he was 51. In 1976, at the age of 60, he fell in love once more, marrying Barbara Marx. They were married for 22 years.

In his last few years, Sinatra retired to his home in California, where Barbara and his children, Tina, Nancy, and Frank, Jr., formed a caring vigilance around him. Sinatra's family, including his wife, was with him when he died.

Sinatra was no saint. But no one can deny that he lived a full life by developing his Talents and expressing them every day. I don't recommend that your Team should include questionable characters, or that you put yourself through three divorces, but I do suggest that you pursue life as enthusiastically and fearlessly as Sinatra did.

Writing your obituary will be a very positive, inspirational, goal-setting exercise for you. It will help you further identify your Talents, who you want to become, what you want to accomplish, and by when. You can plan your life. You can set goals. Let your heart and imagination soar. Don't limit yourself. Plan a grand and fulfilled life. Do this now.

YOUR ASSIGNMENT: WRITE YOUR OBITUARY

Information to include:

1. Name
2. Accomplishments
3. Life statistics
4. Parents
5. Career
6. Education
7. Charitable and political activities
8. Military service
9. Awards and fellowships
10. Professional memberships
11. Religion
12. Marriage
13. Children

_____

_____

_____

_____

_____

_____

_____

_____

_____

_____

_____

_____

By listing your Talents and projecting your life, have you learned a little about yourself? Can you better see who you are? How others see you? What you want to accomplish? How you want to feel about yourself? How you want to be remembered?

Theodore Roosevelt once said, "Far better it is to dare mighty things, to win glorious triumphs, even though checkered by failure, than to take rank with those poor spirits who neither enjoy much nor suffer much, because they live in the gray twilight that knows not victory nor defeat."[2]

Talent License

Your success in accomplishing all you have scripted for yourself in your obituary requires that you have the confidence to go out on the world stage and do it. You will need a Talent license for this journey. These licenses fall into four classes: the BBD, the VST, the BMT, and the C.T. All successful careers belong to holders of one or more of these licenses.

The BBD license is a Bachelor of Brilliance Degree. Most exceptional industry executives (Viacom's Sumner Redstone, former GE chairman Jack Welch, News Corp's Rupert Murdoch, and Intel's Andrew Grove) hold one of these. So does _A Brief History in Time_ author, Stephen Hawking. Being smart will still get you a long way in business. Look at Microsoft's Bill Gates, who maintained his technology brilliance while building one of the most successful companies in the world. And he didn't even finish college. When all is said and done, being smart is a lot better than being dumb.

The VST license is a Very Special Talent, the kind that people will stand in line to see: Jim Carrey, Robin Williams, Jack Black, Will Smith, Tiger Woods, Celine Dion, and Emeril Lagasse. A lot of successful people have had VSTs. You're issued your VST license at birth, but it expires if you don't work hard to keep it current.

The BMT license is a Better Mousetrap, an innovation that people want badly enough to pay for it. The mousetrap in question can be the automobile, the Apple computer, George Foreman's hamburger grill, Microsoft Windows, Pokemon, Ron Popeil's Showtime Rotisserie ("Just Set It and Forget It!")—or a movie, like *The Matrix*, that everyone wants to see. "But everything has already been invented," you say? Well, let's not forget Jeffrey Bezos, who as recently as 1994 moved to Seattle and decided to sell books on the Internet. He named his new company "Amazon.com." He is now referred to as the "King of Cyber Commerce." If Bezos gets it right, one day he will truly own Earth's Biggest Store.

Another Better Mousetrap is illustrated in the story of the origin of Liquid Paper. Originally called "Mistake Out," it was the invention of Bette Nesmith Graham, a Dallas secretary and single mother. Her young son, Michael Nesmith, was later to become famous as a talented singer in the group known as The Monkees.

As a secretary, Bette was used to making typing errors. As an amateur artist, she was used to manipulating inks and paints to create her original paintings. So, combining her experiences, Bette sought a better way to correct her typing errors. She painted over her artistic mistakes on canvas, so why couldn't she paint over her secretarial mistakes on paper?

She used her own kitchen blender to mix up the first batch of her tempera water-based paint concoction. She took it, along with her watercolor brush, to the office to paint over her typing mistakes.

She created the color of the liquid substance to match the stationery. Her boss never noticed. Very soon, another secretary saw the new invention and asked for some of the miraculous, correcting fluid. Bette found a green bottle at home, wrote "Mistake Out" on a label, and gave it to her friend. The word spread fast and soon all the secretaries in the building wanted some too.

From her North Dallas home in 1956, Bette Nesmith Graham started the Mistake Out Company. It would later be renamed Liquid

Paper. She remodeled her kitchen into a laboratory and started mixing up her secretarial product with her electric mixer.

Bette's son, Michael, and his buddies helped out by filling bottles for her customers. She made little money despite everyone working nights and weekends to fill orders. Then one day, disguised as failure, opportunity knocked.

Bette made a mistake at work that even "Mistake Out" couldn't fix. Her boss fired her. She now had time to devote to selling her invention, and business was great. By 1967 it had grown into a million-dollar business, and in 1968 she moved out of her kitchen into her own plant and corporate headquarters. She gave her son and his friends a rest, and hired 19 employees. That year she made a lot of secretaries happy in that she sold one million bottles.

In 1975, Bette moved Liquid Paper into a 35,000-square-foot international headquarters building in Dallas and started producing 500 bottles a minute. The following year, the Liquid Paper Corporation turned out 25 million bottles. Happy bosses contributed to the company's net earnings of $1.5 million.

Bette believed in people and what they could accomplish. She created two foundations to help women find new ways to improve themselves and earn a living. Bette Graham Smith died in 1980, six months after selling Liquid Paper Corporation for $47.5 million. Her life, product and success were "No Mistake."

The C.T. license, or Combination Thereof, is the one everyone wants. A C.T. puts you on the road to Superstardom. A Star is prominent in one entertainment field—say, records or television. A Superstar can move between entertainment media with ease, and can even use a new medium to revive a career when popularity in an old medium is fading.

Barbra Streisand crossed over from stage and recordings to movies. Jennifer Lopez has certainly crossed over from music to movies. There are scores of other television actors, pop performers, and theater performers who've found rejuvenation in the movies, in concerts, and on stage in Vegas. You also can make crossovers of careers in your life with multiple talents

So think about what license you have or want to acquire. I want you to have a safe and prosperous journey on the road to success, fellow travelers. May you reach each and every goal you set, and may your goals be as lofty as your Talents can soar. Where there is Talent and a will, there's a way.

You now know your Talents and your destination. But how badly do you want to go there? How badly do you want to be a Star? Do you have ambition? Do you have passion?

Do you have a Rage for Stardom?

CHAPTER 3
RAGE

Anyone who truly desires to become a Star in his or her own life must possess, or develop, a true sense of "Rage." This Star element is simply an absolute, tunnel vision, maniacal focus on fulfillment and success. Beyond the vagueness of wanting, hoping, wishing, planning, and even passion, presides the certainty of Rage.

Rage is more than knowing what you are passionate about. It is one click beyond mere passion and desire. It is total, head-first commitment every minute of every day. It is what distinguishes the Superstars from the "get alongs" and the modest achievers.

The motivational form of Rage that I'm referring to is not fueled by anger, hatred, revenge, or any negative force. In fact, it has the power to turn those negative feelings into positive action. Motivational Rage is powered by optimism, the belief that nothing can hold you back or stop you, and that when negative events occur, you have the power to turn them into positive energy.

Rage knows no fear. Those who truly have it never, ever give up because failure is not an option. It blocks off all choices. It propels you out of your comfort zone and off the edge in a flying leap without a net.

Academy Award winner Mel Gibson personifies my definition of Rage. In his recent controversial box office phenomena we witnessed *The Passion of the Christ* and The Rage of Mel Gibson. His deep conviction to tell his story allowed him not to simply make a movie the traditional way, but to single-handedly force it into existence. Though people's opinions may differ about the movie itself, most acknowledge and applaud his unwavering belief and commitment to its creation.

When no major studio in Hollywood wanted to finance his script or even distribute the finished movie that he totally financed, he pushed onward. His efforts were ultimately rewarded. It's this level of continuous commitment that you need to be a Superstar.

When you examine Mel's career closely, you realize that his Rage to succeed didn't start with this movie. In 1995 he struggled against conventional wisdom to portray William Wallace, a Scottish common man who fought for his country's freedom from English rule. For this epic *Braveheart*, Gibson won an Academy Award for producing as well as directing.

Nice work, Mel.

Another example of someone who embodies Rage is Ericka Dunlap. Ericka was taunted by the other girls in the halls of Boone High School in Orlando, Florida. "Er ... ic ... ka—Miss A ... mer ... i ... ca!" they'd whine at her, making fun of her for participating in beauty pageants.

Ericka's mother gave her a beauty pageant booklet to read at bedtime when she was six years old. It triggered something in the little girl who was the youngest of five children. She stayed up half the night looking at the pictures and reading about the contestants. Within two years she'd won her first pageant. She won 60 of them through grade school, high school, and college, collecting 1,100 trophies along the way.

And in the fall of 2003, after singing "If I Could" onstage in Atlantic City, New Jersey, Ericka Dunlap, 21, was crowned Miss America 2004 and won $50,000 in scholarship money, on top of the $16,000 she'd already been given for winning the Miss Florida title.

"Ha, Ha, Ha, I *am* Miss America!" she laughingly told her high school taunters when a reporter asked her about her journey.

That was just before she set off to meet with Katie Couric, Regis Philbin and Kelly Ripa, David Letterman, Greta Van Susteren, and Carson Daly. On her schedule there was also a trip to Planet Hollywood, where a pair of her shoes would be enshrined alongside other celebrity memorabilia.

Nobody was taunting Miss America, Ericka Dunlap, anymore. Her raging passion to achieve her goal had carried her to the crown.

Do You Have a Raging Desire to Be a Star?

Mel Gibson, Ericka Dunlap, and others with Rage make any and all fallback positions nonexistent. You can't say, "Well, I'm going to go to that school, or to that city, or to that job, for six months, and if it doesn't work out, I'll return home." If you truly believe you can retreat to less than you desire, that you can stop trying, that you can accept failure, that you can spend the rest of your life existing instead of living, then you lack the level of passion and commitment I call Rage.

You can't get to the edge of your destiny, look down, look back up, start to think about it, and begin to rationalize it all. You have to imagine yourself as Butch Cassidy and your Rage as the Sundance Kid. You have to grab each other, and while screaming as loud as you can, jump together into the abyss. Damn, if that ain't living.

The most talented, driven Stars I have worked with had no real options in case of failure. They couldn't go back to work at the Gap or become accountants. They were not looking for a job or a career; they were being called to their vocation. It was almost like being called to the priesthood or sisterhood. They had to act, to perform, and to succeed. These are the people I worked with and witnessed their becoming Stars.

Barry White was a Talent who chose not to sit around and wait for the door of opportunity to open for him. He went out in 1972, found the door, and knocked it down. Fortunately for me, it was my door.

Jim Barton, a music publishing executive and artist in his own right, had told Barry about me. At the time, I was a young partner in the hot entertainment law firm of Thompson, Shankman, Bond, and Moss. I returned from lunch one day to find this very large, African-American man sitting on the floor in our reception room. He didn't have an appointment. He was just waiting on me. He spoke in a gentle rumble, but I could sense his passion. He wanted five minutes of my time.

He was wearing a gray tattered overcoat and black bedroom slippers. He had nothing on underneath. He had no money. He had a tape of himself singing songs that he had written and produced. He told me he had heard I was the best music lawyer in town, and he only wanted the best. He wanted me to get him a record deal.

He told me he had no car. He had walked from South Central Los Angeles to my Sunset Boulevard office. On the way, he stopped at a grocery store, stole a barbecue chicken, and ate it.

I told him that I would listen to his tape, but that our law firm policy was to have a $500 retainer to open a file and get started. He said, "The only valuable thing I have is this tape. You hold it. I want you to be my lawyer. I'll be back with $500."

Three days later he walked back to my office with five, wadded-up, $100 bills.

"Now, be my lawyer," he said.

By then I had listened to his tape, and my spine was still reverberating. He had created a whole new sound. His voice was aural sex, melodious and deeper than a blue lagoon. Barry White, the Love Maestro, was in full bloom and booming, "I've got so much to give … to you, my dear. It's gonna take a lifetime … It's gonna take years and years."[1]

I took the tape to Russ Regan, who was president of 20th Century Records. He listened but wasn't quite sure. During the company's Christmas party, Elton John heard it being played in Russ's office and asked, "Who's that? He's great." Russ made a deal with me immediately, and Barry White was ready to rumble!

I represented Barry for over a decade, first as his lawyer and later as his manager. He, along with the female singing group Love Unlimited and the Love Unlimited Orchestra, which he created, began to churn out a string of hits that made him one of the most successful artists of the seventies. Songs such as "Can't Get Enough of Your Love, Babe," "I'm Never Gonna Give You Up," and "You're the First, the Last, My Everything," established Barry White and Love Unlimited as the groundbreaking music of choice for many a romantic evening.

No one had more Rage and Talent than "the Maestro," Barry White.

I had fun traveling with Barry, who performed all over the world. He started the whole disco sound, and we opened just about every disco in Europe, the Far East, and South America.

Barry passed away July 4, 2003, and for me and my former law partner and dearest friend, Ned Shankman, who continued to guide Barry's career long after me, "It was the day the music died."

Barry White had true Rage. Most people get fed up and leave before the door of opportunity opens. Will you? Will your Rage hold you over while waiting for it to open? Or will you create your own door of opportunity and knock it down like Barry White?

Aristotle said, "We are what we repeatedly do. Excellence, then, is not an act, but a habit."[2] Those who become Stars in their chosen fields have developed their raging commitment to express their talents fully into an active habit. They habitually strive, push, and seek solutions—all in their drive to develop their talents to their highest use.

The Snowball Motivation Theory

Let your desire to make the most of your talents and to build your life around them fuel your Rage, which in turn will focus your inner motivation into a habit that fuels your success. I refer to this as the Snowball Motivation Theory.

Stand on top of a snow-covered mountain and start to make a snowball of desire. Put it on the ground and start pushing and rolling it downhill. It gathers a mass of snow and momentum as it rolls, and it gets bigger and bigger, rolling faster and faster. One day, like Indiana Jones being chased by a fast-rolling boulder, you find yourself running down the hill in front of the giant, fast-rolling snowball. That's how you get motivated to become an overachiever.

My mother's urging me to get out of town and make something of myself started me packing and pushing that snowball. A couple of other things helped too.

I fell madly in love with Lou Ann Hartgraves in the ninth grade. Her mother, Elsie, was a war widow who taught school and wanted the best for her daughter. In her eyes, I, unfortunately, was not the best. I didn't make the grade. She didn't want Lou Ann to get serious about me. It also didn't help that my family was Italian. In the Deep South at that time, Italians ranked ninth on the Top 10 List of the Social Registry. As I recall, boll weevils were sixth and Yankees were seventh.

Elsie was a Daughter of the American Revolution. That made her number one on the list. She did everything but slash my tires, but Lou Ann and I dated on and off all through high school and some in college. The relationship eventually collapsed under the weight of Elsie's continued pressure and Lou Ann's love and respect for her mother, which I admire to this day. It was painful for me, but motivating. Between Elsie and my own mother, I was one motivated guy.

Sadly, because of Elsie and others like her, I also was embarrassed to be Italian at that point in my youth. I told my father while fishing with him one day that I was embarrassed to have his name, "Angelo," as my middle name. He straightened me out real good with a lecture and an Italian whipping.

So, with my mother's pushing, Elsie Hartgraves's humiliation of me, and my unwarranted shame of my heritage, I started pushing that snowball. I got good at it. I created a huge snowball. And sure enough, one day I somehow woke up running in front of it. Being chased by your own ambition is one hell of a sprint. Of course, I fell down. It rolled over me that night in New York while I was sitting with Donna Mills in the Broadway play *Cats*. Hell, it was the catalyst for my epiphany.

By the way, being the proud Italian that I am and have been since that day my father "enlightened" me, I usually refer to myself as Larry A. Thompson.

So, that's the story of my early motivation. What about yours?

What Is Your Motivation?

Actors draw upon experiences, emotions, and events, good and bad, in their lives to enhance their portrayals of characters in movies, on stage, and on television. When you hear an actor say, "I went inside myself for that role," that is what they mean. They tapped into something within them. Different things motivate different people. How are you going to use your Rage to become a Star and keep the fires burning so you can overcome the challenges and fears and competition you will face along the way?

Rage:

- Keeps your mind alert to possibilities and opportunities
- Works like high octane caffeine to boost your performance
- Inspires you to look for a new path each time one is blocked
- Attracts like-minded, positive people who buy into your dreams
- Propels you into action and keeps you from getting stuck

The desire for wealth, stature, power, knowledge, happiness, joy, fulfillment, respect, and recognition are among the primary things people use to drive their Rage.

I can't tell you which to choose. Only you know what will work for you. The primary drivers listed above can play out in many forms, and even the negatives can be used to drive positive Rage. For example, if you have been hurt or slighted by a boss or coworker, put your anger to a positive use as a performance enhancer. Don't get even—get better. Michael Jordan was known for his ability to do that. In his NBA career, opposing teams learned not to make him angry because it only drove him to turn up the level of his performance even higher. Jordan's positive use of Rage didn't just make him an All-Star, it made him a legend.

Take a few minutes and write down potential events or feelings in your life, both good and bad, that can be put to positive use to motivate you and deepen your commitment to the full expression of your talents. Write down at least five of them:

1. _____

2. _____

3. _____

4. _____

5. _____

Getting Your Motivation

To find your motivation, you have to study your lines and their meaning just as an actor does. But in your case, your "lines" are the internal dialogue that plays out in your mind constantly. Let's study those lines and see if perhaps they need to be rewritten.

SELF-DEFEATING INNER DIALOGUE	STAR-QUALITY INNER DIALOGUE
Other people have held me back.	I take responsibility for my Stardom.
I've screwed up my life.	It's taken me until now to believe in myself.
There's so much work to do.	This is my dream and it's worth it.
I'll never be a Star of any kind.	If I keep the Rage burning, I'll make it.
Getting started is so hard.	This is the most exciting thing!

I'm a disaster!	I'm going to show the world!
I want to be an overnight Star!	Step by step, I'm going to make it!
My friends think I've changed.	If they are friends, they'll believe in my dream and me!

Do you see how just changing the conversations you have with yourself can motivate you and fire up your Rage to be a Star? You've got to get control of your inner motivation and take responsibility for your own success. Consider your Rage an invaluable weapon against mediocrity.

Great achievers understand that success inevitably comes to those who persevere. Learn from the people who did it: Let perseverance keep your goals alive and your dreams real.

In all my years in the entertainment business, those who have the longest and most respected careers are those whose lifelong motivation is to honor their gifts by developing them to their highest level and sharing them with the world. I've known many who have attained wealth and power only to realize after years spent acquiring it that those are rewards that come with striving, not goals to be attained. Greed is like a hungry dog that, after eating everything in sight, begins to chew on its own paws. It is never satisfied, and in the end, it is always destructive. Those who seek to develop their gifts and express them at the highest level are the most fulfilled at the end of their careers.

Stardom Is Not an Accident

Stardom is not a job you apply for. If it were, there'd be high school and college courses you could take on Stardom, perhaps even a B.A. Star program.

Stars become Stars because they have a Rage for Stardom.

Are success and fulfillment something you want or something you need? Need is a substantially better motivator. What level of need do you have? Do you have a drive, an ambition, a passion, or a Rage? A drive will motivate you to move to L.A. An ambition will get you an agent. A passion will get you an acting job. A Rage will make you a Star!

Do you have a RAGE to succeed? Your competition does!!! Stars identify their talents, develop them, and dedicate themselves to expressing and building their lives around them. They are driven every day to find a new way to make happen whatever they need that day.

You have to want it, need it, breathe it, eat it, dream it, pray for it, work at it, sacrifice for it, beg for it, get it.

Stars *are* different from other folks. They're aimed in one direction, and they're running in that direction as hard as they can. They're driven, like human Hondas. Stars are rarely all-around people.

Focus Your Rage

Once you have identified your Talent and decided how you want to express it and build your life around it, you have to develop a raging commitment and focus for doing that. Rage is focus and commitment to the tenth power. To make sure you have the intense focus necessary, I want you to think again about your own unique dream of Stardom and home in on it.

Define *exactly* what it is that you want to do to fully express your talents and build a life around. If you don't define exactly what you want, you'll never know when you've got it, right? So don't be wishy-washy. Don't say "Well, I'd sort of like to." Or, "I might, maybe, could … " One of the major reasons people never get what they want from their talents is because they don't precisely *identify* what they want. Only you can decide what it is that will make you happy and fulfilled and a Star in your chosen field. It is vital that you claim it not only as your goal, but also as your raging right. The more well-defined your goal for Stardom, the stronger your Rage will be.

Be aggressive and demanding of yourself and your talents, but be realistic too. Aim for as high as your level and combination of Talents and experience will take you. And always—always—practice integrity in expressing them.

Realistically assess your level of preparation and qualifications in relation to your age and responsibilities but don't aim too low either. If owning your own business is how you wish to express your Talents and create a fulfilling life, don't be afraid to start small and build as the opportunities present themselves. Remember, your goal shouldn't be to acquire the trappings of success like a mansion or a Ferrari. It should be to *feel* successful by expressing your Talents fully and with integrity.

Here are some questions to help you hone in on *exactly* what it'll take to make you a Star. If you can't answer these questions, then your level of Rage isn't what it needs to be. These are questions that should wake you up at night, keep you standing in the shower too long, and run through your head every mile you drive, walk, or run:

- What will your job title be when you get it?
- What will your income level be?
- Where will you live?
- How will your professional peers regard you?
- What will your workplace look like?
- What sort of awards or recognition will you have earned?

There is so much Talent in Hollywood that in many cases, Rage and drive and passion are the determining factors to becoming a Star. There are so many handsome men and beautiful women, so many talented actors and actresses, so many people who can sing and dance and play their instruments beautifully, that in most casting calls or job interviews, the individual's level of desire is critical. I've also seen a newly stoked passion, or desire, or Rage, elevate someone from a mediocre and plodding career right to the top of everyone's must-have list.

You may not realize that one of the biggest Stars today, George Clooney, spent years and years knocking around Hollywood as a journeyman actor, doing one failed television pilot or series after another. I've followed George's career because his publicist, Stan Rosenfield, who is one of the top publicists in the entertainment business, is a friend of mine. My wife and I tease Stan, who also represents Robert De Niro, Danny DeVito, Will Smith, Kelsey Grammer, and many other Stars, because in nearly every photograph or red carpet interview of George Clooney, you see Stan in the background. He's like Clooney's shadow. Stan has an easy time promoting George today, but it wasn't always so easy.

George was 33 years old before he had his first hit television series with *ER*. He'd had *eight* previous shows! One of his best buddies, Brad Pitt, beat him out for the role in *Thelma and Louise*, which was a small part, but it made Brad a Star. George thought he had that role locked up, but he didn't get it. At that point he'd been an actor for 14 years. After Brad got the part, George was dejected, but instead of giving up, he turned up his level of Rage and aimed for a higher level of performance. George realized then that if he were to move beyond the "pretty boy" roles, he would have to bring more to the table.

He'd always had natural charisma because of his charm and good looks, but he had never devoted himself to working at his craft with integrity. When George landed the *ER* role, he put more into his character than he ever had before. He didn't just take the scripts as they were handed to him. He fought to give his character a dark side and an edge. He went deeper inside himself than he'd ever gone and tapped into emotions and rebelliousness for his portrayal. As a result, his Dr. Ross wasn't your typical television portrayal of a saintly physician. He became *ER*'s bad boy, but one who loved children and small animals, not to mention nurses and other female staff members. George pushed the envelope offscreen too. He convinced the rest of the cast and crew to do a daring live episode that garnered great ratings, even if the critics didn't get it. Some said it failed, but George's drive and daring made him a hot property.

That's another interesting thing about expressing your talents. Powerful people tend to buy into others who are focused and driven. Suddenly, Hollywood was raining scripts and projects down upon the guy who did eight failed television series. George didn't sell out his talents. He continued to push himself to take challenging roles. He didn't always succeed, but he did something that was far more important. He kept stretching. He made romantic comedies and thrillers. He did a very dark *Batman* and he returned to television— again, this guy is fearless—to make a live black-and-white version of a 1960s political drama, *Fail Safe*.

Again, it drew great ratings, though the critics didn't get it. But George Clooney intrigued them, and everyone else. He was in the flow. His Talent and his Rage make for an irresistible force. Even if critics don't embrace his projects, they admire his daring and, to put it bluntly, his guts.

"Clooney, now 41, sticks his neck out on projects that big studios aren't putting down $100 million to make. He finds freedom and flexibility in films with lower budgets," wrote a film critic.[3]

George is now making $20 million for his "big" movies, and he formed Section Eight, a production company, with another daring soul, director Steven Soderbergh. Their HBO series *K Street* and their movies, including *Insomnia* and *Solaris* (the latter an ambitious remake of a highly intellectual Russian science fiction film by Andrei Tarkovsky), are the talk of the entertainment industry. And even if they fail, George Clooney isn't worried.

"If my films go wrong, at least the mistakes are from my taste. I'd really be pissed off if I made the movies everyone in Hollywood told me to make and they ended up bombing," he told one interviewer. "If we succeed, it's going to be a hell of a show," he told another. "If we fail, people will let us know."[4]

Most Stars will tell you that they've *always* been Stars; it's just taken the public 10 or 20 years to catch on. Meanwhile, they've spent their time doing more than telling their friends they were going to become Stars. They've worked hard and acted continuously as though they were Stars already.

The Stages of Rage

To keep your Rage burning, you need to keep in mind that at different stages in your career and life, you will need different forms of motivation, but you will ALWAYS need to stay motivated.

Stage One: The Aspiring Star

Here, you're acquiring knowledge and building experience in your chosen field, so you need a slow-burning motivational Rage tempered with patience. You want to be prepared for the opportunities that are coming, so you keep the Rage on at low to mid-range. At this stage you look to move forward in incremental stages, but you should aim to make each step a little longer or higher or bigger than the one before it. It's good to "keep the end in mind," but if you begin to feel overwhelmed, you can restoke the fires of your Rage by accomplishing smaller goals and moving forward step by step until the momentum swings your way again.

STAGE TWO: THE YOUNG GUN

In this stage, you turn up the heat of your Rage by demanding more of yourself and by looking for opportunities while still honing your unique package of talents and building knowledge. You're still proving yourself, but at this point you shouldn't be afraid to stretch and reach beyond your grasp as long as you stay humble and grateful for opportunities.

STAGE THREE: THE HOT PROPERTY

Now, your Talents are in full bloom and widely recognized. Your Rage should be on full burn as you not only welcome opportunities, but also aggressively work to create them for yourself. In this stage you should begin to think about expanding beyond the limits you set for yourself. For people in the entertainment business, this is when singers look for acting roles, actors look for directing jobs, and directors create their own movie production companies. Push the envelope, resist all limitations, and break through barriers in this stage of Rage.

STAGE FOUR: STARDOM

This is where you begin to collect the rewards of your motivational Rage: the recognition, awards, honors, and material success. It is a wonderful time, but a dangerous one as well because at this stage of Rage you need to turn the flames even higher. Don't rest on your laurels. Set new goals, seek new challenges and motivate yourself to set the bar higher and higher by testing the limits of your Talents and seeing how high they can take you. One more thing, in this stage your Rage should begin to fuel efforts to reach out to others and give back.

STAGE FIVE: MASTERY

At this final stage, your Rage should be driven by the desire to share the rewards of your knowledge and experience by elevating others and contributing to the development of your "art," whether it is acting, fashion, architecture, or landscape work. Your Rage here is still burning but it is directed at leaving your part of the world a better place.

The Power of Rage

In 1987, 22-year-old Eileen Twain's world was shattered by tragedy when both of her parents were killed in a car crash. Returning home from Toronto to take care of her four younger siblings, she began supporting the household by singing and dancing locally in Ontario's Deerhurst Resort. Determined to be a Star, she soon moved the family to Nashville, and as both a tribute to her adoptive father's memory and as an announcement to the recording industry of her commitment to success, she changed her name to Shania Twain, which, in the language of her adoptive father's Ojibway Indian tribe, translates to the phrase: "I'm on my way." She had set her goal and nothing was going to stop her.

Shania won the 1999 Grammy Award for Best Female Vocal Country Performance for "Man! I Feel Like a Woman!" and the 1999 Grammy Award for Best Country Song, "Come On Over." She has been nominated nine times for a Country Music Association Award and won Entertainer of the Year in 1999. *Come On Over* is the biggest selling album ever by a female artist and the sixth biggest selling album of all time, equaling *Back in Black* by AC/DC and *With the Beatles* by the Beatles. Shania has received 22 BMI songwriting awards.

Seven Ways to Positively Focus Your Rage

1. Take Responsibility and Control

When you go after your dream of Stardom with determination and drive, you'll pick up momentum from others who buy into your dream, just as I bought into that of Barry White and other clients. But you will also encounter resistance from people who feel threatened, jealous, or cast aside by your new sense of purpose. Your "old ways" weren't getting you where you wanted to go, and your old friends and old habits may well have been part of the problem. To become the Star performer you want to be, you may have to assert control, take responsibility, and develop more positive relationships with people who have the same passion and Rage.

2. Get Healthy, Physically and Mentally

Taking control and accepting responsibility for your own success also means that you work on both your mental and physical fitness.

Medical researchers are finding mounting evidence that those two aspects of your overall health are more connected than previously recognized. Scientists have discovered that people with optimistic and positive approaches to life live longer, healthier lives. Those who suffer from depression and negative thinking, on the other hand, are at higher risk for heart disease and similar illnesses. If you reduce the stress in your life by taking a positive path, you'll reduce health risks, and if you work to stay healthy by exercising and staying active, you'll improve your attitude.

3. GET RAGINGLY REAL

Dr. Phil McGraw isn't just being a showboat when he tells the guests on his show to "Get real!" He's a psychologist, so he knows the value of putting your emotional baggage in storage and looking at things as they *truly* are. Not the way you *wish* they were, or the way you *perceive* them based on some event in your past, or the way other people with their own biases tell you *they* see them.

We thrive or fail based on the decisions *we* make. If *you* decide to let your mother run your life, *you* pay the consequences. If *you* decide to go along with what your friends want to do, you can't blame them down the road. The blame is yours to bear.

In the same manner, you can't base the decisions you make on tainted information. Nor can you allow other people or a committee of friends and family to make your decisions for you. That's a formula for disaster. It can be very helpful, however, to find someone who has followed a similar path to Stardom in your chosen field and ask them for advice. But you should always understand the biases and viewpoints of any source.

4. CLEAN HOUSE ON BAD HABITS

You'll need a new path to Stardom if your old ways aren't working. You can't keep doing the same old things. That means you have to clean house and dump your old bad habits. If you tend to stay up late and sleep in, dump that habit, except if you happen to work the night shift. If your hanging-out friends are stuck in dead-end jobs and don't care, you'd better look for a more goal-oriented crowd or they'll drag you down too.

How do you tap into your Rage and use it to dump habits that are holding you back? You rewrite your inner dialogue. You learn to measure every action in terms of your goals for that minute, hour, day, month, and year. If you reach over to hit the Snooze button because your inner dialogue says, "I just need another half hour of sleep," you need to rewrite that dialogue. Tell yourself instead: "I've got things to accomplish today."

Learn to consciously listen to the habitual inner dialogue that limits your performance and progress. Rewrite it. Put the new, motivating dialogue down on paper and make it a habit instead. Remember, to change your life, you have to change the patterns of behavior that have held you back.

5. Adjust Your Attitude

Your attitudes develop from the way you've learned to see the world, the conscious or unconscious assumptions you make every minute of the day. Your reactions are based on your unique interpretations of past experiences. You and I might have the same experience, but we often interpret things quite differently. If an acquaintance walks past without saying hello, one of us might interpret it as a snub or rudeness, while the other might think she is preoccupied or having personal troubles or is in a hurry to get somewhere.

Our attitudes spring from our interpretations of events. We generally feel that the way we view things is the way they really are, but in truth, most human beings aren't that objective. You and I are more likely to view things that happen not as they are but as *we* are. That's part of being human. Two people can see the same car accident happen but have entirely different interpretations of what occurred and why. (That basic fact of life keeps many lawyers in business.)

To change attitudes that have not been working for you and develop new attitudes that fire up your Rage and commitment, you need to adjust your assumptions, perceptions, and interpretations. Again, it is a matter of listening to your inner dialogues and eliminating the aspects of it that lead to self-defeating attitudes.

Here are things to listen for and eliminate:

- Blaming others for your mistakes
- Complaining
- Exaggerating problems or challenges

- Playing the victim
- Focusing on past problems
- Fretting over what might happen
- Worrying about things beyond your control
- Venting anger in destructive actions
- Trying to stop the competition
- Ignoring your weaknesses
- Making money your goal
- Holding grudges
- Labeling yourself as a loser
- Becoming overwhelmed
- Being self-pitying

Here are some ways to build a more positive attitude:

- Accept responsibility for your own success
- Deal with challenges as they come
- Work on solutions, not problems
- Know what your competition is doing, then do it better
- Build on your strengths
- Concentrate only on the things you can control
- Eat healthy and exercise daily
- Dress as though you've already made it
- Focus on small achievements first and build on them
- Let go of hard feelings, practice forgiveness instead

6. MAKE A LEAP

To become a Star, you may have to make a leap that involves a great risk. I see this all the time when people give up full-time jobs or leave friends and family behind and move to Hollywood, Nashville, or New York City to chase their dreams in the entertainment industry.

Jake Steinfeld of Body By Jake made that leap. He dropped out of college and moved to Los Angeles so he could pursue his dream of becoming a competitive bodybuilder. He'd pumped iron, and pumped himself up into a powerful physical specimen. It was his dream to be Mr. America.

But as it turned out, once Jake saw that in those days the top bodybuilders were heavy steroid users, he abandoned that particular goal. But he didn't give up on Stardom. Jake worked in movies and television, but he really achieved Stardom as the creator of the fitness trainer industry in Hollywood. Then he went on to develop his own line of fitness products, a 24-hour fitness network, and a global business empire that has made him a very wealthy man.

Jake was my fitness trainer early in his career, but while he was pumping me up, he was also pumping me for information about the entertainment business. He is a great motivator and is also one of the most motivated people I've ever known. Jake has the Rage. He told me that he was a chunky kid with a stutter until he discovered how to take control of his life through bodybuilding.

From the moment I met him at that first workout at my home, I knew this guy had something going for him. For almost 10 years he worked me out three times a week: Mondays, Wednesdays, and Fridays at 7:00 A.M. Boy, did I hate to hear that doorbell ring. But as painful as all those workouts were, it was truly enjoyable to talk with him about his dreams. It was great to see a young man who was so full of Rage. I've known few people who have had the level of Rage that Jake did. You knew this talkative, bodybuilding machine was going to be a Star. He was going to do whatever it took.

In a 35-minute workout, not only did Jake talk to me, motivate me, and train me, but he'd tell me his life story three times and ask my professional opinion about 90 things. By the time he left, I was physically and emotionally drained. But I love him. He's done some great work for a lot of people. So have his brothers, Pete and Andrew. Jake represents the word Rage.

You may not have to move to a place where greater opportunities exist, or press 250 pounds to be successful, but you may have to take a leap of some kind to be a Star in your own chosen field. Maybe you'll have to quit your job and go back to school.

7. CHANGE, CHANGE, CHANGE

Unless you were born into Stardom or fell into it at an early age, the only way you'll become a Star in your own right is to welcome and seek change constantly. I'm not referring to changing partners or cars. It's more a matter of adapting to changing circumstances by changing your approach. You see actors—at least the successful ones—do it all the time when their careers hit a wall.

Change isn't something to fear or resist. If you get a new boss, you'll either have to find a new job or adjust to her or his new ways. Accept that and deal with it. Keep in mind, it's not about kowtowing to the boss or giving up power; it's about moving toward your own goals. Monitor your inner dialogue; be aware of your interpretations, assumptions, and perceptions. Develop more positive habitual patterns that channel negative energy in a positive way. Take that path rather than resisting, complaining, or sticking with your old strategies. Understand that change is part of life, and that if you are going to build a successful and fulfilling life, you have to change.

You can't get to the edge of your destiny, look down, look back up, start to think about it, and begin to rationalize that you don't really *have* to be a Star. You've got to go into this doubt-free and fired up. To change your life for the better, to control your destiny and shine at whatever you do, you need to develop powerful inner dialogues that keep you moving forward, whatever stumbling blocks and challenges you face.

Why You're Not Already a Star

One of the pitfalls you'll encounter as you work toward Stardom in your chosen field is the "unfairness syndrome." You keep working hard and sacrificing, and after a while you begin to feel, "*It's just not fair* that I have to work and sacrifice this hard to get what I want when others get it without doing anything!" And of course, you're right. It's *not* fair that you have to work overtime and put off buying a new car so you can save your money and invest it in the business you plan to start. If you'd been born a Hilton, like Paris and Nicky, you wouldn't have to worry about this stuff. But you weren't, and you do, and when you come right down to it, not much about life really *is* fair. The problem begins when we use our outrage against the unfairness of it all to block ourselves from going out and doing what we really want to do.

Instead, you should sit down with a piece of paper and a pen and make a list of everything in your life that isn't fair. (Better make that *two* pieces of paper.) When you've finished, go down the list and put a check next to all the unfair things that will be rectified by your being outraged about them. You should spend five minutes a day fretting over each inequity that your fretting will actually help you fix. I promise, you won't waste a minute fretting.

You may not like to hear what is about to follow, but it is the truth and you need to face it if you're going to claim a better life.

It's Your Own Fault You're Not a Star!

Nobody else is to blame. Your parents are not to blame. Your teachers are not to blame. The circumstances you were born into or thrown into are not to blame. I'm sure you can cite all sorts of compelling reasons why you are not living your passion right now. And for every reason you cite, I can tell you about a bona fide Star who overcame that obstacle and six others to attain the heights you dream of.

- Was poverty a problem for you?
- Did you come from a broken family?
- Were you abused as a child?
- Were you oppressed as a minority?
- Did you fail early in your career?
- Are you overweight?

I can name a dozen Stars who faced each of the above challenges and overcame them, or I can name just one who overcame *all* of them. How's Oprah work for you? She dealt with every one of those challenges. She overcame them and became one of the wealthiest, most admired, and most successful women on the planet. She didn't make excuses. She didn't play the victim. She didn't blame anyone for her setbacks and circumstances. She just pursued her dreams with a passionate Rage.

So what's really holding *you* back?

Just you!

To fire up your Rage and get you moving toward your starring role, you'll need to abandon bad habits, rid yourself of negative influences, and shed distorted perceptions based on what may or may not have happened to you in the past. You will need to drop all of the woulda's, coulda's, and shoulda's that drag you into living back in your past. Instead, you'll need to power up with a new internal language that is focused on the here and now and the future life you are building, instead of the one you're leaving.

Your beliefs, perceptions, emotions, and internal dialogues can either send you soaring like a Star or drag you down. If you keep telling yourself that you don't have any particular Talent, that you'll never be motivated enough, that you'll never be a standout in anything you do—well, you will live down to that low expectation. But if you turn off the negative self-talk and reprogram your internal dialogues, turn on the passion and Rage, and convince yourself that nothing can stop your Stardom, then you will live up to that sky-high expectation.

The Rewards and Risk of Rage

Rage can push you to the top of the mountain, and if it's not monitored, it can push you over the cliff. It can set you up for success, and if it's not controlled, it can doom you to failure. There is only one requirement to minimize its dangers: common sense.

While I'll admit that in today's scandal-ridden world, common sense is not as common as it used to be, you must maintain it in order to balance the risk-reward ratio that Rage embodies. How do you know if you have common sense? If you have to ask, you don't have it. I'm sure you do.

We will cover the dangers in detail in Chapter 8.

Peak to Peak

I am a member of the Grand Havana Club, a private club in Beverly Hills for cigar smokers. A lot of Stars, celebrities, and entertainment industry leaders belong to the club. In fact, Mel Gibson's private humidor, with his name engraved on it, is next to mine. I see him in the club from time to time, but I run into Arnold Schwarzenegger more often at both the Grand Havana Club and at Café Roma, which has an outdoor cigar-smoking patio. Arnold is another example of a driven, passionate man who has attained incredible heights and never stops climbing.

Arnold always drives up in his huge Hummer, and though he is larger than life both literally and figuratively, he's also a very warm guy, and very smart too. I've come to respect him and to understand that he is a man to be taken seriously.

Growing up in a small Austrian village, the boy who would be dubbed "the Austrian Oak" dreamed of becoming a bodybuilder. Arnold was first introduced to weightlifting during a soccer team field trip to a local gym in Graz. After watching the dedicated bodybuilders there, he was fascinated with the sport.

But his father felt differently. Bodybuilding was not a popular sport in Austria, and he forbade his son from going to the gym to work out more than three times a week. Undaunted, and dedicated to bodybuilding, Arnold made a gym at home so he could continue his sport, and broke a window at the gym in town so he could get in on Sundays. Conditions there were so harsh that more than once his hands froze to the weight bars because there wasn't adequate heat. In time, Arnold transformed himself from a skinny boy into a champion bodybuilder, winning the Mr. Universe title five times and Mr. Olympia seven times.

Once he achieved international acclaim as a performing bodybuilder, he decided to start another career as a performing actor. And there he also succeeded and gathered honors. Arnold has been twice honored in the form of Golden Globe wins for *Stay Hungry* and a nomination for 1994's *Junior*. But no one doubts where his true Talent lies: The man can put fannies in the seats. Among his über-successful films are *The Terminator, Terminator 2: Judgment Day, Terminator 3: Rise of the Machines, Twins, Kindergarten Cop, Jingle All the Way, The Running Man, Total Recall, True Lies,* and of course, *Conan the Barbarian* and *Pumping Iron.*

Now that he's won the governor's seat in California, I'm sure he will bring to that job the same drive, passion, and Rage that he has evidenced in his other careers. It will be interesting to see what other challenges he takes on. I believe Governor Schwarzenegger is truly one of those Rage-driven Superstars who lives not week to week, but peak to peak.

He climbs one mountain and then looks for another.

So will you.

You now know what a Star is. You know what Talents you have to reach Stardom. You have a Rage to succeed. Now you need a Team of believers to help you.

CHAPTER 4

TEAM

Barry White and I were sitting out on a veranda in San Remo, Italy, drinking blood-red orange juice and staring at the diamonds sparkling on top of the Mediterranean Sea. Barry was touring Europe, and he was making an appearance on the Euro Music Awards that night. We were many miles away, and many millions of sold records later, from the first day he knocked on my door.

"Barry," I said, "I've always wondered where you got that $500 to open up a file with my office."

He smiled, leaned into me to get a little closer, and said reverently, "I went to the first man who ever believed in me, a guy in the record distribution business named Larry Nunes. He gave me the money for the music tape I made, and for your $500. He believed in me until the day he died. He was the first person on my Team. After I met you, I had two Larrys on my Team. I knew very early on that to ever get outta the 'hood, I needed a new gang. I needed the best Team I could find."

Why You Need a Fan Club

Stardom is a place you cannot get to alone. No one becomes a Star without help. I know, I know. You are so great, you just hate to share any of that credit with anyone. But the truth of the matter is, none of those four guys on Mount Rushmore got to the summit by themselves. (Even though Cher admitted that for the longest time she thought those monumental faces were just a natural rock formation!)

All Stars have advisers, counselors, spiritual advisers, supporters, mentors, or godfathers. These are supporters, family members, and fans on whom they can rely. You must find others who will pay attention to your needs too.

When you are climbing the mountain of success, the early going on the lower slope is easy to maneuver. The incline is so slight that you can climb it in your tennis shoes. As you continue, the incline will become more steep and difficult, which will require more appropriate shoes. Eventually, the mountain will become so steep that you will require ropes, mountain climbing equipment, and ultimately other experienced mountain climbers who you will literally attach your life to in order to ascend to the pinnacle. You will need these teammates to succeed.

Stars have on their payrolls all sorts of specialized teammates, including agents, managers, publicists, lawyers, personal assistants, fitness trainers, stylists, hairdressers, makeup artists, secretaries, and the mandatory "gofers," who "go for" this or that. Politicians have paid campaign managers, political strategists, lawyers, media buyers, image consultants, fund-raisers, volunteers, contributors, donors, stylists, party loyalists, and gofers of their own. Star athletes have coaches, agents, trainers, doctors, lawyers, publicists, personal assistants, and gofers too. You would not believe how many people work for Oprah or Christina Aguilera, President Bush or New York City Mayor Michael Bloomberg, Tiger Woods or Michael Jordan. Each is like a CEO of a large company. Each is a strong international brand.

Eddie Murphy had the largest entourage I had ever seen. I lived at L'Ermitage Hotel in Beverly Hills for over two years, and he and his entire group would come in and both work and party hard. Boy, am I glad I didn't have that payroll.

No one starts out with a ready-made fan club, but most of us have the next best thing in our parents, families, friends, husbands, wives, and kids. All it takes is someone who believes in your vision for your life. If you are lucky, that person may be willing to sacrifice along with you to help you realize your dreams.

Well, congratulations. You've found your newest supporter and Team member: ME!

You'll recall that I told you earlier that you have to be your own first fan. So, now rest assured that your Fan Club has two members, you and me.

Who else believes in you and is willing to help you achieve your goals? How are they going to help you? How do you begin to structure your own support Team of mentors, professionals, role models, motivators, and reality checkers to help you formulate a plan to promote yourself or your ideas? Do you already have a Team in place? Are they the right Team?

You are going to need parents, family, friends, and even enemies to help you along the way.

In the previous chapters, you identified your Talents and laid out a plan for what you wanted in life. Was it to be a doctor? Lawyer? Vice President? Nurse? Rock Star? Hairdresser? Policeman? Politician? Whatever your goal or definition of Stardom is, you will need to select your Team and solicit their help. Who are they? How do you look for people to help? What kind of people should you look for?

Your Team Players

You will need to fill a variety of positions on your personal support Team. Let's look at the sort of players you'll need.

Mentors

These people are wise guides who are willing to be personally involved in your success. They must willingly to be "on call" for you, which requires that you invest time and effort in developing trusting and mutually respectful relationships with them.

Mentors are not easily found. They may or may not be people who've followed paths similar to those you want to travel. In either case, these are individuals who have made mistakes, learned from them, and are interested in helping you avoid the same pitfalls. They must be willing to share their experience and knowledge with you, and you must be willing to listen to their opinions and advice—even when it may be critical of you or differ from your own. You must heed what they say, otherwise the relationship will not hold up.

Mentors generally are older than you, or at least much more experienced and worldly. Teachers are natural mentors, as are older family members, or successful and knowledgeable people in your field. You are not limited to one mentor. The world is too complex today for one person to know it all.

Your mentors can't protect you from every pitfall, however. You will still have to put in your time at lower level grunt work, proving yourself, and earning your own stripes. But good mentors can accelerate the process and smooth out the road for you by offering wisdom, sharing resources and knowledge and then understanding when the time has come to let you try your wings and fly on your own. Keep in mind that the truly wise mentor will test you along the way to see if you are truly listening and heeding the advice being given to you.

Where do you find mentors? Think of those people you know who seem to share a mutual respect and affection with you. Approach them slowly and feel out their interest. Deepen your relationship, and then beg them.

The truth is, if you are showing sincere promise in your endeavors, often they find you, or they are already there in your network of friends, family, social, and business connections, waiting for you to recognize and recruit them. Not all mentors are naturally extroverted, so be willing to consider people who have quietly encouraged and supported you in the past. You will be required to listen to your mentor, so it should be someone who naturally engages your mind. And remember: Don't demand more than any one mentor is willing to give. You've got to keep in mind that this individual probably has other important duties.

PROFESSIONALS

There is nothing better than having a "pro" on your Team. Someone who is experienced in exactly what you are trying to accomplish. Someone who has "been there, done that" and knows the politics, the pitfalls, and the players. This Team member might be a professional career counselor in your field, a colleague, a boss, a retired executive, an alumnus or professor from your college department, or simply someone who has achieved what you want to achieve and is willing to serve as your guide in the same profession. Whereas mentors give you general advice about most aspects of your life, your pros will offer specific advice in their areas of expertise.

While family and friends are well-intended and will work hard, an expert can bring enormous wisdom and contacts to your endeavors. It wouldn't hurt to create an entire "board of advisers" made up of people you respect and trust. Many entrepreneurs appoint such people to their board of directors or advisory councils. Even if your main product is yourself, you will find it enormously helpful to have a Team of professionals from your chosen field watching your back, front, and both sides.

I'm always flattered and glad to help when someone asks my advice. You might be surprised at how willing the current Stars in your field will be to give you advice and direction as long as you don't take up too much of their valuable time. Never be ashamed to ask for advice. It is always better to ask dumb questions than to make dumb mistakes.

Once you find pros willing to help you, make sure you also pay attention to what they say. If you're going to work with them, or if you're going to ask them to give you advice, you should respect them and listen to them. Even if you totally disagree with their advice, you can debate it with them or maybe get a second opinion, but it's nice to have somebody whom you know is in your corner. Not all the advice is going to be perfect, but it's often helpful. Remember: Listen to those who've been there before. You don't need to reinvent the wheel. Their experiences can save you from making the same mistakes. Chances are, you'll find entirely new mistakes to make, but that's part of the process too. Your professional Team players will be there to remind you that they too made mistakes yet overcame the screw-ups and setbacks to find success. Your most important job is to listen and heed their advice.

ROLE MODELS

It isn't necessary for you to have a personal relationship with your role models. These can be people who have either been successful in your field or have exhibited qualities that you want to emulate in your life. It is not unusual to have several role models from a variety of fields. Often they are celebrities or people you've read about and followed from afar. I would certainly recommend that you read the biographies of people who have succeeded in your field or with similar talents.

If you are an aspiring apprentice and Donald Trump serves as your role model, then in situations that present challenges to you, you might be wise to ask yourself, "What would 'the Donald' do?" The same holds true for any role model whose success inspires you. By studying their lives and careers, you build up extra storage files of knowledge and experience that you can go to when you face a problem or a setback.

Where do you find role models? If you are a businessperson, then *Business Week* and *Fortune* are among the natural reading choices. Professional journals for your field are also likely sources. The alumni magazine from your college department is another good place to find people. You can then study them and their lives by looking for articles or books about them or even their own autobiographies. You can also go to Google.com, enter the person's name, and check out the results. The old-fashioned way is to go to the local library and ask the reference librarian to help you find biographies and autobiographies on men and women who became Stars in your chosen field.

Keep in mind that role models, unlike your other Team players, are not people who likely will be willing to invest their time and efforts in your success. They are people you study rather than communicate with. They come from outside your personal network of friends, family, colleagues, and business contacts. That's not to say that someday when you rise to a Star level of success you won't find yourself standing side by side with a role model at an awards ceremony or professional gathering. If that happens, feel free to share with them that they've played a role in your success, but otherwise be content to study them from a distance.

MOTIVATORS

These can be lifelong friends who serve as cheerleaders and boosters. Or they might be rivals and "sworn enemies" who want to leave you ground up in the dust. It doesn't hurt to have both types of motivators on your Team.

Some people get motivated through encouragement. They respond to supportive advice and constructive criticism. They are likely to seek motivation from loving family members and close friends. If they are athletes, it's likely they look for coaches who've given them pats on the back and pointed out their strengths. Coach John Wooden, the legendary UCLA basketball coach, was known as this sort of motivator. Positive motivators who can inspire you through encouragement or serve as a cheerleader are rare, but easy to spot once you find them. You will find that these unselfish people are among the greatest blessings life can offer, so it would be wise to take good care of them and to return their encouragement and support at every opportunity.

Other people respond best to a kick in the pants rather than a pat on the back. These are generally people who consider themselves tough, streetwise, and underdogs. They will likely seek motivation from hard-nose friends, and in many cases, from enemies or rivals, and anyone else whose "trash talk" compels them to train and work harder. It's just part of their characters that they are more likely to give extra effort if they think they're going to be embarrassed or lose out to competition.

Bobby Knight, the infamous, screaming, cursing, and chair-throwing coach who was fired from Indiana University and moved to Texas Tech, was known as this sort of negative-feedback motivator. Some players couldn't handle his menacing manner. Others thrived under it. NBA legend Isiah Thomas, who is now president of the New York Knicks, played for Knight at Indiana University and led them to a national championship in his sophomore year. Even though Thomas was a high school All-American, Knight rode him hard. He'd often scream at him, curse him, and throw him out of practice. But Thomas, who grew up in utter poverty without a father, responded by saying, "Coach never called me anything that I hadn't gotten worse from my mother."

Consider what sort of motivation works best for you.

REALITY CHECKERS

This is an important Team position but a difficult one to fill, and, be warned, their words are often hard to hear. It requires individuals who have your best interests at heart and know you well, but are not afraid to "rip" on you when you need a reality check.

Uncles, aunts, brothers, sisters, and even grandparents are often good for this position because they generally are devoted and close enough to you to step back and offer unvarnished opinions and assessments. Family members make the best reality checkers because it is necessary for you to have total trust in the motives of these people. Very close friends of many years can also serve in this role, as can your spouse. Whoever serves in this role has the right to expect you to listen and respond without anger or resentment. That is never easy when someone is telling you things you don't necessarily want to hear.

I had a friend who was an alcoholic for many years. He was a famous guy known to millions of people. He ran with a crowd of equally famous, wealthy, and successful men who, as he said, "Had a lot of spare time and a lot of freedom." They called themselves "competitive drinkers," and for years they gathered to drink until they couldn't stand up any longer. They had a lot of fun, but they also caused a lot of emotional and physical damage to themselves and to others. They got away with it for years because they were men who lived as boys. They managed to drink heavily for years without letting it affect their performance in high paying, high profile jobs.

But then that changed.

One day my friend went to a hotel room for a meeting that he'd been asked to attend by one of his longtime best buddies. When he walked in, he was at first shocked and then outraged to see that the room was filled with many of his dearest friends and family members. He realized that it was an "intervention" meeting based on a model from Alcoholics Anonymous. This is a reality check of the most severe kind for an alcoholic. It is when loved ones tell you that they will no longer accept your self-destructive behavior.

Like most people who go through this extremely difficult reality check, my friend at first rebelled. He cursed them. Told them they were wrong. Screamed at them for interfering in his life, and threatened to walk out and never talk to any of them again. And then his own daughter, his favorite child, stood up and said, "Dad, I've always been proud to be your daughter, but it has gotten to the point that I no longer admit to it because of the embarrassment you've caused us all."

That did it. My friend broke down into tears and admitted that they were right. He submitted to the love and caring words of his reality checkers, gave himself over to the professionals at a rehabilitation clinic, and, in the process, saved his life, his career, and his reputation. He will tell you today that he is forever grateful that they were there for him, and that they had the courage to face his wrath and tell him what he didn't want to hear.

Do yourself a favor and put your ego on hold when being submitted to a reality check. Give up your right to be right, your desire to strike back, and your sense of indignation. Practice humility and gratitude in the presence of a reality checker. Tell yourself: "This person cares enough about me to tell it to me straight. I need to simply listen now so that I can understand. I'm lucky to have someone who cares so much."

Some people make the mistake of taking Team members for granted or treating them as "hired hands." If you expect people to invest in your success, you have to give them respect and trust. A strong support Team of mentors, professionals, role models, motivators, and reality checkers are an incredible resource, but they also are a great responsibility.

Putting Your Team to the Test

Let's take a quick look at the quality of your Team right now. Are the people you hang out with supportive of your dreams and goals of Stardom? Are they helpful? The true-false test below will help you gauge whether your current Team members are pumping you up or dragging you down. Circle True or False for each of the statements. Be brutally honest with yourself! Don't let emotions get in the way.

It's one thing to be loyal to a friend; it's another to be blind to the fact that this so-called friend does not have your best interests at heart. A true friendship is win-win. Sometimes one of you may lean on the other, but mutual support is the mark of real friendship. If you are not getting as much as you are giving over the long term, get out!

TEAM TEST

Think of the people around you and then, one by one, apply these True and False questions to each of them.

My Team player:

1.	Always cheers for me when I do well.	True	False
2.	Does things that I no longer agree with.	True	False
3.	Warns me when I'm messing up my life.	True	False
4.	Tries to get me to do things that are not good for me.	True	False
5.	Gives me compliments when I deserve them.	True	False
6.	Supports me when things aren't going their way.	True	False
7.	Helps me prepare for things I want to accomplish.	True	False
8.	Is willing to listen to my problems and concerns.	True	False
9.	Makes fun of my dreams of Stardom.	True	False
10.	Is a true believer in my dreams.	True	False
11.	Resents the time I spend preparing for Stardom.	True	False
12.	Pitches in so I can work on my goals.	True	False
13.	Encourages me to push myself.	True	False
14.	Is a source of positive energy.	True	False
15.	Has goals that are far less ambitious than mine.	True	False

Check your answers for each friend, lover, or Team player, and consider whether this honest appraisal shows that they are helping or hurting your chances for Stardom. You don't have to ditch someone permanently because they may not be an entirely positive presence in your life. But be aware how each person impacts your goals, and accept the fact that some people are better influences than others. Always be aware that if you are going to expect support and encouragement from someone, you have to be willing to give as much as you get.

Your relationships have a powerful impact on your ability to achieve your dreams of Stardom. They affect the choices you make, your behavior, and your ability to concentrate on positive goals. Friends who do drugs, drink excessively, party all night long, and live beyond their means will entice you into doing the same things because they want company. And they don't want to be left behind if you succeed. That's an ugly truth about human nature, but it is true nonetheless. You must learn to recognize which people in your life are holding you back and which will help you soar.

Finding Your Team

Who can you go to for help or advice? Who is willing, and qualified, to be a part of your Team? Who could be one of your mentors, professionals, role models, motivators, or reality checkers? This is important. Think hard. Who likes you? Who believes in you? Who do you like? Why do you want them to be on your Team? What specifically do you want them to do for you? Do they know how to do it? What professionals do you know who can help? How do I start to evaluate and find these people?

DOGS AND CATS

I have met and made friends with many people all over the world. I've spent time with them, talked at length, and truly communicated. I like people. I take the time to get to know them. I listen to what they say. I feel what they mean. I pay attention when they express themselves to me. I watch them act and interact with others.

From all these encounters and observations, I've come to the conclusion that people fall into one of two categories. They are either dogs or cats.

"Dogs or cats?" you ask.

Let's start with people who, no matter how long you've talked to them, no matter how long in life you've known them, you never quite understand what they're thinking, what they're saying, or what they mean. That's their nature: They're cats.

You can be as close to them as you are to anybody, but you know there's something else going on. There's a secret. There's a mystery. Maybe there's a hidden agenda. What did they mean when they said that? No matter how close you want to get to them, they are only going to let you get just so close. You want to know where they are at night? They are out somewhere; but you don't know where. It seems that if they don't have the proverbial nine lives, at least they have two lives, one of them that you don't know anything about. No matter how hard you try, how close you get to them; you know it's just not their nature to be totally forthcoming about anything and everything. They are guarded. They keep their private thoughts to themselves. Can cats be Team members? Yes. Just be sure to recognize them for who they are.

Then there are dogs: loyal, easy to understand people. In essence, they run up to you. They go get the paper for you. They go get the slippers for you. They say what they mean and mean what they say. They just look at you. They adore you. They think you're the most wonderful thing in the entire world. All you have to do is feed them. They'll be there. You call them; they come. You say, "Sit"; they sit. You say, "Heel"; they heel. You know they're man's best friend. They're true blue. You just have to love a dog. You'll find some people who are like that. They're just who they are. What you see is what you get. You trust them. You believe in them.

Now just because I praise the dogs doesn't mean I criticize the cats. Cats are equally lovable, but for different reasons. They are smart, chic, mysterious, cutting edge, sexy, and independent. They are to be respected for always being able to land on their feet, and for having multiple lives.

So, if there were a Star Kennel that boarded Stars showing traits of being either a dog or a cat, how would we separate them?

Star Dogs	**Star Cats**
George W. Bush	Bill Clinton
Jay Leno	David Letterman
Ray Romano	Madonna
Tom Hanks	Angelina Jolie
Sandra Bullock	Cher
Will Smith	David Bowie
Matt LeBlanc	Sean Penn
Billy Crystal	Warren Beatty
Reese Witherspoon	Keanu Reeves
Arnold Schwarzenegger	Nicole Kidman
Paula Abdul	Johnny Depp

WHAT ARE YOU?

In putting your Team together, you will want to create a unit in which Team players rely on each other, are honest with each other, and believe in each other, not to mention being honest, true, and loyal to you. Even though the members of your Team need not be together all the time, they should know, respect, and be able to work together when needed. So, in recruiting Team members, are you going to assemble a Team of dogs or cats? Or are you going to mix them up?

I think the first thing that you should do is decide whether *you* are a dog or a cat. So, consider the characteristics I've cited in describing the two types and ask yourself: "Do I tell people everything? Do I have secrets? Am I loyal and forthcoming? Am I 'what you see is what you get'?" Be honest with yourself.

Don't tell me you're both a dog and a cat, because you're not. You can't be both, sorry. That's not in the rules here. You've got to be either a dog or a cat. Just because you can act like a dog sometimes and a cat at other times doesn't change the fact that your basic nature is one or the other.

In analyzing, "Am I a dog or am I a cat?" ask other people their opinion: "Listen, if I had to be a dog or a cat, what do you think I would be?" Ask 20 people. See what 20 people say. I bet you they would all just about agree.

Now that you know whether you're a dog or a cat, I suggest that you surround yourself with either more dogs or more cats. I don't think you can be a dog and have a lot of cats supporting you. However, if you're a cat, I think you probably could have a lot of cats and dogs supporting you. Dogs will support dogs, cats, kangaroos, giraffes, and any other living species that exited Noah's Ark. Dogs just love anybody and everything. In fact, you can kick a dog and he'll come back to you. So, even if you're a cat and you want to mistreat your dog friends, they'll still keep coming around and supporting you until they have finally had enough—and then they'll bite you.

If you're a dog, try to get other dogs to help you, not cats. If you're a cat, you can have both.

Think about all the people close to you. Which are they? Ask them.

All I can tell you is this: Don't keep secrets from your support Team, and don't ever mistreat or abuse them along the way. An abused cat will slip off and hurt you behind your back. If you kick a dog one too many times, it can turn mean, ferocious, and bite you. Try never to lose a loyal friend, because a loyal friend lost becomes the most fearful enemy you will ever meet.

Parents as Team Players

Most parents will do just about anything to help their children. They would prefer, however, to have a clear understanding of what each child wants and why. That should not be too much to ask. They become concerned when you are vague about what you want, or don't have a plan, or haven't thought through all the dangers inherent in your plan. Be clear and certain when you ask anyone for help, even, or especially, your parents.

Unlike other Team players, who may come and go, parents stay around and can be supportive at different times throughout most of your life.

GUARDIAN ANGELS

Let me introduce you to three beautiful young women whom I like to think of as "Larry's Angels": Drew Barrymore, Tori Spelling, and Shannen Doherty.

I managed the careers of all three when they were child Stars. Their parents played crucial and important roles in each of their lives and careers, but in different ways. The parents' relationships with the three Stars are informative. They illustrate the various ways in which parents can support their children.

JAID AND DREW

Drew Barrymore's mother, Jaid, who formerly went by her first name, Ildiko, instilled into her daughter from day one that she was born into the famed show business family, the Barrymores, and that she was destined for greatness. Jaid had hopes herself of being a Star. She married John Drew Barrymore, Jr., but he could never quite get his life together, either financially or emotionally. After Jaid gave birth to Drew, she took care of her as a single mother and a struggling actress. While Jaid's career never took off, she encouraged Drew to start acting at a very early age, and Drew was a natural. Jaid decided to concentrate on her daughter's future, and she came to me for guidance. She asked me to be Drew's manager.

Once little Drew caught the eye of Steven Spielberg and *E.T.*, she was on her way. We had a lot of success together and we all got along fabulously. It was at my birthday party at Ma Maison, right after *E.T.*

Drew Barrymore started with a Team of supporters at a very young age.

premiered, that the now famous picture of a seven-year-old Drew sitting at a party table allegedly drinking and drunk was taken. I can only tell you that she was definitely not drinking that night, but the more we explained that to the press, the more they wanted to believe she was drunk, as if that confirmed she was a hard-drinking Barrymore.

Jaid dedicated her life to Drew. She drove her everywhere. She went to every meeting. She was the press agent, the promoter. She was like John the Baptist preaching the coming of the next great Barrymore to Hollywood. She breathed, lived, slept, dreamed, and forced into existence what the world came to recognize as the heir to the Barrymore throne. In essence, she promoted her child to be what she herself had dreamed to be. Jaid was Drew's mentor, professional, and motivator all wrapped up as one.

And it worked for Drew. Of course, it's well known that Drew eventually felt smothered by so much motherly attention and such high expectations. As she grew older, she and her mother found themselves increasingly at odds. Eventually, I found myself in the middle. But the fact remains that Jaid set Drew's course, put a Team together for Drew, which included me as the manager, and launched a stellar career. I am so happy for Drew, and I'm always hopeful that the two of them—mother and daughter—will reach a permanent balance of understanding and appreciation.

AARON, CANDY, AND TORI

Tori Spelling's parents are a celebrated Hollywood couple, the legendary film and television producer Aaron Spelling and his wife Candy. Talk about being born to the cinematic purple!

One day, Aaron called me and said, "Larry, Candy and I would really appreciate it if you could take a look at our daughter, Tori. We think she has something special and would love for you to meet her, and if you share our enthusiasm, maybe get involved as her manager." The words, "Sure, Aaron," had hardly left my lips before a limousine pulled up to my office delivering a little Tori.

She was very polite and eager. We worked with her for a while. I remember that she was driven everywhere in that limo. She was trying to figure it all out. She studied. She worked. Then her father cast her in one of his own productions, *Beverly Hills, 90210,* and boom, school was out for Tori Spelling. She became a Star. Aaron and Candy performed every Team player role.

TOM, ROSA, AND SHANNEN

Shannen Doherty's parents, Tom and Rosa, on the other hand, were very dear and well-meaning people who were not remotely connected to wealth, power, or Hollywood. They were a regular couple trying to cope with life, make a living, and survive. As parents, they offered Shannen great support and motivation. They took her everywhere. They were so proud of her.

I was introduced to Shannen and her parents by a wonderful actor, Victor French, who was Shannen's costar on the series *Little House on the Prairie*. I loved her energy and fight. So did Victor and Michael Landon. She worked every day on movie sets. Shannen was a workhorse. At a very early age she learned to be a breadwinner. She worked constantly to help take care of her family and become someone. And she did. In many ways, she was the parent of her parents. I loved them all, and we worked together for quite a long time. Don't believe everything you read about her in the tabloids. Sure, she's a fighter and a survivor, but she's also a fragile soul and a great, and gifted, girl.

Each of these three ladies has grown into their respective Stardoms. Each has loving parents who served as guides and champions. They may have made occasional mistakes, but they were always there for their children. I believed in all three families, and am very blessed to have been a part of their Teams. I have great respect for each of them.

Two-Way Streets of San Francisco

Most parents encourage and support their children not only when they are young, but also when they grow into adulthood.

The critically acclaimed actor, Michael Douglas, was born into a show business family. His mother Diana is a gifted actress, and his father, of course, is the legendary Star, Kirk Douglas.

Michael struggled as much as anyone in the early stages of his career. At 17, to get started, he asked his dad for a job and was hired as a gofer on the movie *Spartacus*. When he was 28, his dad's friend, Karl Malden, offered him his first big break as an actor playing a young, hotheaded detective on the early 1970s TV series *The Streets of San Francisco*. Michael's career since then, as an actor and producer, has also become legendary.

At one time or another over his entire life, Michael's parents have been his mentors, professionals, role models, motivators, and reality checkers. He is always respectful and appreciative of their efforts, and in 2003 showed that the street of support is a two-way street by producing a movie in which he starred along with the other actors he hired, his dad, mom, and son. It's called *It Runs in the Family.*

PARENTS ARE NOT ALWAYS PERFECT

There will be times in your life when your parents support you and times when you feel they are dragging you down or holding you back. Sometimes they are not around at all. Other times they will rely on you more than you rely on them.

It can be difficult to tell whether your parents are supporting your dreams or thwarting them, because our relationships with them are often so complicated and intimate. You may well need to get outside help from an unbiased source, like a clergy member or a counselor, to help you determine whether your parents are acting in your best interests or if they are misguided themselves.

Parental relationships change as you grow older, but they can be just as challenging when you're an adult—or even more challenging— than when you are younger. It is always important to understand that your parents are human. They are also vulnerable to the same emotions and problems as you. Treat them with understanding, and know that as much as they may wish you well, sometimes their dreams for you will be different than your own.

At some point you may have to decide to go against their wishes, however well-intentioned, because they don't have the same grand vision for your life. Don't make that decision without giving it serious thought and without seeking guidance from someone outside the family. If you don't have parental support, or never have had it, I hope that instead of becoming bitter, it motivated you to seek it from numerous other sources, like other family members or friends.

Always remember that parents need you as much as you need them, maybe even more.

Family as Team Players

Who else can help as a member of your Team? Can your husband help? That special uncle may help if you ask. What about Grandpa? Maybe the kids will pitch in. Other than your parents, your closest family and relatives know you best. They love you. If they can help, they will. Do they know anything about what you need? Try to find family members who know something about the thing you are interested in.

FAMILY EINSTEIN

Some women have supported their husbands through law or medical school. Some husbands have worked to launch their wives' Stardom. Take the case of a wonderful couple that my wife and I recently entertained in our home, Bill and Julie Aigner-Clark. Bill had initially worked for his father in a firm that created images for various companies, including their slogans, logos, the whole nine yards. He subsequently worked with Optical Data, a company that created educational software. Julie was initially a teacher of art and literature for both elementary and high school. Later, she worked for Bill as a sales rep for his products. They eventually fell in love and married.

While at home as a new parent, Julie discovered there were no appropriate learning tools for babies. Based on her experiences as a former teacher of art and literature, and her love for classical music and poetry, she came up with an idea for a videotape to entertain and educate small children. From their basement, she made a video. Kids loved it. Parents told other parents about it. Bill shook his head and said, "Well, maybe we can sell this thing." Not only did they sell the videotapes, but shot and sold more and more tapes, and eventually other related products for infants and toddlers. They built the company nationally. It is known as Baby Einstein. In November 2001, only five years after the first videotape, which cost $5,000 to make, they sold the company to Disney for $25 million. Not bad family teamwork.

I GOT YOU BABE

Hollywood has many great family Teams that have reached Stardom together through mutual support and encouragement. Sometimes these Teams come together at first as romantic couples. Eventually the romance fades and they split, but in the best cases, they remain devoted to each other's success. I personally witnessed Salvatore Bono encouraging a very shy Cherilyn Sarkisian LaPierre. His enthusiasm and support made possible the birth of Sonny and Cher. Sonny gave her the courage to eventually become simply *Cher*. I was there. I represented them in the seventies, and 20 years later made a movie of their life for ABC titled *And the Beat Goes On: The Sonny and Cher Story.*

After Sonny and Cher broke up, I continued to represent Sonny. It was tough for him. He was desperate to the point of doing guest spots on *Fantasy Island* and *Love Boat*. Sonny wanted to cut a solo album, so he went into the studio all fired up. My mother was visiting me at the time, and I took her to the studio. After she listened for a while, Sonny came over to my mother, to be nice, and asked, "So, Mom, what do you think?" My mother, who was a natural-born reality checker, answered, "Sonny, I hate to tell you this, but Sonny without Cher is like Sears without Roebuck."

I was horrified! Sonny, as always, was gracious. He laughingly agreed and wandered back into the studio booth.

While Sonny and Cher had their times of conflict and hardship, over the years they grew to become great friends again. In some ways, it seemed they remained closer than either one of them ever acknowledged. When United States Congressman Sonny Bono died in a skiing accident in 1998, Cher grieved deeply for the man who had been such a huge part of her life. At his funeral, she expressed her respect and love for Sonny in a way that brought many to tears.

Friends as Team Players

My father always told me, "A friend is someone you can share your good news with." That's right, good news, not bad. He said that anybody would listen to your bad news. It's a sad truth that many people enjoy hearing that your life is worse than theirs. They say, "Oh, I'm so sorry to hear you lost your job," or that you had to go to the hospital. But a good friend is someone who is truly happy for you and not jealous when you tell them you just got that promotion, got an A on the test, won that scholarship, got elected, or met that "special guy." Pick your friends carefully.

Friends can generally be mentors, professionals, motivators, and reality checkers. That's why they're good to have on your Team. Stars usually have lots of friends. That's one reason why they're Stars. Wouldn't you like to be friends with Nicole Kidman, Gwyneth Paltrow, Sean "P. Diddy" Combs, or Jack Black? Who wouldn't?

Ben Affleck and Matt Damon are two friends who certainly have helped each other. They were living in Boston, cowrote a script, got the movie *Good Will Hunting* made, costarred in it, won awards, and helped launch each other's respective careers. Good work, guys.

In his classic trilogy, *The Lord of the Rings,* J. R. R. Tolkien created one of the most loyal friends in literary history in Sam Gamgee, the Hobbit gardener. Sam protected Frodo, the Bearer of the Ring, on his dangerous journey to prevent Sauron, the Dark Lord of Mordor, from enslaving all of Middle Earth by capturing the One Ring of Power. We all should be so fortunate in our lives to have the type of courageous and loving friendship Sam repeatedly evidenced to Frodo. Lucky for us, we don't have to be Hobbits to be great friends.

I have guided William Shatner's career and been a part of his Team for 24 years. Over this more than two-decade professional and personal relationship, we have become true friends. We've shared life's highs and lows and learned to respect and love each other. It's great when you are teammates and friends.

Over the years, we have transitioned Bill's persona from *Star Trek's* Captain Kirk to television's *T. J. Hooker,* to the popular host of *Rescue 911,* to an icon making fun of himself in the "Get a Life" sketch on *Saturday Night Live,* to the national spokesman for Priceline. Bill has starred in *Star Trek* movies and others, from *Showtime* with Robert De Niro and Eddie Murphy to *Miss Congeniality* with Sandra Bullock. He recently recorded a new album produced by Ben Folds, and is busy working in *Miss Congeniality II.* He is also starring in the new spin-off of David E. Kelley's *The Practice,* titles *Boston Legal,* for ABC. Along the way, he has directed movies, recorded other albums, and written 23 books, not to mention his charity work.

Bill and I have developed that rare type of Team relationship, one that is both personal and professional. We trust and respect each other. We each have strengths that compensate for the other's lesser strengths. It takes time and effort to build that sort of friendship and trust, but it's worth it. True friends are good to have.

Enemies as Team Players

"That son of a bitch! I'll show him."

Meet your enemy and new Team player. He's one of your motivators.

Obviously, you probably won't have a close personal relationship with a rival or enemy motivator. Again, this sort of motivator is generally someone you know all too well, or someone you find easily enough. Or they find you. We all have natural rivals and enemies. Just being around them raises the hair on the back of our necks. Things they say and do almost always hit us the wrong way. Or their success makes us crazy to prove we can do even better.

Channel that negative energy into a positive force by using it to motivate yourself. Also keep in touch with your rivals, competitors, and other "enemies." You can learn as much from someone who hates you as you can from someone who thinks you're the greatest. Why do you think most world powers train and use spies? They want to know what the enemy is planning. Richard Nixon kept an "Enemies List" so he could keep tabs on his rivals and detractors. You may not want to go that far, but it is better to know what they are planning, saying, and doing, than to be blindsided by them later.

Don't block out any information streams that can affect your own performance. Know what the enemy is doing. Remember: Keep your friends close and your enemies even closer.

Learn to Listen

I've always believed that if three people tell you "You're drunk," you should lie down.

Learning to respect people and listen to their advice is crucial. Believe it or not, you don't know everything. Other people's sage advice can save you time, energy, money, and heartache. Learn to listen in order to learn. Not listening to my experienced hotel concierge in India almost got me killed.

We arrived late one night in Delhi, India, on a vacation trip. I told the concierge I wanted him to book a car, driver, and tour guide for 9 a.m. the next day. I intended to take my girlfriend at the time to Agra to see one of the most extravagant monuments ever built for love, the Taj Mahal.

The concierge smiled and replied, "A car and driver? That would be perfectly acceptable, but may I most humbly suggest that you take the very comfortable train which leaves from the station nearby at precisely 7:30 a.m.?"

"No, the car will be fine," I said.

"That is certainly acceptable, but I think most humbly that you would enjoy the very acceptable train ride."

"No, no, the private car," I repeated.

"Maybe you would prefer to fly to Agra on one of our wonderful airplanes? It is such a short and pleasant flight."

"No, I really would like a private car, driver, and tour guide. I read in the guide book that it's only 125 miles to Agra, and I think that would be a nice full-day excursion."

"Yes. May I suggest that if you take a car you leave much earlier, like five-thirty a.m., so that your trip would be most pleasant?"

"No, no. We're exhausted. Nine a.m., please."

"That is certainly acceptable."

Well, it's probably pretty obvious to you by now that in his polite cultural way, he really, really didn't want me to take that car.

But Mr. "Know It All" from Beverly Hills wasn't listening.

At 9 a.m. the driver and tour guide were standing at attention by the car in front of the hotel with very wide, pleasing grins. It marked the start of the most memorable—and very nearly the last—day of my life.

It's true that the road to Agra from Delhi is only 200 kilometers, or 125 miles, but no one bothered to mention the conditions of the road and the difficulty of the travel. We maneuvered on a torn, dilapidated two-way road through poverty-stricken villages, around cows, alongside donkey-drawn carts, by overturned buses, through ambling oxen, dodging snorting water buffalo, alongside fast bicyclists, and avoiding pedestrians hurrying to somewhere. And if you think Indian cabbies drive fast in New York, hold onto your turban when they are on their own turf heading for the Taj Mahal!

That day, I saw India's intimate beauty beaming with life and death. I saw dead bodies off the side of the road with sheets over them. I saw three serious traffic accidents with fatalities. They pulled the bodies off the side of the road and traffic moved on.

It was truly a dangerous journey there, and returning to Delhi that night was sheer madness. They had no lights on the road and the traffic was worse. I thought we were going to die numerous times that day, and that they were just going to go ahead and bury us right there in the Taj Mahal tomb next to Mumtaz Mahal, the Beloved.

My experienced concierge was most humbly trying to save our life, and I wasn't listening. He was trying to help me and guide me in an acceptable manner, but in my desire to get where I wanted to go, I turned a deaf ear.

The same thing happens to many people in their journey to Stardom, whatever their chosen fields. They don't listen to the advice of their well-intentioned mentors, professionals, motivators, or reality checkers, and because of that, they get off track.

That is why it is so critical—absolutely essential—that as you move onto the path to Stardom you develop a nurturing, supportive Team of people who believe in you—your own fan club. You then must learn to listen to their well-meaning advice, as well as their encouragement.

Even Superstars can make the mistake and stop listening when they think they know it all. I have learned that the management of most Talent goes through three stages. First, they listen to you. Second, you listen to them. And third, no one listens to anyone.

Later, when they discover they don't know it all, they find someone new to listen to. And the three stages start again.

An Arabian proverb advises:

He who knows not, and knows not that he knows not, is a fool.
Shun him.

He who knows not, and knows that he knows not, is simple.
Teach him.

He who knows, and knows not that he knows, is asleep.
Wake him.

He who knows, and knows that he knows, is wise.
Follow him.[1]

Once you have learned to listen and gain knowledge, you will learn that the more you know, the more you will learn. What? Think about it. Two people are touring an art museum. One has no knowledge of art and one has studied art. While the one who has no knowledge may discover an appreciation for the beautiful paintings in front of him, the art student, upon viewing the works, will gain an additional level of understanding and appreciation, having prepared for the visit with knowledge of the painters, their lives, techniques, position in the art history world, and so on. Once you have a basic understanding of something, your knowledge grows exponentially. Listen, learn, and grow.

The Tough Part

Building a Team of believers can be difficult at times. It often forces you to make some tough decisions. First of all, you want to build and nurture relationships that fit your new identity, not your old one.

It's a new day and a new you. It might be hard to leave those you were hanging out with but were holding you back. If you are to be a Star, you've got to hang out with Stars: people, like you, who think and act positively about life and their future. If you think that your old crowd was in any way deliberately leading you astray or blocking your efforts, then you've got to say good-bye to them. And chances are, they were holding you back, so be brutally honest in that assessment. It's critical to your future success as a Star. It's great to be loyal to old friends as long as they are willing to be sources of strength and support—as long as they buy into your dreams of Stardom too and want you to achieve them. You can remain friends and support them, but you must replace them for your support.

To achieve Stardom in your chosen field, you must develop positive relationships with people who also truly want you to do well. Their enthusiasm is contagious. Psychologists say that long-term success requires supportive networks that include family, friends, coworkers, mentors, role models, and cheerleaders. The people you know can either support you or sabotage you. It's up to you to tell them what you want for yourself, and what you expect in your relationship with them. If someone is dragging you down, it's up to you to tell him or her that you can't continue the relationship.

Suppose you realize that the very person holding you down is the very person you love, or is even your spouse. Often, such people aren't aware that they are pulling you down. Other times they are aware but haven't wanted to discuss it with you. Now is the time to discuss it. Explain to them how important this is to you. Listen to their side. Commit to working it out. Seek professional counsel if necessary.

Read this carefully: It is *impossible* for you to develop as a Star in your own field if even one of your friends is a dream-buster. People who failed your Team Test are your dream-busters. Don't allow your dream for Stardom to fail because you've let a false sense of loyalty to a false friend hold you back.

In Hollywood, where many people reach the heights of Stardom, it is not uncommon to have the tabloids and gossip columnists report that somewhere along the way a Star cut off a relationship with an alcoholic parent, a predatory boyfriend or girlfriend, or a former friend. Even though the media can make them seem selfish and ungrateful, it was something they had to do, and did.

Sometimes, there are those who just will not believe in you. They have many different reasons. They may be afraid you'll aim too high and hurt yourself by failing. They may be jealous. They may be afraid of a change in the power balance of their relationship with you. They may be afraid you'll move to Success Land and never invite them to dinner. Whatever their reasons, they're not helping you, and they may be helping you to fail. You have to do something about these people, especially if, as is often the case, they're close to you.

How do you deal with them?

You can stand up to them and tell them how you feel. You can take control of your life. You can realize that you don't need anyone's approval to live your life. You can fight approval-seeking behavior by starting your sentences with *I*. You can stop acting in a too agreeable way, and you can start by ceasing to apologize for yourself.

You can fight guilt, the nay-sayer's ultimate weapon, by keeping a guilt journal. When you start to feel guilty, write down the time of day, what you feel guilty about, and how your feeling of guilt will make things better. Chances are, it won't.

If need be, you can deal with negative people by cutting them loose. I know that sounds cold. I know you don't really want to do that. Unfortunately, if someone is pulling you down, you have to let him or her go. You are just saying good-bye for a while, you don't have to call in a favor from Tony Soprano.

List Your Team Players

You should now believe that you need a positive Team to fulfill your quest for Stardom. Your Team should include mentors, professionals, role models, motivators, and reality checkers. These Team players can be parents, family members, friends, and even enemies. Make a list of people who you believe will help you reach your goal. What specifically will you ask each Team player to do? Put your Team together now.

List people who can help you get what you want. What roles will they play and what will they do?

MENTORS:_____

_____

_____

_____

_____

_____

PROFESSIONALS:_____

_____

_____

_____

_____

_____

ROLE MODELS:_____

_____

_____

_____

_____

MOTIVATORS:_____

_____

_____

_____

_____

_____

REALITY CHECKERS:_____

_____

_____

_____

_____

_____

Sign Them Up

Once you know who you want on your Team and what you want them to do, ask them to do it. Don't call them on the phone and say, "Hey, can you help me?" Take them to coffee or lunch and politely discuss it with them. Make it an event. Recruiting is an art. Enjoy it. Show them your Talent. Have them sense your Rage. Assure them of your respect for their accomplishments and offer them your reciprocal efforts in attaining their Stardom. Make it a mutual journey.

I can hear you now: "What if someone says no?" Accept the "no," thank them for their time, and move on. Don't be shocked, mad, or disappointed. Be even friendlier. Offer to help them if they ever need anything. You never know, they may eventually come around. You'll be surprised how people will jump on the bandwagon once you get rolling. Don't get your feelings hurt, cry, and quit. You are on a mission. Go to the next candidate. Rejection should be part of your motivation. Indifference should fuel your Rage. Failure should teach you success. Disappointment should welcome new opportunities. Now get out that black book, identify your Team players, and sign them up for your destiny.

Team Captain

Because this is so important, I put it last to leave it with you forever. Your Team Captain is your God—your spiritual Father. Your spiritual strength is crucial. The more belief and strength you have, the less difficult your journey will be. Your spiritual Team Captain is always there to guide and support you each step of the way, and when the going gets most difficult and the challenges are the greatest, this member of your Team can make all the difference in the world.

> *"No matter how many dreams we dream, no matter how many mountains we see moved ... we never get too big, too strong, too smart, or too old to pray this simple prayer: 'I need help. I can't do it alone. Help me, Lord.'"*
>
> —*Robert H. Schuller*[2]

You've now got a Talent identified. You have a Rage to succeed. You've got a Team of believers to help you. Now all you need is a little Luck.

CHAPTER 5

LUCK

From the first cold, chilling moment of birth, to that final, fateful ride in the hearse, there ain't nothing so bad that it can't get worse.

Luck looms over every aspect of our lives. One second of good Luck can lead to all that you aspire. One moment of bad Luck can undo years of planning and hard work. Lady Luck can make you or break you. She can be the difference between smart or stupid, success or failure, and even life or death.

Some people are lucky. Some are not. In case you're interested, I'm lucky. I'm not claiming I have been, or am, immune to misfortune or failure. I'm just noting that I'm lucky. And I can help you become lucky too. Luck is something you can learn.

What Exactly Is Luck?

Luck is working hard, being prepared for opportunities, and being in the right place at the right time. It also requires the ability to recognize chance events when they strike. Luck you can control. Chance events you cannot.

Shortly after I arrived in Los Angeles, I started taking a night class at the University of Southern California on the Legal Aspects of the Entertainment Business. Elliot Chaum from Capitol Records guest-lectured one night, and I asked him a few stupid questions during class, then followed him out to his car like a stalker and begged for a job. I called him every day, then every week for over four months. Sometimes he took my call, but most of the time not. Then one day out of the blue he called and said, "We've got an opening. It pays eight hundred dollars a month. Do you want it?"

"Done deal," I cried. That was my professional beginning.

When I started working at Capitol Records, I was the newest and youngest lawyer in the legal department. I knew nothing. I worked hard. I was so excited to have the job. There I was, working in the famous, round Capitol Records Building at Hollywood and Vine. I was the first to get to work and the last to leave. I took work off other people's desks and completed it. I wanted to learn, to be prepared. I thanked Elliot once a week for the job.

I also wanted to get noticed. How could I get anyone's attention? I soon realized that the president of Capitol was Sal Iannucci. He was Italian. Well, well, well, so was I. Toto, I guess we're not in Mississippi anymore.

I observed that Mr. Iannucci got into work at about 8:45 each morning. He took the elevator to his office on the "E" floor. It was really the thirteenth floor but I guess somebody in the round building was superstitious, so they called it the Executive floor. My cubbyhole was on the eleventh floor. One day I decided to get lucky, so I devised a plan in which I would just "happen" to arrive at work and ride up the elevator with our president. I did it every morning for about two weeks in a row. I had planned everything I wanted to say, starting on the ground floor and on to the eleventh, where I got off. I even took a few rehearsal runs to time my spiel. For those two weeks I talked faster than I ever had in my life. I was the fastest talking Southerner anyone had ever met.

I introduced myself to him every day. After about a week, he remembered my name. A few days later he invited me to the thirteenth floor to his office. We talked music, recording artists, Mississippi, my real Italian family names—Tomasino and Tuminello—and so on. He liked my youth and hustle.

It seemed the other lawyers were a little old-fashioned and were not relating to the new generation of singer/songwriters and their representatives. Capitol had old school, classic acts like Dean Martin,

Frank Sinatra, Al Martino, and Peggy Lee, but they also were distributing the biggest act in the World: the Beatles. The British band came to Capitol through Apple/EMI in England. Mr. Iannucci, who I now called Sal, wanted Capitol to sign young acts, and he needed a young lawyer to go with him and his Artist and Repertoire (A&R) Team to help make these acquisitions. He suggested to my boss that one of the senior attorneys should give me a crash course in the nuances of negotiating a record deal and get me ready to be on the front line. Well, I certainly was available.

As you can tell, I was working hard, getting prepared, and situating myself to be in the right place at the right time. In other words, I was preparing myself for opportunity, making my own Luck.

As I was taking my cram course in negotiating record deals at Capitol, my best friend, and then roommate, Fred Alias, and I met Virginia Fox Zanuck. She was the widow of famed Hollywood, 20th Century Fox mogul, Darryl Zanuck. We were introduced to her through a woman from our hometown of Clarksdale, Martha Newman, who had married the famous film composer, Alfred Newman.

Virginia invited Fred and me to Palm Springs for a weekend party. She asked us to stay at her magnificent hacienda estate built by her late husband. It was named Ric-Su-Dar after their three children, Richard, Susan, and Darrlyn. We stayed in the Blue and Red guest cottages.

While in Palm Springs that weekend, Fred and I drove over to the hottest hotel in town, where we decided to go to the spa. We were relaxing, roasting in the sauna, and it was HOT. I complained that I hadn't seen much of my boss, Sal, since he'd ordered me to take the cram course on record deal negotiations. I noted that there seemed to be a little envy and corporate intrigue going on with my peers and immediate bosses, as if they were trying to keep me away from him.

The sauna was really baking us, and after about 20 minutes we'd had enough. It was definitely time to get out. As we started to get up and rush out of the blistering heat, who do you think enters the sauna? That's right. Salvatore J. Iannucci!

As overheated as I was, I couldn't walk out of the sauna now! How could I? This was my big opportunity—a chance to sit in the sauna with the president of my company? A chance to tell him I was the "guest of the Zanuck family" for the weekend? A chance again to impress him with my knowledge and gift of gab? So, I told Fred

I'd meet him in the showers and sat back down in the sauna with Sal. As each bead of sweat dripped off my body, I acted calm and cool. I don't remember what I said, but I talked, talked, and talked. And the heat was exhausting me. I thought he would never leave that blistering sauna. Fifteen additional minutes later, or after a total of 35 minutes of sheer torture, I stumbled out of Hell.

I had a chance opportunity. And I took it. I dropped seven pounds and picked up 107 degrees of brownie points. That night while getting dressed for the party, I collapsed from heat exhaustion and never was able to go. Fred went without me and filled me in later.

"Mother," I thought, "I'm working as fast as I can to be important." Sal Iannucci really knew who I was now. Or at least, who I thought I was.

As you can tell, I recognized a chance event and seized it.

I continued to work hard. I became part of the acquisition Team, meeting all the players of the day. Then. It happened: THE BIG BREAK.

April 1970. I get a call in my office. It was Sal.

"Come up here. I want to see you."

I arrived at his office on the thirteenth Floor. Two secretaries sat out in front of his office! "Larry, you know Herb Carp here," Sal started. Herb was General Counsel of Capitol/EMI—my boss's, boss's boss. "Herb, check this kid out. Find out what he really knows versus what he thinks he knows. I want him with me tomorrow. Get him in the files with you. We just found out that the Beatles are announcing tomorrow that they are breaking up. Have we lost them? Can we keep them? Who at Apple or EMI do we need to talk to? How do we have them signed? As a group? As individuals? Jointly or severally? I want them signed individually. I want *four* Beatles! I want Larry to head up these negotiations with me. Herb, get on it. Tomasino, I've never seen you short on words. Get to work."

Tomasino?? He called me Tomasino!! Breaking up?? The Beatles were breaking up?? Holy shit. He wanted me to negotiate the breakup of the Beatles?

Well, that's exactly what happened.

Starting that next day, when the whole known world was stunned by the news, and for the better part of the next year, I delicately and successfully negotiated Capitol's position to distribute in the United States the individual solo albums of John Lennon, Paul McCartney,

George Harrison, and Ringo Starr. That year alone could be a book. That year alone put me on the Hollywood map, gave me the nickname as "the man who broke up the Beatles," and, in 1971, the title of "Showbiz Lawyer of the Year" for Capitol Records which was presented to me by the head of A&R, Al Khoury. It was my chance event, my big break, and to most people who had no way to know, it made me the "luckiest guy on planet earth."

I *was* lucky. Some things I controlled. But I also was blessed with a series of chance events, which no one controls. There were two chance events involved: Sal walking into the sauna, and the Beatles deciding to break up when I was actually working at Capitol Records. But as for Luck, I did work hard. I did beg for the job. I did prepare myself. I did put myself in the right elevator at the right time, and I did recognize a chance opportunity in the sauna when it presented itself—and I was prepared to do whatever it took to take advantage of it.

Sonny without Cher was like Sears without Roebuck.

The Distinction Between Luck and Chance

Chance events are those happenings over which we have absolutely no control. They don't consistently happen to the same person. They may be formative events in people's lives, but they're not frequent.

Luck you can create by working hard, being prepared, being in the right place at the right time, and recognizing chance events when they strike.

When people say that they *consistently* experience good fortune and that they are lucky all the time, I think that by definition it has to be because of something they are doing. In other words, they make their own Luck.

That's right. You have far more control over Luck than you think. Your Luck, whether it be good or bad, is actually manifested by the way you think.

You Can Learn to Be Lucky

Stars of every stripe make their own Luck. Over the years, I've come to know successful people in many fields, including entertainment, law, and finance. Some may claim they lead charmed lives, but whether consciously or unconsciously, these Stars have put themselves in position to make the best of any good fortune that comes their way. They are very creative in the way they find opportunities and jump on them.

I've noticed that most Stars from all walks of life make the most of their own luck by being open to opportunity, creative about responding to it, and energetic in pursuing it. Let's look more closely.

STARS TUNE INTO A SIXTH SENSE FOR OPPORTUNITY

Many people get an idea for a business opportunity or a career move and just let it pass without acting on it. "Lucky" Stars are much more likely to act on those gut feelings and take action. They also work to fine-tune that sixth sense by doing stimulating things, meditating, and hanging out with creative and dynamic people.

Michael Wilson, my very talented buddy and recent partner in a few television productions, is one of those creative people who inspires me. I find that just being around him is like drinking five or six cups of coffee. He gets me charged up. His enthusiasm and energy remind me of one of the great things about Hollywood and this country in general: We are held back only by the limits of our imaginations. His energy is infectious. I pick up his inspiration by osmosis. Rubbing shoulders with his pure energy is an exhilarating experience. Of course, when his energy and my energy connect, we can light up a Tri-State area. Or, at least we think so!

Just recently, Michael came up with a great entrepreneurial idea that we buddied up on and then had a great time selling.

After seeing one of Sony's new state-of-the-art digital movie cameras, he suggested that we send a bunch of them to a number of celebrities around town as gifts. We would include blank videotapes for them to use. We would ask them to tape anything they wanted. There was only one thing we would ask for in return—the tape. We would edit them and put them in a show called *Celebrity Home Video*.

I suggested that we go to Sony Pictures TV, where we had done business in the past, and pitch this as a cross-marketing and promotional project to them. They bought in, and provided not only the digital movie cameras, but several other electronic goodies, which we sent to the celebrities in beautiful Sony Production Kit attaché cases, with the Stars' names engraved on them.

The fun celebrities who have signed on include Coolio, Steven Schirripa, William Shatner, Kelly Hu, Tony Danza, Erik von Detten, Michael York, Orlando Jones, Christopher Titus, Kelly Rowland, Paul Sorvino, Eric Roberts, Mindy Sterling, Chris McDonald, and Gene Simmons. Not a bad line-up.

We're now editing their home movies and pitching the series to broadcasters. If we sell the series, we'll be in high cotton, but if we don't, our special energy at least created an opportunity. Find someone who can spark you. Put them on your Team.

HOW TO STIMULATE YOUR OPPORTUNITIES

Opportunities exist. Often they are right under your nose or banging at the front door but you simply haven't trained yourself to recognize them or to act upon them.

Go Where the Gittin' Is Good

Imagine this guy standing late one night on a street corner looking down at the pavement. Along comes another guy who notices the man looking for something and says, "Hey buddy, what did you lose?"

"A twenty-dollar bill," he states.

"Well, where did you lose it?"

"Down the street," he answers.

"Well, if you lost it down the street, why are you looking here?"

"Because the streetlight is better here," he replies.

If you haven't been finding opportunities that fire your Rage and commitment hanging around the places and friends that provide you with a comfort zone, then you need to get out and expose yourself to new experiences, new people, and new stimulation. Maybe that means moving to a town where there are more opportunities in your field. Just because the street lamp makes it easy to search for the $20 bill, don't continue to look where it ain't.

Entertainers naturally gravitate to Hollywood, Nashville, and New York because that's where the greatest opportunities are. If you want to be a singer/songwriter/dancer/actor, the opportunities are much more limited in Peoria and Dubuque. But if you dream of being a Star heavy equipment salesman or a Star river boat captain, Peoria is home to the corporate headquarters of Caterpillar Inc., the heavy equipment manufacturer, and Dubuque sits on the Mississippi River. If you want a future in technology, maybe Silicon Valley would be a nice place to look around. It takes a commitment to get off your butt and chase your dream by going where opportunities are more plentiful. If you aren't willing to do that, then you need to take a realistic look at whether your dreams of Stardom are real.

Know Where You Want to Go

Opportunities are easier to spot if you know what you are looking for. In the case of our *Celebrity Home Videos* show, Michael and I had long talked about wanting to develop a high concept program together that would appeal to cable broadcasters. We had a framework so when a piece of the puzzle appeared, we saw how it might fit our vision of an opportunity. Spend some time thinking about what sort of opportunities are matched to your Talent levels, contacts, knowledge, and dreams. Prepare yourself by building a framework on paper and in your mind so that when opportunities come along you will recognize them.

Get Sharp

Your eyes see only what your mind can grasp. Once you've decided what sort of opportunities are good matches, prepare yourself to determine which ones to jump on and which ones to ignore. You need to develop an opportunity antenna. Odds are, the opportunity won't come all wrapped up exactly as you envisioned it. And it won't land on your head so that you can't miss it. You have to be prepared to recognize it in whatever form it takes, and to develop it further so it matches your expectations. The way to do that is to educate yourself about your field of interest. Read books, scour Web sites, join organizations and chat rooms, and take classes if necessary.

Stars Make the Most of Their Opportunities

Have you ever been somewhere, and suddenly there stood the very person you need, or with whom you have been wanting to speak. You think to yourself, "I should go up and speak, I should introduce myself, I should … I should … "And you do nothing. Later, in the car going home, you regret your I coulda's, I shoulda's, and I woulda's. You missed a chance event. Stars never shoulda, coulda, or woulda. They seize the day. To create, recognize, and seize these moments, you have to be prepared and anticipate them to happen.

Do you remember when you were in high school and you had a crush on that special girl or guy? You couldn't wait to accidentally bump into her the next morning after biology near her locker. You not only imagined seeing her, but you also imagined the entire conversation in your head that you were going to have. She'll say this and I'll say that. If he asks this, I'll answer that. You prepared yourself for a conversation that you may not even have the next day because you "cared enough to get ready."

The same should be true in all aspects of your life. Think of the 20 most important or influential people in your personal or professional life. Some you know and some you would like to know. Imagine yourself bumping into them and having an opportunity to say hello and introduce yourself. Imagine those conversations. "He will probably think this. I should say that. I would like him to help me do this." Whatever. Care enough. Imagine it through. Be ready. Think of another 20 people and do the same. Eventually you will have a 100 or so "pop in the oven conversations" ready to go. Make yourself knowledgeable and aware of everything there is to know about these people you are going to meet. Know more about the person than anybody. And, as long as you are talking to anyone about themselves, even a stranger, they will listen.

If you died tonight and woke up and God was standing there, would you know what to say? Are you going to stand there and say, "Gosh, I really didn't expect to bump into you, and I'm not really prepared to discuss things right now." Well, you sure as hell better expect to bump into him. And you certainly have had enough time to imagine that conversation. And you surely should care enough to be ready, just like when your heart skipped preparing to talk to your high school first love.

So, if you can prepare these conversations and actions in your life with all the most important and influential people you might, or expect, to meet, including God, you should have no trouble imagining walking up at the office Christmas party to that very powerful and important Senior Vice President of Marketing whom you have never met and who holds your potential corporate promotion in his hands and say, "Bob ... Nancy Collins here ... I head up international media sales in our Montclair office ... " And so on.

Stars Constantly Gather Information

Most successful people often have a wide circle of friends and business contacts. They work hard to stay in touch and network. They are always open to new info and experiences to widen their horizons. They know that information is currency. They find opportunities by being professional and experienced gossipers. They know information is power. They harvest info quickly and distribute it only when they need to. They assemble information.

What they just heard on the phone, which by itself seemed inconsequential, combined with what the limo driver told them he overheard yesterday, confirms to them that Intel is going to make the move. They know they should buy the stock. They act quickly on the opportunity they now have. The stock goes up and they get "lucky."

That's not insider trading, that's well-honed intelligence gathering, which, when analyzed properly, creates opportunity.

Learn to listen. Ask questions. Correlate the raw data. Analyze it. Store it. Use it. Be on the lookout for opportunity.

STARS NEVER STOP TRYING

Overnight successes almost never occur in life; even in that narrow segment of life we call Show Business. When you look carefully at an overnight success, you'll see that the person is almost always well-prepared, like Dustin Hoffman, who washed dishes and waited on tables for almost a decade before he scored his "overnight success" in *The Graduate*. "It doesn't seem," he said at the time, "like exactly an overnight success story to me."[1]

Often, people make the mistake of thinking that if they aren't getting what they want out of life, they just need to keep doing what they've been doing—only do more of it. But the key to "getting lucky" is to step back and expand your vision for what is possible, and to look for innovative ways and opportunities to get what you want. Try a different way.

And don't worry about the no-Talent, unethical, but lucky people who are rising quickly while you're slugging it out the old-fashioned way. Don't think about them. Leave them alone. Don't even try to stop them. In fact, hurry them along. They will eventually be exposed.

STARS ARE OPTIMISTS

I've never met a true Star who was a cynic. All of the long-term successes I know think that the world is loaded with opportunities waiting to be seized. They never see a glass as half empty. It's always half full or higher. Their great expectations lead to high achievement. It's a self-fulfilling thing. If you believe that opportunity awaits, you'll find it. Optimism might just be the secret weapon of the rich and famous.

LEARNING OPTIMISM

You can't buy optimism and you aren't born with it, but you can choose it. It's an attitude and an approach to life that is readily available. It's simply a matter of learning to listen to your inner dialogue, developing the habit of shutting down negative or pessimistic messages, and tuning into more positive or optimistic messages. That doesn't mean losing touch with reality. Most Stars are realists, and one of the things they realize is that an optimistic outlook is the healthiest way to view the world.

Here is how a pessimist tends to view good and bad news:

Good News	Bad News
It is temporary.	This is never going to stop.
It won't happen to me.	I'm going to get nailed.
I didn't play a role.	This is my fault.

And this is how an optimist views good and bad news:

Good News	Bad News
It will go on for a long time.	It's only temporary.
I'm going to benefit.	This won't hurt me.
I made it happen.	I didn't cause this.

Stars have an optimistic sense that they are in control of their lives. Even when bad things happen, they've trained themselves to believe that they will endure and succeed eventually. They rarely feel helpless, and even when they do feel that things are "out of control," they remind themselves that it is only a temporary situation.

To "learn" optimism, you need to tune in to your inner dialogues, the self-talk that guides your thinking, defines your choices, and determines your attitudes. It affects how you see things and act upon them.

Let's say your kitchen catches fire and is destroyed before firemen save the rest of the house. The pessimist or negative thinker will feel overwhelmed and depressed. Let's tune in to the pessimistic self-talk: "I'll never get this cleaned up. My house will never be the same. I'm going to be in debt up to my eyeballs fixing this."

The optimist looks at the same destruction but hears an entirely different inner dialogue: "Well, thank God I have insurance. I couldn't control the fire, but no one was hurt and the insurance money will allow me to build a brand new kitchen with the latest appliances. This is probably going to increase the value of my house in the long run, and it won't take long to clean up this mess if I bring in some professional help."

The pessimist and the optimist stared into the same terrible mess but saw entirely different things. To learn optimism, you must first learn that what happens is one thing—often, you have no choice or control over things that occur—but how you respond is an entirely different matter. You can choose your response, which means you can choose an optimistic interpretation rather than a pessimistic one. It is SIMPLY a matter of choice.

There's a great young actor who appeared on the hit NBC television series *Ed,* in which he played the bowling manager Eli, who was confined to a wheelchair. The actor and rapper, Daryl "Chill" Mitchell, didn't "play" the part of a handicapped person because he too, in real life, relied on a wheelchair. He lost the use of his legs after his spinal cord was damaged in a motorcycle accident in 2001.

He was test-riding his nephew's motorcycle on an unfamiliar gravel road in South Carolina one night when it skidded and threw him off. A lot of people might have become despondent after that tragic bit of bad Luck.

Up to that point, Chill was thriving. He'd been a regular on Kirstie Alley's show, *Veronica's Closet,* and also on *The John Larroquette Show.* Just before the crash, he'd filmed *The Country Bears* with Christopher Walken.

Nobody escapes the grief that comes with losing the ability to walk, and Chill admits to having his "dark days," but in the end his natural optimism won out. He focused on those things he could control instead of the matters that were beyond his control.

One of the things he did, which is amazing, is arrange a meeting with the producers of *Ed,* even though they weren't looking for any new cast members. Chill's raging passion for acting and his strength of character took him right over that hurdle. They wrote him into the show.

Now, Chill is working on producing other hip-hop performers with his own label, and he's established his own nonprofit organization, called All For Wheels, to help other disabled people. He recently told an interviewer: "I don't ask, 'Why me?' I ask, 'What now?'"

STARS TURN FAILURE INTO SUCCESS AND BAD LUCK INTO GOOD

Stars don't get bogged down in their problems because they focus on solutions. They are always moving ahead. They are so determinedly optimistic that when they fail, they just see it as part of the process of success. When they have a streak of bad Luck or misfortune, they accept it as part of life and make the most of it. They never see failure or bad times as a permanent condition because they believe that life will present them with opportunities sooner rather than later. *And*, this is important: They don't worry about trying to control things that are beyond their control. They focus instead on controlling what they can and moving ahead.

Consider the case of the hardworking Kenny Rogers. Kenny was a successful singer with the group The First Edition. He decided his future lay in a solo career, so he quit the group and went out on his own. A few years later Kenny couldn't get arrested. It looked as though his decision to go it alone had been a bad one. Later, his career took off. He got lucky in a way that few people, even few Stars, ever do. All at once it seemed like everybody wanted Kenny Rogers. He signed, at that time, the biggest recording contract in history, and got paid just a shade more than that fellow who won the Illinois Lottery. Today, Kenny's a rich man.

Did Kenny's Luck change? It certainly did. When Kenny wasn't working as much as he'd have liked, it wasn't as though he'd lost his Talent, or decided to switch to a different style of music, or made some other bad career move. Kenny has always been Kenny, with his easy manner, his relaxed country vocal style, and his salt-and-pepper beard. And when America decided almost overnight that Kenny Rogers was what the country wanted, it wasn't the result of a clever publicity campaign or a lucky lottery ticket. In a very real sense, public taste just caught up with what Kenny had been doing all along.

But he kept doing it—he kept standing out in the rain—even when it wasn't producing instantaneous results. Nobody worked harder than Kenny Rogers. Even during his fallow period in the early and mid-'70s, he played benefits and made public appearances and tried out new material and polished up his act. If he hadn't, would he have been standing in the right place when lightning struck? I doubt it—and so does Kenny.

LUCKY STARS HAVE HEALTHY ATTITUDES

Personality tests have revealed that unlucky people are generally much more uptight, tense, and inflexible than those who consider themselves lucky. It's been proven that anxiety does interfere with your observational skills. When you are tense, you simply aren't as tuned-in to what is going on around you.

It's the same with Luck. Those who think of themselves as unlucky are mostly people who miss out on opportunities because they are distracted, uptight, or simply not tuned-in. These are people who don't hear their coworkers talking about a great, better paying job opportunity because they are focused on paying the light bill. They miss the solution because they are dwelling on the problem! Get it?

Luck-Making Formula

Based on the personality profiles of our "Lucky Stars," I've got three suggestions for improving your good fortune.

1. BE OPEN TO "GOING WITH YOUR GUT"

This isn't just about trusting your instincts, it's also about taking action rather than procrastinating, thinking things over, doing intensive research, taking a poll, and seeing what your college roommate's doctor's lawyer thinks about the idea.

Those who consider themselves unlucky tend to be plodders. The tortoise and the hare fable is a nice metaphor, but in real life the race more often goes to the swiftest. If your instincts tell you to make the leap, go for it. If your instincts say "Hold it!" then take more time to think it over, research, and investigate. The key to doing this successfully, once again, is preparation—the not-so-secret ingredient of Luck. When you are fully prepared, your judgment is sound, so you can go with your gut. If you aren't willing to educate yourself about your field of interest by learning the realities of competition and the marketplace, by making contacts, and by joining organizations in your field, then you probably won't be in any position to make the leap.

2. GET OUT OF THAT CAGE!

This goes back to the philosophy of changing your life by changing your habits. If you feel unlucky, break your routine. Go out and meet new people who are already Stars, because they are luckier, more dynamic, and more successful than your current crowd. Open yourself to opportunities by opening up your life. Join organizations that celebrate accomplishments. Volunteer for a charity that attracts successful people. Get involved in community activities that put you in position to meet the movers and the shakers—the people who attract and create opportunities as a way of life.

3. Try on a New Attitude

I've never met a successful Star in any business who thought the world owed him a favor. Nor have I known any "lucky" people who complained of being victims. If your Luck isn't what you want it to be, it's probably time for you to try on a new attitude. Here are a few to slip on for size:

- The Unstoppable Attitude: Nobody can stop me!
- The Attitude of Gratitude: I'm glad to be alive and kicking!
- The Opportunist's Attitude: It's a new day and a fresh start!
- The "Talent Rules!" Attitude: I'm going to take my Talent all the way!

The attitude you carry around doesn't just reflect who you are—it determines what you can become. By adopting a positive, optimistic, proactive attitude, you invite and attract opportunities. It's not simply a matter of putting on a happy face and chanting, "Have a nice day!" It's about believing in yourself and your dreams. It's about focusing on the solutions, living for the future, and expressing gratitude for the gift of life, second by second, minute by minute, day by day. There's nothing sappy or insincere about living like that; in fact, it's the best way to live. And it's more fun too.

Get Lucky!

How do you perceive yourself? Are you lucky or unlucky? Start to believe you are, if you don't. Open up and pay closer attention to what is happening to you.

I have a club called the "Good Luck Club," and I want you to join. To be a member all you have to do is make a list of all the good Luck that comes your way. I want you to keep this list going for one month. I do not want you to put the bad Luck you think you have on the list, just the good Luck. At the end of each week, I want you to review your list, and I bet that you will be surprised at how much good Luck is coming your way. Let's start that list today.

Good Luck Club

List of good things that have happened to me
Date: *What Happened:*

_____

_____

_____

_____

_____

_____

_____

_____

_____

_____

_____

_____

Things happen to you every day. Some are good and some are not. Keeping this list will help you focus, and remember all the good that is happening to you. It will train you to be on the lookout for chance events that may come your way. It will also strengthen you against the bad Luck that also comes with this package we call Life. It will give you a healthier perspective on the life Zorba the Greek refers to as "the wonderful catastrophe." It will also help you feel part of our Good Luck Club.

How to Overcome Bad Luck

When things look bleak, they usually are.

No matter how hard you work, how carefully you plan, or how terrific your support Team is, there are times when your best efforts seem to turn into a carload of Al Gore bumper stickers. There are two kinds of Luck, only one of them good, and all of us have to learn to deal with the other kind.

Luck can be so bad at times that it becomes a no-win situation. There is just nothing you can do.

What's a no-win situation?

A no-win situation is when you work hard, are totally prepared, and even have a chance occurrence, but everything goes wrong. How? Well, I failed to mention to you that all chance occurrences are not necessarily "good" chance occurrences.

OH NO . . . JACKIE O

Quite some years ago, I was making a sales presentation, and when I pitch something, I try not to leave very much to chance. I try to really be prepared. So, before meeting with this advertising agent vice president who was representing General Foods, I thought I was going to get myself ready. I was going to be pitching a two-hour television special called "Remarkable American Women." I was going to have all the living First Ladies celebrate and honor all the great, remarkable American women. I had decided to have Jacqueline Kennedy Onassis host the show.

I had carefully planned where I was going to take this guy to lunch and pitch him. In fact, I even went to the restaurant the day before to have lunch and talk to the maître d' in order to get the seating choreographed. The hot restaurant in town at that time was a place called the Bistro in Beverly Hills.

When you take clients to a high-profile lunch spot, you have to be very careful not to have the activities and the celebrities in the room vie for your lunch partner's attention. I wanted to make sure this guy was focused on what I was selling. So, the day before, I went to the Bistro and told the maître d', "Listen, tomorrow I'm bringing this important guy to pitch this project. I'm bringing him to the restaurant because this is the 'hot spot,' and everybody's going to be here. I want us to walk through the room and shake hands and say

'Hello,' and I'll introduce him to everybody. But I don't want you to sit us in the middle of the room with everybody staring and politely smiling at us. I want you to walk us through the room. Take us to the back. Take us to a quiet corner and slide me into the bistro seat. Put him on the outside, in a chair looking in at me so the only thing he can see is me and a wall behind me, the wall to the left of me, and whatever is to the right of me. I need to hold this guy's attention." He understood exactly what I meant. He replied, "Don't worry Mr. Thompson, we'll take care of everything."

The next day, sure enough, my client met me at the restaurant. We strolled through as planned. Things were jumping, and everything was great. I introduced him to this person and that person. The maître d' slowly walked us to the back and slid us in the corner banquette. I could tell that Mr. VP was a little disappointed. He thought we were going to be sitting out in the middle of the room, holding court. Instead, he was in the corner, staring at a wall and me. He couldn't move to his left and there was nowhere to go. It was just as I had planned. I had a captive audience.

As soon as we sat down, I pulled out my papers with the list of Talent that I was going to deliver for the two-hour special and started to make my pitch as to why I thought Jacqueline Kennedy Onassis would be the perfect host of the show. I had spoken to someone in her office, I said, and felt sure she would do it. I also would arrange for all the First Ladies to be in the audience. I thought it was going to be pretty great. I just sat there selling, doing my best, promising him the world. He was sort of interested.

Then suddenly, an uncomfortable hush fell over the room. Then a murmur rose, becoming louder and louder. An excitement filled the restaurant. I finally tore my eyes away from my buyer, and walking straight toward me, coming to my corner, I saw the maître d' leading no one other than Jackie O herself! The one person whom I'd been sitting there telling this guy not to worry about, that I was going to deliver on this project. And, of course, I had never remotely talked to or met this woman in my entire life.

They brought her over to the corner. The maître d' pulled the table back and motioned her to sit on the bistro cushion right next to me. She sits, politely nods her head to me, and turns her attention to her lunch date, seated across from me. Now, the guy that I was pitching could only see the wall to my left, me, and with a slight look to his right, maybe twelve inches, Jacqueline Kennedy Onassis herself. He could not take his eyes off her. Try competing with that!

It was tough to continue the pitch while eating crow. It was obvious that I had never talked to her, because she didn't speak to me and I didn't speak to her. Mr. VP got the picture very fast, and I slowly realized I was in a no-win situation.

Bottom line is, he did buy the project. We did put it into development. But he eventually got fired and the project never got made.

But here's the tip regarding no-win situations: All you can do in life is all you can do, and all you can do is enough. And when all you can do is not enough, learn from it and move on.

Has anyone ever won a no-win situation? Only once. In the original *Star Trek* series, every Starfleet Academy student who was given the Kobayashi Maru simulator test lost. Captain Kirk, while studying at the Academy, was the only student to ever win. How? He discovered that the simulator test was programmed as NO-WIN. He snuck in and reprogrammed the test. He won.

Don't count on winning yourself, and remember, *Star Trek* was fiction.

Here, however, is a four-step exercise for dealing with real setbacks. When things go wrong: stop, breathe deeply, and ask yourself:

1. WHAT'S HAPPENING TO ME?

It's important to separate what is truly happening to you from the emotions attached to it. It's those emotions that can overwhelm you more than anything else. For instance, if you don't get the promotion you've been seeking, the event that occurred was this: You didn't get the promotion. Often, people attach all sorts of emotional baggage and loaded language to bad luck events so that not getting the promotion becomes: "I was rejected." Or, "They think I'm not good enough." Or, "Someone stuck a knife in my back."

2. WHY IS IT HAPPENING?

It can be difficult to form a truly objective opinion on why bad things happen to you. It's wise to seek the opinions of others rather than jumping to conclusions. And it is also important—always—to remember to focus on solutions and those things that are within your control, rather than obsessing over problems and things that are outside your influence.

3. How Can I Minimize the Bad Consequences?

Again, you must separate the emotions stirred by negative experiences from the reality of what happened to you.

Your emotional response might be: "My boss passed me over, I'll never get promoted."

But the truth is "I didn't get the job I wanted this time."

When you force yourself to strip the emotions from a negative event, it helps you see things more clearly and with greater optimism.

4. Where Do I Go from Here?

You walk away from the box marked "Problem" and reach into the box marked "Solution." You focus on positive goals that are easily implemented step by step and you don't worry about those things you can't control.

Superman, Christopher Reeve, knows what bad Luck is, and how to turn it into something very positive. He was paralyzed from the neck down in an equestrian competition in 1995. He had to ask himself the hard questions above. Never a quitter, he has become an activist for people with spinal cord injuries. He is constantly lobbying on behalf of various national health issues. In 1999 he became the Chairman of the Board of Christopher Reeve Paralysis Foundation. He learned that adversity gives us the opportunity to consider what we're doing, and to think whether we should be doing something else. An inspiration to us all, Reeve maintains a rigorous speaking schedule, traveling across the country giving motivational talks to numerous groups, organizations, and corporations. Thank you, Superman.

Lucky in love

A lot in this book is about learning to have confidence in yourself. Learning to believe in yourself. Learning to love yourself. Loving yourself will attract others who will love you.

To win the love of another, you must do two things:

1. You must love yourself, which isn't always as easy as it sounds.
2. You must *want* the other person's love without *needing* it.

There are exercises you can do to practice loving yourself. You can walk into a restaurant and order your favorite entrée, regardless of the price. You're a Star, aren't you? You *deserve* it! After a hard day's work, you can tell the husband and the kids, "I'm taking an hour for myself so I can sit in a nice, hot bath"—and then *do* it. You can stop drawing that fatal equation between your career performance and your worth as a person. You are not your *job*. This last one is a tough lesson to learn, especially for men.

How do you stop needing another person's love? By realizing that your happiness isn't dependent on another's approval. In this case, the effective technique isn't so much to *do* certain things as it is to *stop* doing them. Some of the things you can stop doing are:

*   Eating poorly prepared food in a restaurant. You're *paying* for the food, aren't you? Why be afraid to send it back?
*   Agreeing with opinions you secretly disagree with because you want the people who hold those opinions to like you. You won't fool them for very long anyway.
*   Trying to impress others by pretending to know things you really don't. One of the smartest guys I know is never a bit reticent about saying, "I don't know much at all about what you're talking about. Could you please explain it to me?" Since so few people ever come right out and say this, you can imagine the impression it makes. Nobody ever thinks less of him for it. And most people are thrilled to be able to explain something to my friend, who, as I said, is a very smart guy, and well known for being one.

Being Lucky in Love is a wonderful lottery that you can win.

A Very Lucky Time

Good and bad Luck seem to come in spurts. Gamblers know this best. Always be ready for the good runs and braced for the dry periods. Some of my "luckiest" years were spent at Capitol Records, where I had many great experiences and made wonderful friends.

Since I may not ever write that Beatle book I mentioned, I thought you might find it interesting that when George Harrison delivered his first post-Beatle, solo album to Capitol Records, *All Things Must Pass*, I went downstairs to Studio B and Harrison was there. He played his new single for us. I was privileged to be one of the first to ever hear "My Sweet Lord." This was a great moment in my life. This was history, and I knew it! Harrison gave me an acetate copy of the single. It had a plain white label. He initialed it *G.H.* I still get a little choked-up thinking back on that moment. Wow.

The day Sal Iannucci left Capitol, I felt worse than he did. I went to his office, but he had gone home. I went to his house. He was with his wife, Eileen. I cried. They consoled me!

With his departure, my heart was no longer there. Capitol offered me a raise and a new title in business affairs, with a promise for crossing over into the coveted A&R department if I wanted, but emotionally it would have been difficult to stick around. ABC TV offered me a job in their West Coast Business Affairs department, but I had worked for someone else long enough. My father had always encouraged me to try and be my own boss and not work for anyone else. He used to say, "There are two kinds of people: People who work for other people, and people who work for me, but I don't work for anybody."

There's one thing I know for absolute sure, and I want you to always remember it about Luck as it relates to success and Stardom: You must work like a dog. You must position yourself for Luck. As I said earlier, "You can't get hit by lightning if you're not standing out in the rain!"

Be the "last person standing" in the rain, and when you are so drenched you think you are about to drown, you will get hit by an electrical bolt so hard that it will shock you silly, and all will become very clear to you why your mammy had you in the first place.

Break a leg!

CHAPTER
6

STAR POWER

'm often asked, "Of the Four Elements—Talent, Rage, Team, and Luck—which one is the most important?"

All Four Elements are necessary, and each is equally important. How much you need of any one element depends on how much you have of the others. The more Talent you have, the less Luck you will probably need. The more Rage you have, the less Talent you may need. The more Luck you have, the less Team you will need ... and so on.

Thomas Cruise Mapother IV, better known as Tom Cruise, struggled to find his talents as a teenager. His parents divorced. He and his mother moved more than a dozen times. But Tom's raging desire and passion kept him focused and driven. He attended the St. Francis Seminary in Cincinnati, where he studied for the priesthood. He eventually decided that was not right for him, and after his athletic career ended with a knee injury, he found a new direction. He signed up for the school play *Guys and Dolls*. There, he found his Talent. He gave himself 10 years to succeed in the movie business. He matched his Talent to his Rage.

In 1981, at the age of 18, he landed his first film role in *Endless Love*, followed by a string of increasingly important roles in *Taps*,

Losin' It, and *The Outsiders.* His big break came when he slid across the room in his skivvies in the movie *Risky Business*—an acting opportunity that was loaded with Luck. He soon became a teen cult favorite, and he claimed major Star status in 1986 with *Top Gun.*

With a Team that includes his production partner, Paula Wagner, and his agent, Rick Nicita, Tom has taken his acting to higher levels over the years to shed his "pretty boy" image and earn critical kudos for performances such as those in *The Color of Money* and *Rain Man,* in which his costars were veteran Stars Paul Newman and Dustin Hoffman. Afterward, he went on to star in top-grossing films such as *The Firm, Born on the Fourth of July, A Few Good Men, Mission Impossible, Jerry Maguire, Minority Report,* and *The Last Samurai.* He has become one of the highest paid and most sought after actors in screen history.

This hardworking kid who went Hollywood is proof that any mission is possible when you have all Four Elements of Star Power working in harmony.

Jennifer Lopez is another example of someone who amassed Star Power in all Four Elements. She was born to Guadalupe Rodriguez Lopez, a kindergarten teacher, and David Lopez, a computer operations specialist, in the Bronx. Their family moved from Ponce, Puerto Rico, to New York. After graduating from Preston High School in 1987, where she ran track, she attended one semester at Baruch College in New York City. But Jennifer's first love and real Talent was in the arts, especially dance, and when she read about a scholarship to a dance school in Manhattan, she went down and grabbed the opportunity.

At the time, she was taking a full-time course load at Baruch, working in a law office, and taking her dance classes. Eventually, this would lead to a falling out with her mother, who didn't want Jennifer to pursue dance as a career. When her mother gave her the ever-popular "you live by my rules as long as you live under my roof" speech, Jennifer's Rage kicked in and she broke out on her own. Not having anywhere else to live, she took up residence in the building where she took her dance classes. A year and a half of auditioning with no success brought Jennifer to the verge of a breakdown. But salvation would come in the form of a tour that sent her dancing across Japan.

Luck arrived in 1990 when she won a dance contest to become a Fly Girl on the Fox television comedy series *In Living Color*. Further television work ensued, including appearances in the series *Second Chances* and *Hotel Malibu* (credited on both as Melinda Lopez), the short-lived *South Central*, and in 1993, a television movie, *Nurses on the Line: The Crash of Flight 7*. She made her first major big screen appearance opposite Wesley Snipes and Woody Harrelson in 1995, in *Money Train*, before working with director Gregory Nava on *My Family, Mi Familia*. Her experience on the latter led indirectly to the high-profile role of murdered Tejano Star Selena Quintanilla in the 1997 biopic, *Selena*.

With her hardworking Team of representatives, Jennifer is now considered a major player in Hollywood. She is the "American Dream." A rags to riches story that is proof that anyone can do great things with Talent, Rage, Team, and a little Luck. With charisma and charm, Jennifer Lopez—or J. Lo, as she is now referred to—has been able to reach almost unparalleled success in both her acting and singing, career. Her acclaimed appearance opposite George Clooney in 1998s *Out of Sight* made her the highest paid Latin actress in cinema history.

These two Stars have all Four Elements working for them. There are many less known, potential Stars who have Rage, a great Team, and Luck, but without true Star-level Talent. They can get hot and hold the stage for a time, but then they tend to burn out like shooting stars, as so many of the "survivors" on all these new reality game and talent contest shows have done. Other contenders for Stardom lack the Rage to persevere. Some never assemble the right Team to help and guide them. And some failed to work for their Luck.

Some Stars, even Superstars, can have all Four Elements working for them, and unfortunately fall prey to one of the dangers we will discuss later in the book and self-destruct. John Belushi, for instance, was a great Talent whose work as a *Saturday Night Live* comedian led to starring roles in hit movie comedies like *Animal House* and *The Blues Brothers*. Belushi may well have progressed into being an even bigger Star, possibly continuing to stretch into serious acting roles had it not been for his self-destructive use of the drugs that killed him. His very talented brother, Jim Belushi, has not had that problem. He is working very hard right now on his popular series, *According to Jim,* and even performs with his musical group, the Sacred Heart Blues Band. Jim's career looks great.

So, in order to become a Star, what is the right formulaic mix of these Four Elements? And how many and much of these elements do you need? I continually tell potential Stars that the formula to success is not an exact, scientific equation, but being the eager hopefuls they are, they never quit asking me, "How much of each element do I need?" The more I tell them it is not an exact science, the more they demand a fuller explanation. So, I finally developed the following numeric example.

Regis Philbin may not stand out as having the most Talent, Rage, Team, or Luck, but he has strong measures of each and it adds up to Star Power.

100 Points of Starlight

Assume it takes 100 points of light to be the Ultimate Superstar. Also assume that each of the Four Elements were valued at a total of 25 points. Therefore, if you have 100 percent of each element, your points of light will total 100. Few people are blessed from birth, or at any one time in their lives, with 100 points.

So, let's assume it takes a minimum of 80 points to be a Star in your chosen field. Each point you add to that intensifies your level of Stardom. Superstar status starts at 90 points.

As you can now tell, since it takes a minimum of 80 points to be a Star, you need points from all Four Elements, because if you had 100 percent of three of the Four Elements, you would only total 75 points.

The following illustration will create a visual in your mind's eye of the task before you. Let's examine each element and study how they need to balance each other out. Every individual is different. Varying combinations of each of the Four Elements lights each Star. What combinations do other people have? What is yours?

Stardom's 100 Points of Star Light

Talent (25 Points)

Rage (25 Points)

Luck (25 Points)

Team (25 Points)

Stars have a minimum of 80 points from various combinations of the Four Elements. Superstars have a minimum of 90 points. How many total points do you have, and from what combination of the four elements? Let's take a look.

TALENT

The more Talent, abilities, trades, skills, and ideas you have to offer the world, the better jump you have on success.

There are some people who just have high-wattage Talent. Its brilliance blinds you. These people may be mental geniuses like the Big Bang's Stephen Hawking—or they're blessed with great artistic

Talent from the get-go, like child prodigies who can sing or play the piano or the violin like angels from heaven.

There are also those with less easily discerned talents. Being charming may not sound like much of a gift until you see it applied at the level that former President Bill Clinton uses it. Knowing how to cut hair skillfully becomes more than a trade craft when it is as artistically done as José Eber does it. Some Stars are masters at building cabinets or are masterful inventors and telemarketers like Ron Popeil. Others are savvy in money matters, mathematics, and finance in the way of Warren Buffett. A wonderful doctor can save your life. A scientist can discover a cure for a disease. All these unique Talents are very important and a serious part of the formula in creating success.

Even though it's only one of the Four Elements you need, Talent is certainly something that, if you've identified it, and if you're working at it, will take you toward Stardom in leaps and bounds.

Keep in mind that you shouldn't fall into the habit of comparing your talents to those of others. That's a waste of time and energy. There will always be people who seem to be blessed with more natural ability than you. Some are simply prodigies. Some have worked from birth to develop their natural gifts. Tiger Woods may be an imposing and dominant figure in golf, but there is always room—and a chance—for other gifted golfers. He doesn't win every tournament. Michael Jordan was a superior Talent, but his teams didn't win every game. Picasso may have been one of the great artistic Talents of his time, but that doesn't diminish the Talents of other great artists.

Those with lesser talents can prevail given the right combination of the other elements, timing, and circumstances. I don't want you to watch others, feeling you have less Talent, and think, "Well, gosh, I've got a little Talent but nothing like that." When you compare your talents to another's, you overlook the fact that your talents are unique to you, and your challenge is to fully develop your own abilities, not be jealous of someone else's.

Once you have identified and developed your Talent, it will get stronger and stronger the more you use it, just like a muscle. So, keep working because it only gets better. Your Talent may not have arrived fully developed as a gift from God, but that doesn't make it any less a gift. It is still Talent, and while you may have to dig very deep to discover your particular gift, that may be part of the blessing. You may come to appreciate it all the more once you've uncovered it, or realized it was there, unrecognized, all of the time.

Sometimes, you have to search for something that's deep within you. In some cases, people don't recognize a Talent because it is so much a part of them. They've had it so long they've taken it for granted. Maybe you assume it's just a part of you, but you've never really recognized it as a viable Talent nor taken time to develop it.

That's a key point that I often stress to my clients: Even though you may think you have just a bit of Talent, the more you develop it, the more you work at it, the more you strengthen it, the more you put into it, the more you focus on it, the better it will get, continuing to bloom to a point where you exceed even your own wildest expectations! Know that you do have Talent. In all likelihood, you probably have several Talents. Dig for them, identify them, work at them, develop them, and build them into something you can wrap your life around.

Of the 25 points that Talent represents, the total may vary from time to time depending on how fully developed the Talent is at the moment. Have you identified your Talent by now? How developed is it? Later, I am going to ask you to score your Talent level from 1 to 25. What does it take to score a perfect 25 points in Talent? Let's use the following Stars as a benchmark.

We know there are certain actors, for example, who are just incredibly gifted—Robert De Niro, Dustin Hoffman, Meryl Streep, Al Pacino, Cate Blanchett, Sean Penn, and Jodie Foster, to name a few. Some actors have an enormous amount of Talent, which they developed and polished over the years. These Stars certainly rely on Talent more than the other three elements. Let's score them with the full 25 points of Talent.

How does the level of your Talent, at this time, compare to the perfect score of 25 given to those listed above?

RAGE

Rage is like a force of nature that cannot be denied. Truly driven people can overcome negligible levels of Talent, buckets of bad Luck, and a mediocre Team simply because they don't let anything stop them or stand in their way. I can't emphasize enough how important Rage is.

Again, I'm not referring to simple ambition, hopes, wishes, and idle dreams. This is the *Raging Bull* kind of Rage. To be a Star in your own life takes maniacal, tunnel vision, burning passion, over-the-top, make the leap, and buy a one-way-ticket RAGE! Think of the Incredible Hulk going green, or Stallone on steroids. You've met those people. Maybe they even make you uncomfortable. You can feel their energy bouncing off walls. Their ambition makes windows rattle and buildings sway. They commit themselves head first over the edge.

Rage is not something you can develop as easily as Talent. If you work at Talent, it will improve; but Rage has to be something that's burning within you. I could go on and on about Rage for 10 more pages, but the truth is: If you don't have it, I can't give it to you. I might be able to get you excited for a week or two, but Rage is something that burns from an inner flame. Either you have it or you don't. Either you will light that flame from within or you won't.

I have met people who are very talented and have a great Team, but I can tell they don't have enough Rage. There is no fire in their bellies. They're indifferent, blasé, or nonchalant. They may have Rage and ambition for other things. They may love their families or they may be avid travelers or athletes, but they aren't willing to put in the effort that it takes to be Stars in their chosen fields. Some people just don't like to work. But you can't be totally successful at anything—anything—if you're not willing to work. To work that hard, you've got to be motivated. There's not enough money to pay people if they're not motivated. Rage comes from within.

So, I ask you to dig deep, maybe pray, maybe not, and ask yourself: "What is it that I really want? Am I willing to pay the price?"

Everyone has a Rage for something. Let's start with the basics. You have to breathe, right? So, if you couldn't breath, if there were no longer any oxygen in the room and you started to gasp for air, I'm sure you would have a Rage to find air. You would do anything, go anywhere, and knock over any table, to get to fresh air. You would feel a Rage to survive. Now, can you imagine desiring something else in life as much as gasping for that fresh breath of air? NOW, do you understand what Rage is? That is 25 points of Rage.

Lance Armstrong, world champion cyclist, two-time Olympian, renowned humanitarian, role model, cancer survivor, and now five-time winner of the Tour de France, is clearly an example of someone applying Rage to Talent. He is the most celebrated and charismatic contributor to the sport of cycling. Armstrong made world headlines in Paris on July 25, 1999, with the most stunning comeback ever in the history of the sport. But his athletic accomplishments paled in comparison to his personal achievement. To say that he is an emotional athlete is an understatement. To say that he is a passionate and fearless competitor is evident. He is a great man who embodies a Rage for excellence. Let's give him 25 points here for his Rage.

I've identified Rage for you. I've attempted to motivate you, but that's something you have to take responsibility for doing on your own for the rest of your life. I think the more Talent you identify, the better the Team you assemble, the more focused you are, and the better plan you have, the stronger your Rage will burn. It's like going on a diet. You hate it. You dread it. You don't want to do it. Then you lose five pounds and you look in the mirror and your pants feel a little better around your waist. You get a little tingle of excitement. You get motivated. Someone says that you look good. You decide to lose another five pounds. You start to get support and reconfirmations from family and friends along the way. You really get motivated now and you're going to lose 20 pounds! Of course, as we know, you wind up losing a total of 12 pounds, and then a month later you gain back 15. You've got to keep the Rage going to keep the weight off. The inner flame can burn off pounds too!

Go for it! Live life with gusto. Get your plan together. Sheer Rage has taken many people a long way in their careers. Madonna may be the poster girl for raging success. Jake Steinfeld, who was a chunky kid with a stutter back in Long Island, raged his way to a multimillion dollar business empire. Oprah? All she could do was talk, but after a childhood marked by abuse, abandonment, and poverty, her inner flame made her a billionaire. Surely all three of those examples have Talent, but each of them would gladly tell you that they know scores of more talented people. They are proud that their drive and determination carried them to such heights. They Rage. Talent is 25 percent. Rage is equally 25 percent. How does your Rage level compare to the Stars discussed here? How many points are you thinking about giving yourself?

You need to remind yourself that the form of Rage you'll need is a controllable drive and commitment, not some blind fury. Athletes learn to successfully channel their Rage to achieve peak performance, and you must do the same, or else you'll crash and burn, or you'll be so obsessed that others might take advantage of you. Stay focused on your goals, but also remain alert to your circumstances and the influences around you at all times.

TEAM

You can have all the Talent and Rage you want, but without help, you couldn't go the total distance. Team is another 25 percent.

I encourage you to sit down and think carefully about selecting people who can add value to your life. Then, before you go to any of them, give thoughtful consideration to the roles you want each of them to play on your Team. Every Team has role players who specialize, who bring unique skills to the game. Your challenge is to put together a Team in which each individual offers something that complements and enhances your own Talent, Rage, and Luck.

Once you've outlined your plan and you know what specific help and experience you need, you can go to your family, your friends, the professionals, and everybody you've identified who can be helpful. Put together an organization—your Team. "Your Organization, Inc." That's why I call my company Larry A. Thompson Organization, Inc. I'm not afraid to let the world know that I welcome all the help I can get.

Hold on. Don't pick up the phone yet. There is something else you need to consider before you call that first team member. You are about to reach out to people and ask for their help. You are going to request that they invest time and effort in YOUR dreams of Stardom. Before you do that, you need to think about each prospective team member and ask yourself these questions:

- Have I earned the right to ask this person for help?
- Have I invested my time and my effort in THEIR dreams?
- Have I been loyal to them?
- Have I encouraged them?
- Have I earned their trust?
- Have I been there when they needed me?

I'm sure you've heard and read about the importance of networking. It is an extremely important tool for success, but one that is probably more misused than any other. Networking isn't just about knowing valuable people and using them as resources. The most important aspect of networking is serving.

It's great to know people in all different fields, with all different skills, abilities, personalities, and traits. And it is fine to ask them to sign on as teammates, but only AFTER you've earned their trust, loyalty, and good graces. If you want them to work for you, it's necessary that you show you are willing to work for them. It's got to be a win-win. You can't expect to draw on their bank of goodwill and hard work if you haven't made any deposits in their account. Your mother and father may be willing to selflessly work on your behalf, maybe your spouse too. But other talented, busy, time-constrained people will require proof of reciprocity. You scratch their backs and they'll scratch yours. You watch out for their best interests, they'll do the same for you. Then, and only then, can you ask them to work for you. That is how you motivate them. That is how you instill Rage in them.

We all know people who have had moms and dads, aunts and uncles, brothers and sisters, friends, and even rich relatives supporting them, and giving them a boost as teammates. We've all said, "If I had that kind of help … if I had that … " Well, maybe they've got more of a Team but less of something else. You've got to put your own act together. If you don't have a Team, you better have a lot more Talent. If you don't have Rage, you better have a lucky horseshoe on your wall.

When it comes to Team, put the very best people together because you are only as good as your weakest link.

The world of sports has had many great team builders, including Vince Lombardi, John Wooden, "Bear" Bryant, Casey Stengel, Joe Torre, and Joe Paterno, just to name a few. Military leaders who assembled, trained, and led men into battle included Generals George Patton, Dwight D. "Ike" Eisenhower, Norman Schwarzkopf, and Tommy Franks.

While you may or may not have agreed with the jury's verdict, most people readily concede that O.J. Simpson assembled one of the greatest legal defense teams in the history of American jurisprudence. In fact, if you remember, the Team of Robert Shapiro, Johnnie

Cochran Jr., Barry Scheck, F. Lee Bailey, and Alan Dershowitz, among others, were referred to as the "Dream Team." They were the right people for the right job. This example alone should show you what a good Team can help you achieve.

Hopefully, you will never need a legal defense Team, but you will need a Team of qualified believers to help you reach Stardom in whatever career or quest you have for fulfillment.

When putting your own Team together, remember:

- Don't be ashamed to ask for help.
- Don't be embarrassed to approach people you respect.
- Show your willingness to be supportive in return.
- Listen more than you talk.
- Give as much as you get.

Start thinking about your Team members. Are they helping? How many of the 25 points are you considering giving yourself later?

LUCK

Okay, so we all know people who can fall into a pile of you know what and come out smelling like a rose. And it gets worse. These people get up to 25 points for smelling like that.

Working hard and being prepared will allow you to rack up a lot of Luck points, and you won't even have to smell like that. That alone makes you lucky.

Think about it. You should give yourself a few Luck points right off the top just for being healthy, living in America, and having a job. Everything good in your life after that adds big points in your Luck column.

With the realization that maybe you already are a bit lucky, you will eventually come to know that True Luck runs very deep. The truth is, most people share the same basic, human needs and objectives: to love, to be loved, to give, to be fulfilled, to be the best at who and what they are, to be happy, to feel accomplished, and to leave footprints in the sands of time. If you don't take care of those basic, internal wants and needs, no amount of external Luck or chance events that may bring you wealth, power, and fame will ever fulfill you. That's why I've encouraged you to simply make your own good Luck by identifying and developing your Talents, adding your Rage, finding your Team, and working hard with integrity. When you focus on building a life like that from the inside out, you generate momentum that, I believe, can make you feel like the luckiest person in the world.

Charting the Stars and Their Star Power

All of these Four Elements of Star Power are important, and for different reasons for different people at different times. Therefore, let's not diminish the importance of any, or emphasize the importance of one over the other. What matters is the balance of the four: Talent, Rage, Team, and Luck.

15 Successful People

Let's take 15 successful people and attempt, at this time in their lives, to estimate their Star Power. Study the chart carefully and see if you agree.

STAR	TALENT	RAGE	TEAM	LUCK	TOTAL STAR POWER
1. George Clooney	23	22	23	22	90
2. Prince William	15	15	25	25	80
3. Bill Gates	25	25	22	20	92
4. Ashton Kutcher	20	20	20	20	80
5. J. K. Rowling	25	24	19	18	86
6. Tiger Woods	25	24	25	23	97
7. Jennifer Lopez	23	24	22	21	90
8. Stephen King	25	25	20	20	90
9. Oprah Winfrey	24	24	24	24	96
10. Shania Twain	22	24	22	20	88
11. Jack Welch	25	22	25	19	91
12. Ozzy Osbourne	22	21	24	20	87
13. Regis Philbin	22	22	21	22	87
14. Senator Ted Kennedy	13	13	25	25	76

Now, let's take number 15—you. I want you to honestly take inventory and ask yourself, "Of Talent, Rage, Team, and Luck, how much Star Power do I have? How much Talent? Rage? Team? Luck?" These are tough questions, but I do want you to score yourself. Take your time. Write in how many points you think you have at this time in your life.

15. _____   —   —   —   —   —

(Your Name)

I want you to fill out your Star Power scorecard so you can better identify what you have and what you need. It will help put it all in perspective, give you direction, and define your mission.

What was your per-element and total score? Are you already a Star? Are you close? Do you have a lot of work to do? Are you excited? No matter what your total score is today, with focused hard work you can reach Stardom level. How? By turning up your Star wattage capability using the Three Secrets to Gain Star Power.

Three Secrets to Gain Star Power

If you truly want Stardom in your chosen field, and you are willing to work for it, you can and will continue to grow in power. The following three power secrets will help you focus your efforts.

1. Focus on Strengths, Not Weaknesses

We all would like to be great at everything. Unfortunately, our DNA genetic structuring usually provides each of us with the ability to do some things better than others. Our individual aptitudes, or inherent abilities, differ from person to person. Most people make the mistake of struggling to improve themselves in areas in which they don't have a natural aptitude, rather than in perfecting themselves in those areas in which they do have natural aptitude.

Unfortunately, we learn to make this mistake early in life. While our parents mean well, most of them teach us this bad habit. For example, if a child brings home a report card and it shows an A– in English, a B in History, a B– in Geography, and a D– in Math, the parent panics and says, "Every night, I want you to crack that Math book and get that grade up. I don't care about those other grades, you better not bring home that report card again."

Well, it's true that this student may need to focus a bit more on Math and improve her grade up to at least a C, but not to the exclusion of continuing to do well or improving on what she is already doing well in. It may be a lot easier for her to go from a B in History to an A, or from an A– in English to an A+, than to go from that D– in Math to a B. Maybe she just doesn't get the numbers in Math like she gets the words in English. She probably will grow up to be a famous novelist with a gang of employed accountants adding up her money.

Similarly, I want you to look at your Star Power score and commit yourself to working on all the areas, but focusing more on those areas where you are already doing well in. For example, if you scored 18 in Team and 20 in Talent, work harder, not exclusively, at Talent than Team. Once your Talent starts to soar, it will be easier to pick the right Team. Likewise, if you scored 20 in Rage and 22 in Luck, commit to working even harder to get lucky, and ask your Team to help you with your Rage. Get great at one, and the others will become less hard. Remember, you have to average a 20 in each of the Four Elements to total 80, which qualifies you as a Star.

2. Make Yourself More Visible

One of the quickest ways to jump-start and increase your Star Power is to physically venture out of your comfort zone and make yourself more visible to others. Being around and known by more people will help you either identify or inspire your Talent; enhance your Rage, find your Team, and possibly cause good Luck.

It's okay to want people to know who you are, and to like you. In fact, it's a natural and necessary thing if you want to stand out and be a Star. From the beginning of time, man has sought to make sure that people knew of his existence, that they knew who he was as a civilization, that he was here; that he lived, that he meant something. We see paintings on walls of cavemen telling their stories of hunting, living, and dying. They wrote their names on walls. They told of their lives. It was important to them that they said, "Hey, I'm here. I live here on planet Earth. This is who I am. This is what I do. Don't forget me."

Most people think that the opposite of love is hate. It's not. The opposite of love is indifference. There is nothing worse than feeling that people are indifferent to you, that they ignore you, that they don't recognize that you're alive. There's a certain need in people to want to be identified—to be special. That's why you have a name. That's why people refer to you by your name. It's something that's individual. It's something that's yours.

I've always thought it was sad that people could feel they were wallflowers—that no one saw them. A former client, Paul Williams, who is a wonderful soul, wrote a very sad and poignant song about this feeling called "When I Was All Alone."

There's also this wonderful song in the musical *Chicago,* called "Mr. Cellophane," where the sad-sack character, who feels he is invisible and even inconsequential, sings that "Mister Cellophane shoulda been my name ... 'cause you can look right through me, walk right by me, and never know I'm there, never even know I'm there."[1] Nothing is worse than to feel you don't exist; that no one cares, that no one even knows you're there. How sad.

It's human nature to want to be cared about, to be known, respected, and loved. Becoming successful requires you to make yourself visible. Make yourself or your product known. People who know you know your Talents. They may even know them before you do. They can help you discover your innate gifts. They can also inspire you to use your talents properly. Their good feelings about you may even increase your confidence and Rage.

If you have a great product and you want to sell it, but people don't know you have that product, you're not going to sell it. You are your product. So, the marketing and promotion of you is very important. That is what I'm referring to when I talk about making yourself visible.

In Hollywood, Stars have a Team of publicists, also called public relations people or media consultants. These people create images, modify them, feed them to the media, or keep them from the media—whatever the situation requires. Their job is to get you "ink"—getting your name or picture in the paper for doing something, whether it's marketing a movie or just being at a party. So, once you've established what your image is, you need to start making yourself known. It's time to step out.

There's a song lyric by the group Dr. Hook, in which the singer bemoans the fact that no matter what they do, they can't seem to "get our picture on the cover of the *Rolling Stone.*©"[2] Well, that basically says it, doesn't it?

Maybe you don't need your picture on exactly the cover of *Rolling Stone*, but you know what? It's nice to have your name in the local newspaper, or the company newsletter, or, hell, a Most Wanted poster. There's nothing wrong with getting your picture or name in the paper. In fact, in order to be successful, it's helpful.

People like winners. People like famous people. Famous people like other famous people. People like powerful people. Powerful people like other powerful people. We live in a society where if people read about you in the newspaper, they feel like, "Well, if the newspaper thinks they're important enough to put their name in the paper, they must be important!" So suddenly, getting your name out there, becoming visible, and having people talk about you, having newspapers and magazines write about you, being on local television, marketing your product—which is you—all of this is very important.

How do you apply this to your life? If you're living in a small town and you've decided that you're going to open up a store, you've got to talk to the newspaper. You've got to tell them what it is that's unique about your store. Tell them why the local people will enjoy coming out and patronizing your business. If you live in a town where there are publicists, or where there are media experts or public relations firms, go talk to them. Find out what it is that they do. Explain to them what you're trying to do. See if they can help you get done what you need. You want them to be a part of your Team. These people work on a monthly fee basis, ranging from $1,500 to $5,000. You lay out a campaign and goal with them concerning what you want to accomplish, and they will help you accomplish it.

I remember when I first came out to L.A. and I had been hearing about publicists. I finally met one and asked him, "What does a publicist do?" He was with one of the top PR firms in the business. He said, "Well, if you have to ask what a publicist does, you don't need one."

Think about that. Have you ever heard of a publicist, or a PR firm, or a media expert? Maybe you need one. So, don't be embarrassed if you've never heard of one. I'm giving you the clue that these people exist and everybody you know and read about uses them. You might want to check into it and see if they can help.

For those who can't afford a publicist, there are many less expensive alternatives. Here are a few ideas for increasing your visibility:

* Create a good Web site on yourself that offers interesting or useful information and links to other good sites.
* Start a newsletter to publicize your service or products.
* Be a "blogger." Web diaries are a great way to attract attention.
* Write guest editorials or letters to the editor of your local or national newspapers to establish your credentials as an expert in your field.
* Join professional organizations in your field and be active on committees and at conventions to raise your profile.
* Become a member of community service organizations such as the Lion's Club, Kiwanis, the Jaycees, the PTA, and the Republican and Democratic parties.
* Offer your services as a public speaker to local organizations, schools, and nursing homes to raise your profile.
* And finally, here's my top-secret tip for raising your visibility as a Star in your own field: WRITE A BOOK!!!!

So, get out there. Get exposed. Make yourself visible. Promote your product. And get *your* picture on the cover of the *Rolling Stone*.

3. CREATE AFFINITY

Affinity is the ability to enter someone else's world and make them feel that you understand them, that you have a strong, common bond. It is the essence of successful communication.

Regardless of what you want to achieve, create, share, promote, sell, or experience in life, there are people who can help you accomplish your goals. Someone else knows a shortcut. Other people have followed similar paths. They can serve as your guides, educate you, and help you find the way. They can be part of your Team.

To attract these valuable people, you must achieve an affinity with them—some magical bond that unites you in a common goal.

As you identify yourself, get out into the public arena, and start networking and talking to more and more people, and as you interview and ask people to help you and be a part of your Team, you'll need to develop excellent communication skills. You'll need relationship skills. You'll need to be able to get your message across quickly and specifically.

The ability to quickly establish an affinity with others is a vital skill. Unless you plan on being a hermit, a monk, or a lighthouse keeper, your success will depend a great deal upon your ability to connect with your customers, clients, and coworkers.

How do you create an affinity with people? By communicating with them in such a way as to discover or create things in common.

When people are like each other, they tend to "like" each other. Take any relationship between any two people and you'll discover that the first thing creating the bond between them was something they had in common. The more things people have in common, the more they tend to like each other, because they are a reflection of themselves.

So, when we meet people who we want to befriend, love, influence, sell, or recruit as part of our team, we need to create an affinity with them. There are many ways to discover commonality with another person. Here are four obvious ways:

- Common *interests*
- Common *associations*
- Common *experiences*
- Common *beliefs*

Common interests run from "You like to ski too?" "I also collect stamps," "Don't you just love Sandra Bullock?" and "I can't believe we both like ketchup on our scrambled eggs," to "I'm so excited I found someone who likes *Queer Eye for the Straight Guy* like me."

Common associations range from "I went to high school with his sister," "His family knew my family," "We go to the same clubs," and "I can't believe we have so many friends in common," to "We have the same bookie."

Common experiences can include "I went to Camp Tallahatchie too," "We stayed at that same hotel in Paris," "He colored my hair also," "I dated him too!" (That's a real affinity-getter.)

Common beliefs touch the soul: "I'm Italian too," "I voted for him too," "I'm definitely prolife," " I'm also a vegetarian," "I also believe in the Easter Bunny."

All of these commonalities can be discovered through communication.

While speaking seems to be the most common form of communication, studies have shown that less than 10 percent of what is communicated between people is transmitted through words alone. Almost 40 percent comes through the tone of voice. When you were a kid and your dad raised his voice and said your name—often your full name—in that certain tone, you knew he meant more than dinner was being served.

Over 50 percent of communication is the result of physiology or body language. The facial gestures, expressions, and type of movements of the person delivering the communication provide us with much more of what they're saying than words alone. This explains why a hilariously talented comedian like Chris Rock can get up and say outrageous things and make you laugh your butt off. Is he funny or what? Next time you see Chris Rock on TV or in a movie, just watch his body movement, his expressions, his delivery, and listen to the tone of his voice. If he were speaking Portuguese, you would still laugh. Bernie Mac breaks me up too. It's not only the words, it's the delivery, the tonality, and the body language that make you laugh.

To further confirm my point, go rent a classic, silent movie and discover how you can totally understand the story with no dialogue. Long before "talkies," the world flocked to see movies without any sound. Great actors were able to express a feeling or story point with facial expressions, body movement, hand gestures, and a few written words that occasionally appeared on screen. Charlie Chaplin was a master.

When you are talking to someone, don't stand there with your arms crossed: body language that says you are guarded or closed off. Drop your arms and you will appear more open and receptive to their ideas and comments. Do you remember Michelle Pfeiffer's body language in the movie *The Fabulous Baker Boys*, when she was lying on top of the piano and singing? I'm not suggesting you try that on the conference table at your next staff meeting, but then again, why not?

Everyone communicates the same, but differently. What I mean by that is, research has shown that people receive and give out information through one of three different primary thought processes. They use all three, but primarily use one:

1. Visual (Steven Spielberg)
2. Auditory (Quincy Jones)
3. Kinesthetic (my wife)

When you identify and access their thought processes, you mirror and anchor them and create instant unconscious affinity. What exactly are these thought processes and how can you access them?

If one's thought process is primarily Visual, when they speak, they use phrases like "This is how it looks to me," "I just can't picture myself doing that," "I see your point," "Am I painting a clear picture?" or "I want you to take a good look at this." Visual thinkers speak quickly and their breathing is usually high in the chest. The vocal tone is high-pitched, nasal, and often strained. When asked to describe an image, they will access the image in their head by physically looking up and left, as if it is in their memory bank, or up and right if they are constructing a new image. Meet Steven Spielberg.

If another's thought process is Auditory, they will use phrases like "It sounds good to me," "That doesn't ring a bell," "I hear what you are saying," "I want to make this loud and clear," and "Does what I'm saying sound right to you?" Their speech is usually more modulated. The tempo is balanced. The voice tends to have a clear, resonant tonality. Breathing tends to be even and deep, coming from the diaphragm of the whole chest. When asked to describe an image, they will access the image in their head by physically looking laterally to their left if it is being remembered or laterally to the right if it is being newly constructed. They may also physically look down and to the left. Meet Quincy Jones.

Those who have a Kinesthetic thought process use phrases like "It doesn't feel right to me," "I'm just not in touch with things," or "I feel that I am in touch with what you are saying." They speak in a slow tempo. Many times they take long pauses between words and have a low, deep tonality. You can tell they're thinking, that they're feeling. They seem to be more relaxed musclewise. When asked to describe an image, they will access the image in their head by physically looking down and to the right. Meet my wife.

It's important that you understand these three thought processes because if someone primarily is an auditory processor and you're trying to persuade him to do something or ask him about something, and you're asking him to picture how it will look and you talk very, very fast, you probably won't get through to him. He needs to hear what you have to say. He needs to listen to your proposal and notice if it clicks for him. In fact, he may not even hear you simply because your tone of voice may turn him off.

So, if someone hears information and uses verbs to express it, mirror that. If someone sees things, see them also—paint them pictures. If someone feels things, feel with them. I call this "changing channels" or "matching frequencies." Observe the person. Mirror him. Speak the same language as your friend.

I once dated a girl who would put her hands over her ears during the scary scenes in movies because the music frightened her. I put my hands over my eyes instead, because I was afraid to watch. Well, I guess it's obvious that she is an auditory processor and I am visual. We eventually broke up. She heard me say, "I'm not prepared to get married now," and I watched her walk out the door.

The only way to communicate well and create affinity is to begin with a sense of humility and a willingness to change. You can't communicate by force of will. You can't bludgeon someone into understanding your point of view. You can only communicate by constant, resourceful, attentive flexibility.

There are no resistant people, only inflexible communicators. Creating affinity and communicating better will increase your Star Power.

Ready for Your Close-Up?

When the director asks a Star if she is ready for her close-up, a hush comes over the set. Everyone watching knows this is the money shot, and the Star knows she had better be good. At this distance, the camera doesn't lie.

You have now identified your Talent, conjured up your Rage, gathered your Team, and prepared for your Luck. You have learned the formulaic, required mix of these elements, and the secrets to power them up. You are ready for your close-up.

Stars live for this moment. It probably wasn't easy getting here, but then again, it's not easy getting anywhere.

CHAPTER 7

IMAGE

There's a saying in the movie business, "Open big or you're dead!" Well, that pretty much holds true for life in general and Stardom in particular.

Give 'Em the Old Razzle Dazzle

If you are starting to roll your eyes, let me assure you that this is not superficial nonsense. It's true that "it's what's inside that counts." And no one should be judged entirely by appearance. But in the real world, the fact is, how you present yourself is every bit as important as how you present your products and services.

APPEARANCE

One of the first steps toward Stardom is to present yourself in a way that says, "I'm a Star."

If you want people to buy into your Stardom, whatever your field, you should dress and act as if you're already a Star. Why do you think everyone is interested in what all the Stars are wearing to the Academy Awards? "Look at Ashley Judd's dress. Can you believe Nicole Kidman's shoes? Denzel Washington looks great. Michelle Pfeiffer's Armani pantsuit is so classy. Charlize Theron is so elegant. That Jack Nicholson guy looks like a hoot."

Hollywood is definitely a town, and an industry, where looks and style are critically important. But don't kid yourself, in any town, in order to make the most of your Talent, Rage, Team, and Luck, you've got to present yourself in the best possible manner that is appropriate for your working environment. The influence of appearance in the courtroom, for example, is so great that an entire subindustry has developed to provide advice to lawyers, plaintiffs, and defendants on how to dress and comport themselves in front of judges and juries. In fact, that's how Dr. Phil McGraw made a living before he became a television talk show host.

Hollywood Stars are often fashion trendsetters. That may not work if you aspire to be a Star accountant, lawyer, or corporate executive. So you'll need to tailor your "look" to the standards of your profession. Your appearance is extremely important. Everything about your appearance is crucial, including your hair, teeth, complexion, nails, hygiene, clothes, accessories, jewelry, and shoes. It doesn't have to cost a lot of money to appear stylish and confident. It does, however, require some thought and time.

Dressing like a Star is also a matter of what you want to Star *at*. You should dress accordingly. A good bartender's wardrobe isn't necessarily appropriate for a banker. A teacher's hair coloring should probably be different from a female wrestler. A Wall Street broker dresses differently than the foreman of a dude ranch. You must learn how to pick a look that fits your model for success. The clothes don't make the man, but they do make the image of the man. Or woman. The manner in which you dress affects your self-image, just as it impacts the way people treat you.

DRESS FOR THE ROLE

I was making a movie for NBC called *Original Sin,* and it was going to star Ann Jillian and Robert Desiderio. We needed a mafia don in the movie to play Desiderio's father. I didn't really want to cast the stereotypical actor to play the mafia don role. I wanted something larger than life but different. Over the years, I had befriended Jack Gilardi, an agent who represented quite a few important clients, among them Charlton Heston. I thought, "Wow, Charlton Heston! Gosh, he played Moses, Ben Hur. I mean he was a big name, and is a big name. Wouldn't it be interesting for him to play a mafia don?" Now, I know he's not Italian or anything like that, but you know, with a mustache, different hairstyle, maybe this could work.

I talked to Jack about whether Mr. Heston would be interested in playing a mafia don. He said, "Well, you know, let's send a script up there to him and let him read it, then I'll put you two together, and you guys can talk about it, and we'll see where it goes."

"Great!" I beamed.

Sure enough, we sent the script to his house, and five or six days later, Charlton Heston called and said, "Let's meet."

So, there I was now driving up Coldwater Canyon to this beautiful home sitting on a cliff overlooking the world, and there was Moses, Charlton Heston, just bigger than life. He answered the door himself, and I stared up at his famous face. "Larry, come on in. I've read your script."

As we were sitting down, he said, "You know … it's interesting that you thought of me for this role. I want you to know that I'm very appreciative of it, but I don't actually see myself playing the part. Meaning, I'm certainly not Italian. I don't look Italian, and I'm not the classic mafia don. I just don't know if this is something I can make believable. Not to mention the fact that I have never really played the heavy in a movie but once, and that's when I played Cardinal Richelieu in *The Four Musketeers*. Other than that one bad guy in a period classic, I have never really played the villain before. So, to play a contemporary mafia don, who is a villain, who is Italian, I just don't see myself playing it, but I appreciate you thinking of me and coming up here. I just didn't want to summarily say no and sound unappreciative. I wanted to meet with you because Jack has told me a lot about you, and I wanted to say, 'Thank you, but pass.'"

He started to walk me out of the house, and as he did, we were walking along a hallway that had these wonderful pictures of him in movies he had starred in. I don't know if these were all of his movies. There is probably not a hallway long enough for him to put pictures up of all of his movies, but there were pictures of him as Moses in *The Ten Commandments,* Ben Hur on the chariot, and Cardinal Richelieu in *The Four Musketeers,* among others.

As we looked at his photographs, Heston said, "You know, Larry, as an actor I have always enjoyed wearing costumes. I like playing characters where costumes are involved. The reason is a lot of actors get into a role by internalizing the character first then externalizing the performance. I sort of call that inside out. But I work outside in. I have to see myself as the character in full costume before I can start to become that character. That's why costumes have always helped me."

I pondered that and something struck me. I said, "Listen, what about this? Suppose we costumed you as a mafia don. Put you in front of a mirror fully-clothed and made up as the don, and let you see if you could begin to feel that role?"

"Well, most of the costumes I am talking about were period pieces, like robes or togas," Heston responded. "Your movie is a contemporary story. How exactly would you do that?"

"I tell you what I would do," I replied. "A lady I am dating is in the fashion business. She is a friend of the famous Italian designer, Valentino. I'd like to have him design for you two beautiful Italian suits. That's probably not the type of clothing you normally wear, but let's have him design and make for you two double-breasted Italian suits. They will be a gift to you from me whether you do the movie or not. I think we also need a contemporary wig and maybe a mustache. We will get you totally costumed and have you take a look at yourself in the mirror and let's see what happens."

"Well, I'd be open to that," the great actor said, "I just don't want to promise you anything."

I told him that I totally understood: "The fact that you would even do this thrills me, and just continues to confirm to me the gentleman Star that you are."

Sure enough, Valentino created two double-breasted Italian suits: one black and one gray. They were gorgeous. We went to the greatest wig maker in town and had a hairpiece styled for him with a matching mustache.

I drove back up Coldwater Canyon to visit my would-be mafia kingpin.

I went in with a dresser and hair stylist. We dressed and costumed Charlton Heston to be Louis Mancini, the mafia don.

He walked in front of his mirror in total costume and stood there and studied his image. He stared into the mirror for the longest time.

Total silence. And then I saw a miracle. I saw a man change his entire essence: his stance, his look, his expression, his hands, his attitude, and his entire demeanor. I saw an artist look at himself and transform himself into something that he was not. From the moment he walked in front of that mirror, a master went to work. He eventually walked away from that mirror transcended—walking differently, looking differently, speaking differently, he had become the character, Don Louis Mancini. He looked at me with Sicilian stillness and with a deep sense of power, and with a voice I had never heard come out of his mouth, he said, "You've got yourself a mafia don!"

Once he dressed the part, he became the part. That was a lesson that I will never forget. That is why I want you to dress for the role in life you want to play, so that you become the person and Star you wish to become.

Heston was magnificent in the movie, by the way. Just as I'm sure you'll be magnificent in your own starring role.

LET'S SEND YOU TO WARDROBE

Before you can dress for your starring role, however, you must be certain of the role you're playing. Decide who you want to be. Then, just like Charlton Heston, dress the part.

What you wear says a lot. It says whether you have style or not. It says whether you have taste or not. It says whether you know how to dress for your age and your specific body or not. It says whether you are a slave to fashion or your own style-maker. No matter what age you are or what body size, you can always look great.

Wear clothes that flatter you. Don't wear clothes just because they are in fashion. If snakeskin is in, you don't have to wear the whole snake. You can just wear the shoes and the purse. Don't overdo it. Don't try too hard. Don't try to impress too much. Be aware, be confident, be natural, and be consistent. When you dress with a certain intellect, you will be surprised at how much you say.

Take a few minutes and come up with an image that fits your dream of who you want to be. Look through some magazines. Write down what you think is necessary to create "the look" of Stardom that suits you.

You might start by selecting a "role" model whose style of dress you admire.

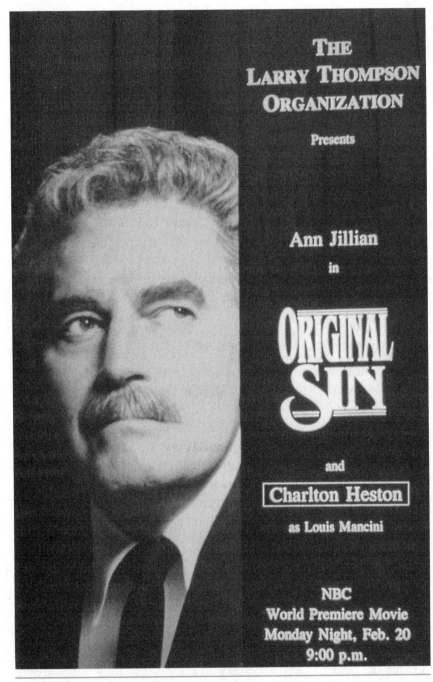

THE
LARRY THOMPSON
ORGANIZATION

Presents

Ann Jillian

in

ORIGINAL SIN

and

Charlton Heston

as Louis Mancini

NBC
World Premiere Movie
Monday Night, Feb. 20
9:00 p.m.

Charlton Heston understood the importance of Image when he became my Mafia don.

My role model is:

_____

Here is "the look" I want to create for my own Starring role:

_____

_____

_____

_____

_____

How you look is always important, at all times, even when you are alone. How you think you look is how you think. You must train yourself to look good. You must get in the habit of looking good. Dress for yourself. Take pride in how you look. If you think you already look good but would like an update, maybe hire a stylist to shop for you and give you a more modern look. Always change your appearance to add freshness. Cut your hair. Give it a different color.

Have you ever needed to run to the grocery store to get something fast, and thinking you probably wouldn't bump into anyone you knew, you didn't comb your hair and you slipped on that comfy, but dirty, jogging suit? Sure enough, you ran into everyone you ever knew. Has that ever happened to you? It has? Well, it rarely happens to a Star. They try to never put themselves in a position to be seen or photographed looking less than their best.

Even when Colin Farrell, Brad Pitt, Johnny Depp, Orlando Bloom, and other young Stars look like they've just been dragged along 10 miles of dirt road, they are usually making a statement about their style and their attitudes that appeal to their young fans. On those few occasions they do slip up, the paparazzi have a field day and you wind up reading about it at the supermarket, or seeing them on E!'s _Celebrity Uncensored._

Even if it's a Saturday and you are wearing jeans or casual clothes for a trip to the farmer's market, make sure you look neat. Make sure you look clean. Make sure if anyone knocks at your door and wants to come in, you're not embarrassed. Looking your best is not only about what others see, but also about making you feel better about yourself.

Let me ask you this: What are you wearing right now? Would you want me to see you like this? Are you sitting in bed with some big flannel pajamas on? Does the top match the bottoms? Do you have chocolate ice-cream stains on your top? Do you have on goofy slippers? Is your hair in curlers?

Hey buster, don't laugh. Are you in your boxer shorts? Do you have on jeans that haven't been washed in two weeks? Are you just hanging out casual? Do you have a pizza stain on your T-shirt?

Better yet, let me ask you this: Let's assume you knew that we were going to have a meeting tomorrow and that you were going to ask me things about this book, talk to me about what you're planning in your life, where you want to go, how you should go about it, sort of a personal one-on-one meeting about you. How would you dress if you came to see me tomorrow? What would you want me to see? How would you want me to perceive you? Who is it that you're presenting yourself to be?

Do me an important favor. No matter what you have on right now, and I'm sure it's nice, I'd like for you to put the book down and get up. I want you to go to your clothes closet. I want you to dress as if you're going to have a meeting with me tomorrow. I want you to present yourself to me as the Star you want to be. Present to me an image of who you are. I don't want you to go out and buy anything. I want you to go to your closet. I want you to take a bath if you need to. Wash your hair if you need to. Do whatever you need to do to prepare yourself for looking a way that you want me to see you. Clean up. Polish up. Get dressed. Get ready for our meeting tomorrow. Do this now. I'll be right here on the page.

Welcome back. Well, wow, you look great!

How was your experience? Was it tough to decide what to wear? Did you need to get one of your Team members to help? That's allowed, you know. How did you enjoy getting dressed? Did you have everything you needed in your closet? Did you have a lot of choices? Or did you think to yourself: "Oh my God, where have I been? I hate these clothes! I have nothing to wear."

If you like the way you look now, and you wanted to look that way every day for at least five days to present yourself to your coworkers or to your future employers or to people who could help you out, could you go back to your closet now and pull five or six other outfits that create the same image?

Do you have a lot of different clothes with different looks, but not one specific look? Does it look like Sybil's closet with clothes for every one of your 16 multiple personalities? Would you wear all those clothes if you were going to be dressing for Stardom and on a focused direct path?

Maybe you need to take an inventory of your closet. You know the look you want. You know the image you want to present. You know the style that is right for you. You understand what is flattering and what is not. Now, go back to your closet and start asking yourself: "Do I need this? Do I need that? What the hell is this? What is under this pile of dirty old clothes? What was I on when I bought that?"

You might want to clear out your closet and simplify your belongings to just those precious, specific clothing articles that show you in your best light. It's not about how many clothes you own, it's about how many appropriate clothes you can wear.

The other thing you should do while you are looking around in your closet is asking yourself, "Am I organized?" Could you find everything in the closet that you wanted? Were all the slacks together? Were the dresses together? Were the blacks separated from the blues or the reds from the greens? Were the shoe boxes and tennis racquets falling all over the place? Did you have tennis shoes scattered all over the floor? Well, however you've organized or cluttered your closet is how you've organized or cluttered your mind. Think about that. If your closet is clean, organized, and displaying the proper attire, you're ready to go. Your mind is focused. Focused not only on how you look, but also on what you're going to say and what you're going to do.

On the other hand, if your closet looks like a tornado hit it, I suggest you get busy cleaning and organizing that closet as well as your mind.

Clear your mind. Create your own appearance style. Create your Star image. But be aware of the difference between fads, trends, and values.

FADS, TRENDS, AND VALUES

The Republican party conducted a survey several years ago to determine what influenced people most when it came to voting. Three things were prominent: fads, trends, and values. The way respondents described it was to explain: When one looks out over an ocean and sees a wave, the first thing they see is the frothy, whitecapping, top of the wave as it is breaks. That's the first thing that catches the eye. It's breaking. It's there and it's gone. That's the fad.

The second thing is the wave itself, moving in a certain direction. It's what's moving. That's the second thing they see. That's the trend.

The third thing, which they don't even see, is the deep current underneath the water that's moving the wave in the direction that it's breaking. This deep current of water is the values.

The wave represents a fad, a trend, and a value. People will listen and be influenced by candidates who are the hottest thing, talking the talk, personifying the fad. They will also listen with eagerness if a candidate is evidencing a trend toward a certain truth. But then, when they get into the voting booth and pull the curtain behind them, and they're all alone and about to cast their vote, they vote the candidate with values.

They don't vote the fad. They don't vote the trend. They always vote the values. The deep undercurrent of values is the most important thing to them. That's what touches them the deepest. That's what they feel will give them security. That's what they feel will give their children a future.

You may say to me, "What do I need to know about fads, trends, and values? I'm not running for political office. I'm not trying to get anybody's vote here." Well, the truth of the matter is that every day when you make a choice, you choose a fad, a trend, or a value.

Start with what you're you going to wear today. Will it be low-waisted jeans that seem to be in style right now, with no regard to whether you weigh 200 pounds or 99 pounds? That might be a fad or it may be a trend, but is it a value? You may look into your closet and find that all you have are bell-bottomed jeans from the seventies. Do you have at least one pair of good old 501 Levi's jeans? My point being, even when you dress, are you either dressing the hottest, hippest way, the trendy way, or are you dressing with values? Now, you can dress all three, and you should. You dress the appropriate way for the specific occasion. But at least be aware of it. You shouldn't be caught up in the fad and living only in the fad. You shouldn't be caught up only in the trend, or only in the values. What you choose to wear states who you are.

The same holds true about whom you hang out with or work with. Fads, trends, and values influence how you feel about everything. If you're out at a cocktail party or a dinner and someone raises a social issue, before you open your mouth and start having it flap, you might want to consider if you're just saying what's popular, as in: "Oh yeah, let's do this because everybody is doing this." Ask yourself: Is this a fad? Is this a trend? Is this a value? If you speak in a way that demonstrates that your thought process is reflective, and how you feel about life in general and subjects in particular show a deep respect for values, people will see you as a more creditable person. They're going to see you as thoughtful and intelligent. They're going to see that you can look beyond the immediate moment.

Don't misinterpret what I'm saying here. I don't want you to be some old fogey. You should be trendy, fashionable, hip, hot, and fun. I want you to be all those things. Some days I want you to just be a fad. Then you'll be a trend. Then you'll be a value. All I'm saying is, when you make your choice, about anything in your life every day, be aware of what you're choosing and why. Put it in perspective. Put your day in perspective, your choices in perspective, and eventually your life will fall into perspective. So, think about it: choosing fads, trends, or values.

THE IMAGE OF A SOLDIER

I had been living in Los Angeles for less than a year when the letter arrived from the United States Army suggesting pretty strongly that I come to serve my country. They ordered me to report to Philadelphia, Pennsylvania, where there would be a bus waiting to transport me to Fort Dix, New Jersey.

I had been inducted as a reservist into the Army's Judge Advocate General's Core (JAG) with orders to do six months basic training at Fort Dix and then five and a half years of reserve duty in California.

In 1969 the war in Vietnam was in the headlines every day. I felt a sense of duty even though it was difficult to leave California and the good life. My instructions were to bring only a toothbrush, toothpaste, and one change of clothes. No jewelry, luggage, or other valuables were allowed. Well, I thought that was a bit limiting and certainly not applicable to me. After all, I was a lawyer. It was only going to be six months. It wasn't active duty. Fort Dix was pretty close to New York. I thought that on the weekends I would be going into the city and seeing a Broadway play or meeting some people—you know, getting away for the weekend, so I certainly had to have my clothes.

Disregarding the letter, I packed a beautiful suitcase with suits, shoes, and my best clothes. Then I headed for Philadelphia and basic training boot camp. I arrived at the airport there wearing a three-piece blue suit, white shirt, striped tie, a fob watch across my vest, and black shoes. There were a few younger kids around. Some looked eager. Others scared. I was feeling relaxed, thinking that it was nice to get out and see the rest of the country. We were told to board a bus that was going to take us to Fort Dix.

When we arrived at Fort Dix late that night, we saw this big illuminated sign at the entrance that said, "The President of the United States Welcomes You." It was nice to be welcomed so warmly. It made it feel a little personal. I thought that was pretty cool. The radio on the bus had broadcast news of a historic event that day: the moon landing by our astronauts. It was July 20, 1969, about 10:56 P.M., Eastern Time. On the radio, the man said that Neil Armstrong was stepping onto the moon, saying, "It's one step for man, and one giant step for mankind." There I was, stepping off the bus about to go into the Army, and I thought, "Whoa, that's pretty heavy. He was stepping on the moon, an astronaut, in the Armed Services, and I was stepping off this bus at Fort Dix, New Jersey, with the President of the United States welcoming me." I will never forget that the landing on the moon and my landing at Fort Dix occurred simultaneously. History was being made.

We entered a small building. They had this little Quonset hut barracks set up, sort of an orientation area. There must have been about 35 guys there. Of course, I was the only person wearing a three-piece suit and carrying a suitcase. Most of the others had on jeans and a T-shirt and were carrying toothbrushes. There I was, looking good.

We all sat in the Quonset hut behind these little desks, like you did in elementary school. They had forms and pencils to pass out. I used my Mont Blanc fountain pen. While we were sitting there filling out forms like third graders on the first day of school, I thought, "This isn't too bad either."

This drill sergeant came up and said, "Whatcha got in that suitcase?"

"Clothes," I said.

"Clothes? Whose clothes?" he asked.

"I've got my clothes, my suits, other clothes, because we're near New York and I'm sure that at some point you guys are going to let us go into the city. I wanted to make sure I had my clothes," I explained.

"Oh, I see. You were thinking, even though the letter said, 'Don't bring anything,' that you were an exception and that you could bring your clothes?"

"Well, you know, I've never done this before," I replied. "I'm not sure who all you're bringing here. Some of these recruits here are younger kids. I didn't know, but I wanted to have it here anyway."

"Well, we told you not to do it. ... What do you do for a living?"

"I'm a lawyer."

"Oh, you're a lawyer?"

"Yep."

"Where?"

"In California."

"Oh, you're a lawyer in California."

"Yeah, I've been out there about a year. I'm a member of the Mississippi Bar, and now I'm out there studying for the bar in California, but you know, I'm a lawyer." I figured I had his attention now.

"Oh, okay. You must be a pretty smart guy."

"Well," I said, "I don't know. I think I am. I did pretty good in school and all."

"You sound like you could be a leader."

"I don't know. I sorta think I could."

"Well, let's see. Stand up."

I stood up thinking he had already selected me as some model soldier. Obviously the Army knew what they're doing, and they had quickly zeroed in on me.

"I want you to walk to the front of the class," he ordered.

"Okay."

I walked to the front of the class thinking I was going to be a leader here.

"Okay, everybody. Listen up. See this guy here? His name is Thompson. He's a lawyer from California. See how he's dressed in his three-piece suit? He looks good. He's got his suitcase for his clothes to wear to 'the city' for when we have our weekends off. He's a pretty smart guy.

"Listen, Thompson; do me a favor, why don't you take off your coat. You're a little dressy for this group. Why don't you just take your coat off?"

"Sure." So I took my coat off.

Then he said, "Why don't you take that vest off and put that watch in your pocket. It looks a little tight and restricting."

So I took off my vest.

"Take your tie off too. And while you're at it, your shirt."

I was starting to wonder, "Where is this going?" I took my shirt off and stood there holding my coat, my vest, my shirt, my tie, and my fob watch.

"I'll tell you what," the drill sergeant said, "why don't you just go ahead and take your pants off."

"You're serious?"

"Oh … I'm serious. I'd like for you to take your pants off."

So I took my pants off. Now, I was standing there in my white boxer shorts with my calf-high black socks and my black shoes.

He said, "I'll tell you what I want you to do now. I want you to take your underwear off."

"No, I can't."

He snapped, "Take your underwear off, Thompson."

This was a new one on me. I took my underwear off. I was now standing up in front of 35 or 40 young guys, totally naked except for my calf-high black socks and black wing-tipped shoes.

He said to the eager recruits, "See this guy? He's pretty smart. He's a smartass too. Everybody, I want you to see this. This is what a lawyer in California looks like, but when you work for Uncle Sam, you are all going to look alike. You are all going to look like a soldier. He's going to get a haircut tomorrow just like all of you are going to get a haircut tomorrow. He's going to wear the same fatigues that you wear. He's going to wear and polish the same boots that you do. He's going to be issued the same type of weapon and ammunition you will get.

"One thing that you have to learn about joining the Army—you lose your identity and you become a soldier, and we all become one unified soldier fighting for the United States. So, whatever image you have of yourself, you're going to park it at the door, and by the way, Sergeant, pick up that suitcase for private Thompson and let's lock it up for him until he's out of here. Now, you go sit down, and don't move until I tell you."

I walked back to my desk humbled.

The Army knows how important a soldier's obedience and image are. There's not much room for individuality.

As humiliated as I was, and for something I will never forget, it was a lesson well learned. When you work for Uncle Sam and you're in the Army, you're going to look like a soldier, think like a soldier, and fight like a soldier and a soldier only; I don't care who you think you are.

When I arrived at Fort Dix, I was still in my role as an entertainment lawyer. My drill sergeant, in his own special way, helped me adjust to my new role by demanding that I dress like a soldier even though I wasn't, by any means, a soldier at that point.

The fact is, you too should begin to dress for the starring role you're training to play, even before you feel you're ready. Abandon your old style of dress just as you will abandon the life that came with it. Take on your new role immediately by adjusting your appearance as well as your attitude. Don't worry if you aren't mentally there yet. As soon as you start to look the part, you'll be on your way.

Making the Right Impression

If you have exquisite taste and lots of money, you can skip to the next chapter. A lot of people have one or the other, but few have both, which is a good thing for magazines like *Vogue, Allure, In Style,* and *GQ*. If you have only one of these qualities, or neither of them, maybe someone in your support Team can help.

What's the secret to dressing well on a limited budget? It's the old Bauhaus motto: Less is more. Better to buy one very good suit than several not so good ones. People will say, "Gee, that's a terrific outfit," when you wear the one good one. If they see you in it more than once, they'll remark on what solid fashion sense you have. If you rotate your cheap suits, they won't comment on your extensive wardrobe of tacky clothes. They'll just think it.

I have been with my friend, former client, fashion supermodel, and cosmetic entrepreneur, Iman, all over the world, and whether I saw her dining in New York, working in Los Angeles, marrying David Bowie in Florence, or relaxing on David's yacht anchored at St. Jean Cap Ferrat, she always looked fantastic. She can wear anything and look great. When asked once about how she thought women should dress, she said that the one outfit a woman could wear every day, anywhere, is a pair of gray slacks or skirt, with a black, long sleeve cashmere top, accented by a single strand of pearls. It's classic and timeless.

We can recognize Stars even when they're off-screen because the people around them treat them like Stars. Learn how to impress. There's nothing phony about creating an impression.

Every day, people sit in judgment of us, and in many cases the impressions we make have an impact on our lives. And it isn't simply the way you look that affects the impressions that people form. It is also the way you feel about yourself, the mastery you have over your talents, the knowledge you've accrued in your field, and the commitment you have to your work and your goals.

As you pursue your place as a Star, it is important to understand that you are on stage every day in some way. You are always marketing yourself and your package of talents, knowledge, and experience to others. Marketing is simply the process of determining what it is that others want and then convincing them that you've got the goods. If you are uncertain as to how you come across in the marketplace, try this exercise:

Ask six friends/acquaintances/neighbors/coworkers/customers to fill out this form. First, have them write down for each item how you "rank" in each category by putting a check somewhere along the dotted line between the two descriptive terms, and then have them circle five characteristics from the list that best fit a description of you.

Shining . . . . Dull

Charismatic . . . . Unappealing

Attractive . . . . Not attractive

Empathetic . . . . Uncaring

Interesting . . . . Boring

Sophisticated . . . . Unsophisticated

Motivated . . . . Unmotivated

Easy to be with . . . . High maintenance

Enthusiastic . . . . Low key

Disciplined . . . . Unfocused

Intelligent . . . . Unintelligent

Street smart . . . . Naive

Mature .... Immature
Patient .... Impatient
Lucky .... Unlucky
Talented .... Untalented
Warm .... Cold
Fun .... Serious
Charitable .... Selfish
Extroverted .... Introverted
Giving .... Demanding
Honest .... Dishonest
Speedy .... Slow
Trendy .... Conservative
Timely .... Late
Sharp .... Dull

Now, study the responses you get and evaluate where you need to work on creating a better image. Undoubtedly, you will be surprised at some of the responses. Often, we make impressions that we are not aware of. You should keep in mind that these impressions are commonly formed instantaneously, for better and for worse. People make quick rulings based not only on who YOU are, but who THEY are. Their own experiences, prejudices, likes, and dislikes come into play.

Haven't you ever taken a liking to someone quickly because they resembled someone else whom you once had a good relationship with? We've all done that, as silly as it may be, and it just shows you that sometimes, no matter what you do, people will form their own opinions. You can't control how they feel about you, but you can control how you react to it. And the type of reaction you have depends primarily on how you feel about yourself.

That is why it is important to form the most positive self-image you possibly can by always trying to look, do, try, and feel your best. Maybe if you don't think you look good physically there are other parts about you that do.

One of the nicest compliments I ever got was from my brother Marshall. We were at a taping of *Battle of the Network Stars*, and all these great-looking girls with tight bodies were running around. One pretty woman in particular was wearing short shorts and displaying a stomach so tight you could bounce a quarter off it. When she ambled by, I whispered to Marshall, "Damn, look at that body ... I wish my body was in that kind of condition." He said, "Larry, if you really wanted your body in that kind of shape, you'd have it. You made other choices. She spent the time training her body to look like that. Take one more look at her body. See it. Well, that's what your brain looks like."

Reputation

Sticks and stones may break your bones but the wrong words can put your lights out. It is difficult to shine when others are casting shadows over you. Work at earning a stellar reputation.

How? You can start by developing the demeanor, and the manners, of a Star. Don't be negative or self-destructive. At work, compliment your peers and your bosses whenever you can honestly do so, and look for such occasions. Act like the kind of person you'd like to be around. Soon, you'll have the reputation as that sort of person.

Look for chances to do favors for others, and be prompt in acknowledging favors done for you. When someone's gone beyond the call of duty to do something nice for me, I like to send a small gift. I *never* send that old business standby, the bottle of liquor. Send someone a bottle and he may think of you the next morning when he's hung over—if then. Instead, I try to send something permanent: a Tiffany key chain, a Mont Blanc pen, even a book I think the recipient would like. If you have no idea what sort of book someone would like, send something a little loftier than the current newsstand best-seller. That way, even if it's a bit over your recipient's head, he'll be flattered at your high opinion of him. The litmus test I try to bear in mind is: "Will my friend still have this gift in five years?" And if you don't have much money to spend on gifts, a handwritten thank-you note can be just as meaningful, if not more so. In our e-mail era, handwritten notes are becoming as rare as seeing Pamela Anderson wearing a bra.

I am not suggesting here that you become a phony. I'm simply saying that you need to be sensitive and kind to others. Be aware and recognize that there are other Stars in the universe than you, and if you let them know that you see and appreciate their brilliance, they will speak about you in glowing terms and help you shine as brightly as you deserve.

At the professional level of Stardom, Stars pay people to speak kindly about them. They pay publicists to spread the good word, to get their name and picture in the paper, to in essence create an image and reputation. In a regular business, it would be called the marketing department. You want your family, friends, and acquaintances to serve as your own marketing department.

Confidence

It might have surprised you that confidence was not one of my Four Elements of Stardom. I know that many self-help gurus insist that this is a mandatory requirement for success. I too think it is enormously helpful if you have it, but you know what? You don't necessarily need total confidence.

The gurus tell you that "the more prepared you are, the more confident you will be," but no one can tell you how to gain confidence. No one can give it to you. You can't buy it and you can't fabricate it by repeating affirmations like, "I am getting more and more confident every day." Either you got it or you don't. Even when you got it, you can lose it, and get it back to yet let it slip away again. If you are totally confident every day about everything, you are a righteous bore. If you have Talent, Rage, Team, and Luck, just feeling pretty sure about yourself most of the time is all you need. More than that becomes vanity, and that's one of the no-no's.

Yes, being prepared for something makes you more secure and confident about that one thing you have prepared for, but you can't prepare for everything in life. As the saying goes, "Life is not a dress rehearsal."

Even though you can't teach anyone how to be truly confident about every thing in his or her life every day, I can offer you one simple guideline to apply in each scary situation of your life: The way to gain confidence is to lose fear.

Everybody loses fear differently. Some get right back up on the horse when they fall off and "face the fear." Others give it a rest and start again after the horse has had some time to think about it. Whatever works for you. But at some time identify how you prefer to lose your fears, and work through them—one fear at a time. As you lose each fear, you will equally gain confidence.

Confidence comes from experience. Or it can come from the Great Pyramid of Egypt. Let me tell you how I gained some confidence by sleeping with the spirits of Alexander the Great, Julius Caesar, and Napoleon Bonaparte.

A NIGHT IN THE PYRAMID

I've always had a fascination with Egypt, maybe because I used to hear stories as a kid about living in the fertile Mississippi Delta where the soil was rich for growing cotton from the overflowing sediments of the river. They used to say that the only other place on earth that was as fertile was the land in Egypt along the banks of the Nile River. "Hell," they would say, "they even named that town Memphis up the river after one of them old, fancy cities in Egypt." This place called Egypt, which I seemed to have a connection or kindred spirit with, was in an exotic galaxy far, far away from the cotton fields of my youth.

I remember being in the Ole Miss law school library late one night. I had been studying for quite some time and was looking to take a break and read something lighter than Monahan's *Real Property*. So I found this book about Egypt and the pyramids and started going through it. And I learned that the Great Pyramid of Giza was built around 2600 B.C., in the reign of the Pharaoh Khufu (known as Cheops to the Greeks), as Khufu's burial tomb. So much mystery still surrounds the site. I was mesmerized by everything I read. I couldn't learn enough about this tomb where Khufu thought he could start his mystic journey to the afterlife.

One of the most fascinating things I read was how Alexander the Great, in the fourth century B.C., at the age of 26, having conquered Egypt, slept alone overnight in the king's burial chamber of the Great Pyramid. Allegedly, lying there all night long, with no lights on, he came out early the next morning a transformed individual, claiming he had experienced an enlightenment that explained to him life and his destiny. He never shared that information with anyone. Whether he needed that information or not, he did go on to rule the known world. The story became legendary.

Centuries later, Julius Caesar conquered Egypt, and when he went there to meet Cleopatra, having heard the story of Alexander, he too attempted to duplicate the experience. So he lay in the burial chamber overnight, with no lights, alone, and of course came out the next day and also proclaimed that he had experienced an enlightenment that no man had before, other than Alexander the Great. Whether that was Caesar actually experiencing some divine enlightenment or his just not wanting to be outdone by Alexander, we don't know, but Caesar also ruled the known world, and that was something special he had shared with Alexander.

Interestingly enough, centuries later Napoleon conquered Egypt, and of course he had heard the story of Alexander the Great and Julius Caesar. Napoleon wasn't going to be outdone. So, one afternoon in 1799 A.D., he arranged the same thing and spent the night in the burial chamber alone. He came out the next morning like the two previous rulers and proclaimed that he understood the same thing now that Alexander and Caesar understood, and of course he practically controlled the world. Maybe he should have stayed in a little longer and gotten the rest of the information, I don't know, but ...

The bottom line was that these three men claimed they had shared this experience, and that was good enough for me. I wanted to be next. I guess if you have Rage, and you want to succeed, and you're looking for that edge, or you're looking for some special knowledge, or you're looking for whatever it is that someone else claims to know that you don't, or you're looking to overcome a fear of the unknown, you say, "I'm going for it."

So you can imagine that once I read this story of the Great Pyramid and its famed overnight visitors, I vowed, even though it seemed a little scary, that I too would lie in that burial chamber and summon the divine truth to answer the mysteries of life.

And so, it came to pass ...

There I was, standing at the base of the Great Pyramid on the Giza plateau in Egypt in 1994 A.D., only about 5,000 years after it had been built. I was negotiating with an Egyptian archives custodian for the opportunity to sleep alone overnight in the granite sarcophagus in the king's burial chamber in the Great Pyramid.

Even though I had a good translator, I didn't understand everything the custodian was saying, but in looking at his shocked expressions and body language, I got the feeling that he was saying something like, "Who in the bejeezus do you think you are?"

Well, I made a few phone calls to some diplomats, and they all had sort of that same bejeezus thing going on, like you know … for safety reasons, security reasons, liability reasons … if we let you, then everybody blah … blah, blah. So at some point I realized that this wasn't going to happen—legally.

Late that afternoon, I entered the Great Pyramid with the lady I was seeing at the time. We crawled down the Descending Passage, then up the Ascending Passage to the Grand Gallery, which leads to the Great Step, which presents the king's burial chamber. Holy Moly! There it was! It truly was eerie. Inside this small, royal, rectangular, granite, lonely, quiet, empty room, there was nothing but a granite, rectangular, empty, burial sarcophagus where the king, Alexander the Great, Julius Caesar, and Napoleon had lain.

It was now later in the afternoon and we were in the burial chamber alone. I asked her to go watch the entryway to make sure there were no other tourists, guards, guides, or administrators coming. She stood guard at the door.

I carefully climbed up and into the cold burial chamber and lay on my back with my arms crossed in front of me as I imagined it was done by an Egyptian king waiting to be transported to the afterlife. For about 20 minutes I lay still in that burial chamber. There was coldness in that room and a stillness that I have never ever experienced. My body became heavy and numb. My feet got cold. The chill moved up my body to my chest. I felt totally paralyzed. For a moment I felt as if I weighed nothing and could have floated out of my earthly body.

I must admit it was scary. And there was a small light on! Yikes, if the lights had been off, I couldn't have stayed two minutes, not to mention overnight! To lie in the burial chamber of the Great Pyramids overnight with no lights on and nobody around, I was surprised that those other guys hadn't come out crazy. Or maybe they did.

But I know that it was truly a calming, confidence-inspiring experience for me. I didn't have any divine visitation from the spirit of Alexander the Great, but I did get a sense of calm, and I did get a sense of peacefulness, and I did get a sense of accomplishment that I had done something pretty special. And, most important, I lost a great deal of fear of the unknown. It takes a lot to scare me after I faced my fears that day.

When I left that chamber and climbed down that staircase and back up into the fresh air, I felt good. I didn't have a legion of soldiers standing there to salute me, but I saluted myself. I learned that I could conquer my fears that day. And that has given me all of the confidence in the world, and the netherworld too.

Did it give me an edge from an informational point of view? No. Did it give me an edge of confidence that I had accomplished something and faced a fear? Yes. And is that confidence something that I carry on in my life? You betcha.

I don't think you have to do an overnighter in the king's burial chamber in the Great Pyramids to become confident. But there is great value in learning to face your fears. You can buy the finest clothing and groom yourself for success, but if deep inside you are fearful of taking life on, it'll show. That fear and hesitancy will come through. You can't hide that, even with Armani.

So when you are stepping into your role as a Star, remember to leave your fears in the closet. No one is better than you.

The Bible says that God made us all in his own image. Imagine that.

CHAPTER
8

DANGERS

There are obviously dangers inherent with Stardom. Too much of anything, including Talent, Rage, Team, and Luck, can drive you off the straight path. Arrogance, greed, need, a lack of common sense, and having it all can throw you out of whack if you aren't paying attention. Boredom, isolation from people telling you the truth, and plain hubris can get you in deep trouble.

It's easy to wake up one day, as many Stars have, and humbly whisper *Citizen Kane*'s last word of regret, "Rosebud."

I have never known success and fame to improve anyone's sense of reality or fairness. When one reaches an elevated level of respect, and there's no one around to say every once in a while, "Hey, you're out of line here, buddy," it isn't uncommon for a little brat to emerge.

Take, for example, Martha Stewart. Truly on a roll, she had worked hard and smart for a long time. She had driven herself and everybody around her to the top. Then suddenly she was indicted and convicted in a federal trial for lying to prosecutors about trading her ImClone stock. Stewart is a personal friend of ImClone Systems, Inc. founder, Sam Waksal. He pleaded guilty to securities fraud and was given a seven-year prison sentence.

Oddly enough, I know Sam also. I first met him at my three-day fiftieth birthday party in Monte Carlo. He was the guest of my friend, Alexandra Dwek, who introduced him to me as a doctor. Later in the day someone said, "Oh, you must talk to Sam, he's discovered a cure for cancer." I thought, *Well, I should probably seat this guy at a pretty good dinner table.* As it turned out, he was very gracious and a delightful addition to the festivities. I never bought any stock in his company, however.

There are many who feel that Martha Stewart's high profile and stunning business success contributed to her being targeted by federal prosecutors. What happened to her is a powerful example of the price of fame. Those put on a pedestal are often knocked off unless they are careful to establish strong principles and values early on and stick with them throughout their lives.

Winona Laura Horowitz, also known as Winona Ryder, was sentenced to three years probation and 480 hours of community service for theft and vandalism convictions related to her $5,500 shoplifting spree at Saks Beverly Hills. Though she could have faced three years behind bars, the sentence came as no surprise since prosecutors early on did not seek jail time for the actress. Lucky her. At least we got to see her performance on videotape.

Hugh Grant and Kobe Bryant were out prowling, and got busted. Both of these guys were embarrassed, and rightly so. One could argue that it helped Hugh Grant's career. It certainly made him more known, but I doubt if it helped. I'm sure he wishes he had never gone out that night. Kobe is in a fight for his life now. No matter how it turns out, this is one big loss for his record books.

With success, fame, and Stardom comes RESPONSIBILITY. That is something you have to prepare yourself for. Everything in life has a price. God giveth and He taketh away.

No matter what level of success you achieve, you never rise above your fellow man, or the law. When you are successful and famous, you have less freedom to screw up, and receive less forgiveness when you do. You have an obligation to be a role model of appreciation. If you don't, you can lose it all pretty fast. Unfortunately, just as the press likes to build you up and tear you down, so does the public. Lose your bearings and sense of responsibility, and the police will come and lock you in a room and throw away the building.

The Road to Success

The following series of quotes depicts the five stages of an actor's career:

"Who is *Brad Pitt*?"

"Get me *Brad Pitt*!"

"Get me someone *like Brad Pitt*!"

"Get me a young Brad Pitt!"

"Who is *Brad Pitt*?"

"Who is *Brad Pitt?*" occurs when you're starting out and no one knows who you are. "Get me *Brad Pitt*" is when you are in demand. "Get me someone like *Brad Pitt*" is when they want a knockoff of you because you've gotten so big they can't afford you. "Get me a *young Brad Pitt*" is when you are getting old and they want a younger version of you. And "Who is *Brad Pitt?*" comes full circle to the start, when they didn't know you, and now they have just plain forgotten you.

One minute an actor is the hottest thing going. The next, he's forgotten. It can happen that fast. Fame is fleeting, which is why that should not be your only goal.

On the road to success, you want to live minute by minute in the joy of expressing your Talents and pursuing your interests, whether it's on a stage, in the office, on the field, at the hospital, or in a quiet room of your home. You also want to express them with integrity.

Success isn't such a rare commodity. Its visible symbols are as close and tangible as the nearest Mercedes, Malibu beach house, or *People* magazine cover. What is rare are those people who manage to achieve success with their integrity intact.

In a celebrity-oriented place like Hollywood, what you're doing and how well you're doing it can be a matter of intense public scrutiny. That's what causes people to sell out. They trade their souls for another day in the spotlight, another dollar in hand.

The newspapers and television reports are full of examples of people who traded their integrity for status and wealth. Corporate fraud and corruption are at epidemic levels, as represented in the fallen empires at Enron, WorldCom, Global Crossing, Rite Aid, Adelphia Cable, Tyco International, ImClone Systems, and others.

It takes guts and determination to do what's right. I've always found the story of John Galt, the protagonist in Ayn Rand's famous novel *Atlas Shrugged*, to be helpful, even inspirational, in this regard. In the book, Galt achieves greatness through intelligence, ability, and hard work, while retaining his integrity. And in the world today, that's enough to make anyone a hero.

It's not so very difficult to succeed. The difficult task is to survive the constant emotional bombardment to succeed quickly and immorally, and to come through life with our ideals and integrity intact.

We all have our own challenges. I've already discussed some of them, and I'm sure you know your own. Fortunately, we don't have to be heroes out of novels to succeed. In real life, the heroes are simply ordinary men and women who were challenged by extraordinary situations and met the challenge.

If we meet our challenges, if we preserve our integrity while swimming in the transparent fishbowl of success, we'll have really done it. It's still possible—though not easy—to succeed, and to do so in a way that makes us happy and proud. And that's the only true success. Anything else is tinsel.

Deep

Hollywood is more than a place; it is a state of mind. Hollywood and Vine is more than a street corner; it is a sense of personal arrival. Everyone's state of mind and personal arrival are different. But the temptations and entrapments of power, money, and fame are the same. And they are formidable. It's often, sadly, joked that Hollywood is where people rush to spend money they don't have, to buy things they don't need, and to impress people they don't know.

When famous, successful people fall from grace, it makes headlines. And it should. If we have to read about their professional triumphs, love lives, and favorite chili recipes, we should also read about their emotional breakdowns and felony charges. We learn from their good and bad behavior.

Using Hollywood Stars as role models for success may seem absurd and vapid to people who think of all celebrities as self-absorbed, immoral, and of shallow character. They are entitled to their opinions, of course, but I have learned firsthand that celebrities as a group are no different in character than any other group, in that you will find a mixture of good and bad, shallow and deep. The bad apples in their group, however, do make the 11 o'clock news more often than those in other groups.

It's true nonetheless that people who strive for accomplishments and success face more stress, meet more fear, attract more temptation, and possibly fall more publicly than others. A fall from grace can happen whether you are a Star celebrity or a Star in business, or in any occupation or pursuit. Keep in mind that you should be careful about stepping on others in your climb to success. That's not just a trite saying to make you play nice. It's a reminder that humility is only one false step away.

In my 36 years in Hollywood, I have seen all the vices, opportunities, trappings, and trapdoors it has to offer, and I am truly blessed that they didn't appeal to me as a lifestyle. Don't get me wrong: I'm no saint. But I'm a fairly decent guy.

Recently I had a thought about how fortunate I am that I came to town and zigged to success when I could just as easily have zagged to ruin. On that very same corner of Hollywood and Vine where I got out and cried the night I arrived there, the place where I started my career at Capitol Records only months later, there now stands a very hot and edgy nightclub that is the present rage. It's called "Deep." *Oceans Eleven* shot a few scenes there, as have a few other movies. On New Year's Eve past, my wife and I, along with my brother Marshall, celebrated the evening there with some unusual gusto. As we pulled up, Marshall said to me, "Larry, this is your old stomping ground." I looked around and smiled fondly.

When we entered the club, our senses were assaulted with music and sexy images. Above, and behind the bar, there were large windows with seminude couples dancing and simulating sex. Our VIP booth was situated directly in front of all the action. It was as if we were voyeurs watching their private acts. It was a little artsy, and a lot sexy. This sure wasn't here when I first came to town, I thought. But if it had been, and if I had zagged into this lifestyle instead of zigged into Capitol Records and the future I chose, how different would things be?

As I sat in the club, I couldn't help but picture some of the people who did make it big, but zagged into a life I'm sure they didn't bargain for when they set out to find Stardom. Some of the better-known tragic stories ran through my mind. Jim Morrison, Marilyn Monroe, River Phoenix, Janis Joplin, Kurt Cobain, Judy Garland, John Belushi, and Elvis Presley. All had the elements I've been talking about. Each was

supremely talented, had the Rage to make it, had at least some elements of the right Team (although some notably had less than helpful
Team members), and lots of Luck, at least in their professional lives.
What happened to them? And for the purposes of this book, how can
you be sure it won't happen to you?

Balancing Health, Love, Money, and God

You don't have to take a satirical, Divine Comedy trip with me to
know right from wrong. I know you already know that. I also know
that it would be negligent on my part to tell you all the great things
about working hard to become a Star and not warn you of the possible dangers. Unless you have established some guidelines for yourself, it will be difficult to tell when you may be getting off course.
Many of my friends have cars with navigational systems that have a
little voice to tell them when they're driving off the course they
entered into the trip computer. Your guidelines serve the same purpose. They plant little voices in your head that tell you when you are
en route or headed for trouble—when you are zigging or zagging.

In your journey with Talent, Rage, Team, and Luck, you must
maintain a balance between Health, Love, Money, and God. Without
Health, you will find Love and God. Without Love, you can find
Money and Health. Without Money, you can find Health, Love, and
God. Without God, whatever you find is the food that dead men eat.

Now shake it off. The spooky things won't happen to you. Once
you've been warned, you will never go there.

99 No-No's

I've discovered that you cannot always do the right thing in life, but
you can always not do the wrong thing. There are quite a few wrong
things. I call them "no-no's." They apply to every profession and every
person. These are the certain "small" and "big" things to avoid on
your way to Stardom. You also can't forget them once you've attained
Stardom. Here's the list of 99 no-no's to remember:

1. Wishing for someone else to fail
2. Speaking like Ozzy Osbourne in a corporate staff meeting
3. Forgetting about God

4. Denying pain
5. Leaving a job undone
6. Comparing yourself to someone else
7. Lying about your age
8. Failing to return someone's call
9. Dismissing your hunch
10. Dressing like Anna Nicole Smith at your daughter's piano recital
11. Believing you are ugly
12. Having bad breath
13. Thinking you are alone
14. Expecting anything free
15. Complaining
16. Blowing your nose in your napkin while eating
17. Doubting your ability
18. Giving up
19. Giving in
20. Not loving *Oprah*
21. Being rude
22. Forgetting the less fortunate
23. Underestimating your competitor's abilities
24. Saying no to anyone who wants to help you
25. Pressing your Luck when it's running bad
26. Having dirty fingernails
27. Expecting too much
28. Giving too little
29. Thinking the hip-hop group OutKast are outcasts
30. Watching Janet Jackson's Super Bowl performance on TiVo over and over
31. Saying yes when you mean no
32. Letting someone else always operate the TV remote control
33. Not facing your fears
34. Not singing along in church
35. Refusing to work late with your boss

36. Spotting more than 14 points in a pro football game
37. Not grieving a loss
38. Wasting time
39. Wasting someone else's time
40. Thinking that rapper Eminem is a chocolate-covered candy
41. Leaving home without "it"
42. Not staying in touch with family and friends
43. Saying, "I can't"
44. Believing fame will solve your problems
45. Disrespecting your parents
46. Putting someone down
47. Feeling sorry for yourself
48. Thinking it's ever over
49. Talking like you know everything
50. Not believing Dr. Phil
51. Putting yourself down
52. Dropping out of school
53. Worshiping any person or thing
54. Not caring what people think of you
55. Threatening "Over my dead body"
56. Not learning from your failures
57. Leaving home without looking your best
58. Sweating the small stuff
59. Not getting enough rest
60. Wishing that both Madonna and Britney Spears would kiss you
61. Doubting the healing powers of chicken soup
62. Losing your sense of humor
63. Saying you hate computers
64. Smelling your armpits
65. Not embracing who you are
66. Being unappreciative
67. Not being there for a friend

68. Being indecisive
69. Spewing anger
70. Trying to figure out Michael Jackson
71. Following the pack
72. Being lazy
73. Overindulging
74. Not reaching for the brass ring
75. Taking that last ski run
76. Not sharing the load
77. Trusting just anybody
78. Not listening to a child
79. Taking no action
80. Naming your son after Billy Bob Thornton
81. Getting too full of yourself
82. Believing everything or anything has to be fair
83. Hogging the spotlight
84. Shaming someone
85. Wearing unpolished shoes
86. Believing you can do it alone
87. Not believing
88. Not laughing
89. Feeling guilty
90. Thinking that the rap artist Bow Wow is a dog
91. Being unprepared
92. Taking too many shortcuts
93. Holding a grudge
94. Never saying, "I love you"
95. Doing anything half-assed
96. Taking anything for granted
97. Having regrets that outnumber your dreams
98. Not remembering Mister Rogers and his Neighborhood
99. Catching the fire truck

My dear friend Cicely Tyson once wrote me, "Let Go. Let God." It's the best advice for avoiding the dangers that can come with being a Star in any field.

Those Who Caught the Fire Truck

It's always exciting and scary to see and hear the fire truck scream by. It also sort of makes you smile to see the proverbial dog chasing it. He seems to be having the time of his life. He exemplifies the thrill of the chase. He runs and sprints, barks and pants, and finally says to hell with it and turns to hurry home as another of his species picks up on the hot trail and takes off down the block. While this makes us shake our head with pleasure, I've often thought what would happen if the dog actually caught the fire truck.

I imagine he suddenly finds himself standing there with a mouthful of the back right tire in his mouth, and the truck has stopped. He opens his mouth and the truck doesn't move. He looks around, and starts to walk proudly around the big red machine, sniffing it. He eventually climbs aboard, sits in the driver's seat, and looks around, quite pleased with himself. Then what? He climbs down, continues to look around, sniffs some more, and finally pees on one of the tires. After going up and down, around and around, in and out, he looks down the street, sees no one, and sits. Later he checks it out again. Then lies down. He becomes totally bored with his new toy and finally craps on it, leaves it in the middle of the street, and goes home.

Jim Morrison, Marilyn Monroe, River Phoenix, Janis Joplin, Kurt Cobain, Judy Garland, John Belushi, and Elvis Presley caught the fire truck.

For different reasons, on different days, by different means, all these Stars did the same thing. They extinguished their lights. They wasted their Talents, lost their Rage, devastated their Team, and ran out of their Luck. *The End.* This is an ending you should learn from. Always chase the fire truck, but catching it is a big no-no.

How Do You Avoid the 99 No-No's?

You don't need a long list of things to remember to avoid the no-no's. The answer is short. I received it in a telegram in my hour of need from a dear friend and exceptionally gifted actress, Cicely Tyson. She wrote simply, "Let go. Let God."

If you let God work with you, all you need to be fulfilled will manifest itself. If you attempt to accomplish everything alone, you will struggle, and your attention can easily be diverted. It's pretty easy when you think about it.

Now, brighten up. It's Showtime.

CHAPTER 9

SHOWTIME!

It's Showtime! Don't be nervous. Opening night butterflies are good for you. You've prepared well and you're ready. The only thing left to do is to do it. Break a leg.

In this chapter, you will

* *Review* what you have learned.
* *Apply* it all to your life.
* *Rise and Shine* to star in your role of a lifetime.

Review What You've Learned

You've identified your Talent and your dream. You've developed your plan to achieve that dream. You've summoned your Rage to ignite your action. You've identified and solicited a Team of believers to help you, and you've learned how to create Luck to prepare you for chance occurrences when they kiss you. You've created your image and you know how to avoid the dangers.

You've learned how to deal with the impulses that were holding you back. They sounded something like these:

"I can't."

"What would my friends, husband, kids, parents say?"

"I'm not sure."

"But I'm not beautiful like Ashley Judd."

And all the rest of them. You've seen how to plot out your goals, how to go after them, how to leave a profound impression on the people you meet, and, in the bargain, how to be a swell person instead of a Mike Tyson.

You've seen how today's top Stars followed their own dreams, experiencing successes and setbacks along the way. You've read some amusing and revealing stories about your favorite Stars and realized that, at the end of the day, they are pretty much like you.

By now you should have a good feeling about yourself, your potential, and your chances of realizing your aspirations. You were already a Star. I only showed you how to switch on the light to see yourself. As the group America sang: "Oz never did give nothing to the Tin Man ... that he didn't ... didn't already have."[1]

Summarizing the Success Secrets of Stars

1. Stardom begins at the intersection of Humility and Egomania.
2. Make time to reach your goals.
3. Being a Star is being fulfilled—in whatever aspect of your life you choose.
4. Be yourself and no one else.
5. Nobody is born a Star.
6. Hollywood is not a place—it's a state of mind.
7. The Four Elements crucial for Stardom are: Talent, Rage, Team, and Luck.
8. Everyone has a Talent.
9. Square peg in a round hole? Don't fit in? You could be on your way.
10. Believe you are deserving of Stardom.
11. Become your own first fan.

12. Prepare for adversity.
13. Catch self-defeating behavior before it starts.
14. Set realistic goals and set a date to achieve them.
15. Decide what you're willing to do to achieve your goals.
16. Aim in one direction and run in that direction as hard as you can.
17. Learn to see yourself as you want others to see you.
18. Start acting like someone who has already achieved his or her goals.
19. Match your talents with your work efforts.
20. Proceed with integrity.
21. You must have a Rage for success.
22. Stardom is not an accident.
23. Get over the feeling that life isn't fair. Move on.
24. Make a leap.
25. Move from peak to peak.
26. Stardom is a place you cannot get to alone.
27. Recruit a Team of believers.
28. People are dogs and cats. Learn to identify them.
29. Listen and learn from parents, family, friends, and pros.
30. Get out and network.
31. Lose the dream-busters.
32. Never forget who your Team Captain is.
33. You must take risks to attain Stardom.
34. Confront the unknown.
35. You don't need anyone's approval to attain your goals.
36. You can learn to be lucky.
37. Focus on the solution, not the problem.
38. The harder you work, the luckier you get.
39. There's a distinction between Luck and chance.
40. Make disadvantages work for you.
41. Recognize opportunities.
42. Be an optimist.

43. Go with your gut.
44. Try on a new attitude.
45. Be lucky in love.
46. Love yourself and others will love you.
47. Seize the day.
48. Stardom is too important to take seriously.
49. Know your 100 Points of Starlight.
50. Unlock your Talent.
51. Create an affinity with others.
52. Open big or you're dead.
53. Be concerned with your image.
54. Dress for Stardom.
55. Improve your appearance, reputation, and references.
56. Avoid the Dangers.
57. Keep a sense of balance with health, love, money, and God.
58. Avoid the 99 no-no's.
59. The real standard of success is personal, internal, and unique to each.
60. You're already a Star. You just need to switch on the light.

Apply What You've Learned

In our Results Workshop, you will apply this new knowledge to your personal goals. We have worked through each of these success secrets individually. We are now going to put them all together and create your own map to the Stars.

THE FIVE STEPS TO STARDOM

1. DECIDE EXACTLY WHAT YOU WANT

(*Select specific, realistic, and achievable goals*)
First, decide exactly what it is you want in life. Be specific. Don't wish vaguely, "I want to be enormously rich." Instead, wish, "I want to earn $100,000 a year," or "I want to open two Krispy Kreme doughnut

The Starmaker paints your map to Stardom.

franchises." I want to become a vice president at work. I want to graduate from college. I want to go on *Survivor* and win! I want to open a
hair salon. I want to win the Pulitzer Prize.

Your goal has to be obtainable and sustainable. "I want to be King
of France by September 12, 2010," just won't do it. The result of setting
unrealistic goals is frustration and self-recrimination. Your goals should
be custom-fit for you, like a tailored suit. As you grow in Talent, knowledge, and experience, you can adjust your goals, just as you'd alter a
suit to fit bigger muscles. So, if you're just starting out as a clerk in the
shipping room, it's okay to set a goal of moving up to the purchasing
department, but probably not wise to make it your immediate goal to
become chairman of the board. Make an honest assessment of what
goals your Talents, knowledge, and experience suit you for *at this*

point, then adjust your goals as you grow in each area. Write your specific goal down now.

2. DECIDE THE EXACT DATE FOR ACHIEVING YOUR GOAL

(*Don't say "in a couple of years"—say an exact date.*)

I want to be promoted to the purchasing department by August 31, 2005. I want to open my own salon before my twenty-sixth birthday.

3. WHAT ACTIONS AND SACRIFICES WILL BE REQUIRED?

(*This is your Map.*)

I will take a professional course at night to prepare myself for the VP job. I will go to cosmetology school, work two jobs, and save the money to open my own shop. I will even embarrass myself and ask my parents to help.

4. ACT AS IF YOU ALREADY HAVE WHAT YOU WANT

(*This will be fun.*)

Knock yourself out. Develop a successful attitude. Start living as though you've already achieved your objective.

5. BE PREPARED TO MODIFY YOUR PLAN

(*If something isn't working, don't quit, change the plan.*)

If it isn't working, go back to the drawing board. If it is working but your goal has changed, modify your plan. It's okay. It's your plan, after all.

As you follow these steps you'll notice something happening. As soon as you achieve one goal, you'll immediately want to set yourself a new one. You'll find that your goals, your own personal definition of success, are always changing. If you don't keep this in mind, if you don't remember that success is a journey and not a destination, you run the risk of being terribly disappointed when you finally achieve your objective.

There are as many ways to be a Star as there are Stars in the heavens, but these five steps will allow you to create your own personal map to Stardom.

Read the following corresponding explanations for each step in the Results Workshop, and then fill in your Map:

Searching for the Star Within You

RESULTS WORKSHOP . . . YOUR MAP TO THE STARS

Step 1. My goal for Stardom is to:

_____

_____

Step 2. I will achieve Stardom by the following date:

_____

Step 3. My plan to achieve Stardom is:

_____

_____

_____

Step 4. What talents do I have to help me achieve Stardom?

_____

_____

List of my special qualities:

1._____

_____

2._____

_____

3._____

_____

4._____

_____

5._____

_____

List of my special accomplishments:

1._____

_____

2._____

_____

3._____

_____

4._____

_____

5._____

_____

Step 5. How much Rage do I have to achieve Stardom?

_____

I am willing to:

_____

_____

_____

Step 6. Who are my Teammates to help me achieve Stardom?

_____

_____

_____

Step 7. How do I handle Luck?

How I will attract good Luck:

1._____

_____

2._____

_____

3._____

_____

4._____

_____

5._____

_____

How I will overcome bad Luck:

1._____

_____

2._____

_____

3._____

_____

4._____

_____

5._____

_____

Step 8. How can I start to act as if I were already a Star?

_____

_____

_____

_____

_____

Step 9. What changes do I need to make in my plan for Stardom?

_____

_____

_____

Step 10. How will I help other people when I am a Star?

_____

_____

_____

Your Map to the Stars

STEP 1. MY GOAL FOR STARDOM

Each individual's idea for Stardom is unique. We've noted that being a Star is a metaphor for being fulfilled in your life. Therefore, everyone's sense of fulfillment is going to be different. Whether you are a musician, an actor, a secretary, a housewife, a student, a marketing executive, a newscaster, or a schoolteacher, each of us has different dreams. Each of us has different aspirations, and what you want in your life is going to be different than what some other person wants.

Early in the book we went through the exercises to identify what it is that would fulfill you. If you remember, you filled out an obituary, where you identified exactly what it is you wanted to accomplish in your life, how you wanted to be remembered, how you wanted to be perceived. And, no matter where you are in your life, you projected further, to what you would accomplish, what you would do, what things people liked about you and what they didn't. Now, I'd like you to clearly state your goal for Stardom.

So, if you are a schoolteacher who has always wanted to be principal, it's time to say outloud, "I want to be principal." If you are a secretary, but in fact would rather be a hairdresser and own your own beauty parlor, then it's time to tell the boss to take this job and shove it. It's time to change careers. No matter what you are or where you are, you now have to set a goal of who you want to become. That may call for making some changes.

In Step 1, I want you to clearly state what it is you see yourself doing to lead a more fulfilling life. Accordingly, we've called this step My Goal for Stardom. Fill out exactly what it is that you want.

Maybe you've accomplished one level of Stardom and you want to get to that next level, like an actress who has performed in off-Broadway musicals but wants to move up to the Broadway stages. Or maybe you've been out working for a while and just don't feel fulfilled on your current path. Perhaps you feel that you've accomplished a lot but that even greater things are possible. If so, you will find that doing these exercises will reenergize you. They will remind you of things that you probably knew but have forgotten or failed to recognize.

Sometimes we suffer setbacks and failures and lose sight of the fact that what has happened to us in the past affects our future only if we allow it to defeat us. There are countless Stars out there who have suffered humiliation and defeat but regrouped, refreshed themselves, and kept climbing. So if you are more of a battle-scarred veteran than a fresh-faced rookie, don't worry. These exercises will be useful for you too if you consider this: If you are a Star still on the rise and looking for new heights to achieve, understand that even the biggest Stars realize that they must prove themselves every minute of every day. As long as you are willing to be flexible in adjusting your plans and goals, and as long as you stay ever alert to opportunities wherever they may arise, you will find fulfillment by staying committed to expressing your talents to the highest possible level.

STEP 2. I WILL ACHIEVE STARDOM BY THE FOLLOWING DATE

It is very important to establish a specific time frame for achieving your goals. You can't just say, "You know, I want to be president of the United States," or "I want to be a professional baseball player," or "I want to be a ballerina." Tomorrow never comes. You've got to set a *specific* date. Even when you write a check, you date it, don't you? If you want to be principal of that high school, or if you want to be quarterback on that football team, or if you want to be on *American Idol*, you have to say, "I want to be on the very next *American Idol*," or "I'm going to be a principal by January 2007." In Step 2, I want you to fill in the exact date that you will accomplish it.

STEP 3. MY PLAN TO ACHIEVE STARDOM

Now, we've talked about thinking through those things in life that you want to accomplish, and how to formulate what it is that you want to do. We've also discussed people who are going to help you along the way. So, having had some time to think about that, in Step 3, I want you to lay out your plan, as specifically as you can, for how you're going to accomplish your goal by the date that you established.

STEP 4. WHAT TALENTS DO I HAVE TO HELP ME ACHIEVE STARDOM?

When we dealt with Talent, we went into detail in asking you to identify your Talents and the Talents people perceived you to have. What things do people compliment you on? Do your friends praise you for certain things you do well? "She's always good at helping other children," or "She's great at math," or "He certainly can run."

Your talents are those things you do well—your innate abilities. Some of those talents will help you implement your plan to achieve your goal by a certain date. If you are that secretary who wants to have a hairdressing salon, this is the time to put it in writing. Whatever your dream is, it's time to stop dreaming and to start going after it.

So, in Step 4 list all the different talents you have—but I want you to do more than that. List not only the Talents that you have achieved for Stardom, but also list your special qualities and accomplishments. Don't be shy here. The accomplishments you write down don't have to be big. Accomplishments can be big or small. I note that because if you set out to do a very, very small thing and you don't finish it, or you don't achieve it, you feel really bad about yourself, even though it's a small thing. And if you can feel really bad about yourself when you don't finish or achieve a small thing, why would you not feel good about yourself if you did finish it or achieve it? So, an accomplishment is an accomplishment, big or small.

List all of your special qualities, all the things you feel good about, and all the things other people feel are good about you. Also, list your accomplishments, big and small. Your accomplishments, qualities, and Talents are your ammunition. Putting together a stockpile of all your assets and abilities will help you implement your plan to achieve your goals by a certain date.

STEP 5. HOW MUCH RAGE DO I HAVE TO ACHIEVE STARDOM?

Think about this before you fill it out. I want you to take the word *Rage*, take the concept *Rage*, take the emotion *Rage*, and translate them into something specific that you are willing to do to add to your talents, implement your plan, and achieve your goal.

If you decide you want to open that beauty salon and be a hairdresser, you may have to go to cosmetology school or quit your job. You may even have to borrow some money. How much Rage, how much chance, how much risk, how much craziness, how much desperation is involved: How much do you really want it? You've got to write this down. You've got to be willing to pay the price, whatever it might be, financially or emotionally.

Obviously, you can't predict what challenges you will face, but it helps to prepare yourself and commit to doing whatever it takes, as long as you stay within the boundaries you've set with your guiding principles and values. You can hardly go wrong if you dedicate yourself to always putting your talents and knowledge and experience to the highest use—that is, to the use that offers the greatest benefit to the world you live in.

So, think about this. You may say, "How do I say *Rage*? How do I write down my passion?" Well, right now we're going to transform Rage, passion, ambition, need, desperation, wanting, desiring, wishing for, hoping for, and praying for into action. Let's translate, "Okay. You want it? So prove it. What are you going to do? *Exactly* what are you going to do?"

You've now identified your goal. You've now identified your talents. You've now identified exactly when you're going to get there. What are you going to do to make this real? What's your Rage? How much Rage do I have to achieve my Stardom? I'm willing to do what? Write it down.

STEP 6. WHO ARE MY TEAMMATES TO HELP ME ACHIEVE STARDOM?

We noted earlier that nobody gets to Stardom without help. None of the presidents carved into Mount Rushmore achieved greatness without assistance and support. There are few things in life that you can do by yourself. So, you need help.

We've talked about Teammates. Are yours dogs or cats? Who are the support people in your life? Who are those who will step up and truly support you? Who has the expertise you need? This is important. You may have friends who want to help you but don't know shinola from shinola about what you're trying to accomplish. So, you have to be careful taking advice.

Your Team is only as good as your selection process. Then, you've got to listen to them and welcome their support. You've had some time to think about your selections. Now is time to make your list of choices. Who are your Teammates, Mentors, Professional Role Models, Motivators, and Reality Checkers going to be? Write them down.

STEP 7. HOW DO I HANDLE LUCK?

I mentioned earlier that you could learn to be lucky. You cannot learn to control chance, but you can learn to be lucky. What are you going to do now to start attracting good Luck?

Remember how I stood in that elevator every day and waited on my boss, Sal Iannucci? I put myself in the right place at the right time. I worked hard and I was prepared. Are you going to prepare yourself? Are you going to work hard? Are you going to be standing in that elevator? Are you going to create lucky opportunities? Are you going to go where you need to go? Are you prepared to stand in the rain so lightning can strike you? How will you attract good Luck? How will you overcome bad Luck?

Remember, you're going to have bad Luck. You have Luck every day. How do you perceive it? Do you perceive it as good or bad? No matter how you perceive it, even if you were the most optimistic guy in the world and everything you did you perceived as good, there's going to be some Luck one day—trust me—that there's no way you can put a positive spin on it. It's going to be bad Luck. As I said earlier, "When things look bleak, normally they are." What will you do? How will you handle it? Are you going to quit? Are you going to stop? Are you going to cry? Are you going to burn this book? Or are you going to overcome it? Are you ready for it? Are you braced for it? You've got to create good Luck and overcome bad Luck.

Think about this: You now have a specific goal. You've got people to help you. You've got a timeline. You've got a date with destiny.

You are determined to be prepared. How will you track this Luck? How will you overcome bad Luck? Write down your plan for dealing with Luck.

Tell how you plan to prepare yourself for it by developing your Talents; acquiring knowledge in your chosen field by reading related books, newsletters, journals, and visiting Web sites; building a network of contacts by joining organizations, volunteering, speaking to groups, writing newspaper columns or letters to the editor; and doing all of the little things that can lead to big things down the road. Remember that the secret to cultivating and attracting good Luck is to prepare yourself for opportunities and develop a sixth sense for spotting those opportunities where others may not see them.

Step 8. How Can I Start to Act as if I Were Already a Star?

Start acting today as if you've already achieved your goal. Remember the Charlton Heston story? "If I see it, I can believe it." I want you to develop an attitude. I don't mean an arrogant attitude. When you reach your goal, you're not going to be pompous. You're not going to be arrogant. You're not going to be ugly. You're going to be fulfilled. You're going to be nice. You're going to smile. You're going to be happy.

So, I want you today to start being happy, start being fulfilled, start getting that certain swagger in your walk, start getting that certain smile, start getting that look in your eye that says you know something that nobody else does. Feel good. Feel the part. Know the part. Be the part. When you act as if you're already a Star, people will see that and reflect it back to you. You will constantly be bombarded with confirmation. What you put out will bounce back to you. Therefore, if you walk around gloomily with your head down and you're moping or crying and people see you, they will turn away. They don't want to talk to you. They don't want to hear your problems. Instead, beam out good news. Beam out smiles. Beam out promise. Beam out hope. It will come back to you.

So, how do you start acting like a Star? Well, let's identify what your Stardom is. If you want to be that principal, if you want to be that *American Idol* winner, if you want to be captain of the football team, president of your company, or vice president of marketing, start looking, dressing, acting, and being that part.

Now, in Step 8, let's look at how you can start to act as if you were already a Star. Let your imagination soar. If you think one day that you're going to win an Academy Award as an actress, then prepare your acceptance speech. If you're in acting class and being beat up by your acting teacher and peers because you didn't do a good scene on Thursday, don't let it bother you. Drop it. Forget it. Let it go. It's history. You're going to win an Academy Award. Go write your speech. Practice it in front of the mirror and thank the Academy. Shout it out! I want your neighbors to hear it. Next Thursday, when you are asked to prepare another scene for your class, deliver your Academy Award acceptance speech. Be happy. Be effusive. Be fulfilled. I want you to tell me, the class, and the Academy how thankful you are. I want you to know what it feels like to win that Oscar.

Be there. Act the part. Act it every day. Act it when you put this book down. Act it when you're on the phone with someone. Act it when you're alone in your apartment. Feel good about yourself. Start living the part. Remember, as your action is, so is your reality. Congratulations. May I have your autograph?

YOUR ACCEPTANCE SPEECH

Whatever your chosen field, write down your acceptance speech for its highest award.

_____

_____

_____

_____

_____

_____

_____

_____

_____

(I was going to give you more lines but the orchestra started playing and cut me off . . .)

Step 9. What Changes Do I Need to Make in My Plan for Stardom?

Okay, so you've laid out a goal, a date by which you will reach it. You put a plan of action together. You've identified all your Talents. You've got all your people to work for you. You put a Team together, started acting like a Star, but it didn't happen for you. Why didn't it happen? Something went wrong. Maybe, from the time you put the plan together to the time you wanted to achieve Stardom, you decided you wanted to do something else. That happens. Trust me, it's going to happen probably a few times in your life. You're going to change. You're going to grow. You're going to want to do different things.

Maybe some of the people on your Team weren't the right people. Maybe you need to replace those Team members. Or maybe the date you set was a little too ambitious. Or maybe you thought you had Rage but you didn't express it. Maybe you did have Rage but not at the level of desperation or need or ambition or assertiveness you really needed. Maybe, on your Team, you need to find somebody who will motivate you and help you build up a higher level of Rage.

Now is the time to modify. By the way, there is nothing wrong with constantly modifying. You set a goal, you put it in ink, you make it specific, and you set out to do it—but sometimes it happens and sometimes it doesn't. Not all plans work. What definitely doesn't work is if you fail to make a new plan. Do you need to make changes in your plan? Maybe this is something you don't need to fill in today, but three months from now you might want to review where you are. You might look at it and say, "Okay, what changes do I need to make? I need to replace this Team member. I'm not acting as if I were already a Star. Something is wrong here. How do I get some help?"

If you continuously try to get through a door and find it locked, and you stand there, banging on that same door year after year after year, you're an idiot! You've got to walk around to the back of the house and find a window and climb through, or come in through the chimney, or come in through the back door, or get a bulldozer and knock the damn house down! You can't stand there in front of that door and keep knocking on it.

When the plan is not working, you need to change your plan. What changes do you need? At some point you may have to back off, take a breather and put things in perspective. If you are feeling frustrated and need inspiration, look to your role models, mentors, and even professional advisers in your field. Find out what worked for them in similar situations. This is where groups like the Young Presidents Organization, Chamber of Commerce, Jaycees, and other professional clubs can offer invaluable resources. Often, there are retiree groups in your chosen field that offer mentoring to younger people and even mid-career people who might feel stuck. Take advantage of their services instead of beating your head against the wall.

I have made many changes in my life and career. In fact, constantly reinventing yourself is necessary for professional survival in Hollywood, where there is constant pressure to find the next new Star or to take your career to higher levels. There are two things you can't be in Hollywood when you are striving to reach the top and they are: (1.) cold and (2.) Boring.

You have to project "heat" or at least "warmth" to an audience and the people who can put you in front of an audience. And you have to offer something of interest, whether it's an irresistible beauty, animal magnetism, intelligence, or high level energy. You can't afford to let the level of any drop for very long if you want to stay in the entertainment business.

I have changed from being a lawyer at Capitol Records to a partner in an entertainment law firm. I then moved my talents from law to management of other people with Talent. I managed the careers of Stars with my own company employing very gifted managers such as Erwin More, David Brody, Michael Oursey, Brian Medway, J. P. Hinraux, Jodie Knofsky, and David Stuart. I also managed Stars with other Team members, including Jay Bernstein. As a Team, Jay and I got HOT very fast. Jay was the sizzle and I was the steak. I would make him rich. He would make me famous. Our partnership lasted a total of three years. Nearly everyone in the business thought it was 15. But I thought it was closer to 100.

Raging on, I bought and quickly sold out of New World Pictures with Harry Sloan and Larry Kuppin and started independently producing movies and television.

While still producing, I write books, lecture, and conduct seminars. I'll also wash your car on Thursday afternoons if it isn't raining. After all, I am the hardest working man in Show "Business."

Not only have I changed careers with my Talents, I have changed Teams, the intensity of my Rage, and the degrees of my Luck. On top of all that, I have had four major epiphanies in my life.

MY FOUR EPIPHANIES

First Epiphany, 1967: Valley of the Dolls

As a 23-year-old law student, I went to see the movie *Valley of the Dolls*, starring Barbara Parkins and Paul Burke. They were entertainment lawyers for movie stars. Patty Duke was their client. I decided before the end credits rolled that I was going to Hollywood to be an entertainment lawyer like them.

Second Epiphany, 1983: Cats

Sixteen years later, sitting in the Broadway musical *Cats*, a giant Snowball of Ambition rolled over me and made me realize I had built a House of Cards.

Third Epiphany, 1991: Lucy and Desi

Eight years later, during the making of *Lucy and Desi: Before the Laughter,* I finally got the chicken bone out of my throat, the monkey off my back, my mother's dress out from under the bed, and I felt important enough to think about what I wanted for myself, instead of helping everybody else get what they wanted.

I had represented over 200 stars. I had taken care of their problems and wishes. I looked around and discovered someone new. He was right under my nose. He was a person that I really believed in. Someone who I thought was talented. He had a lot of Rage. He even was lucky. He listened to me. He went to every meeting I went to. He always showed up on time. He was respectful and appreciative of my advice. He paid me on time. I knew he was never going to leave me. I decided to sign him.

I SIGNED ME!

In one moment I went from someone representing Talent to being Talent—from an Artist representative to an Artist. I could now use all the knowledge and experience I had gathered over the years and apply it to myself.

I have been one of the best clients I have ever had … now that's an epiphany.

Fourth Epiphany, 1999: Sonny And Cher

Eight years later, while planning to get married for the second—and last—time, and during the filming of a movie I had lived 20 years earlier, *And The Beat Goes On: The Sonny and Cher Story*, I got the idea to write this book.

As you can tell, "change happens." Embrace it. In fact, maybe you should use a pencil in filling out this form. It's okay to change your direction to get where you are going. Where you are going will even change. You too will have epiphanies.

In filling this form out, you may have already filled out the first eight steps and it looked good. Now, go back and look at the others and say, "That's right. That might not work. That might work." Maybe you need to make some changes. Or, as I said, you can leave it blank and can come back to it at a later time.

STEP 10. HOW WILL I HELP OTHER PEOPLE WHEN I AM A STAR?

Now, you may say, "Oh, we didn't talk about this a lot. What is this all about? What do I have to do? Who do I have to help?"

You have to give back at some point.

"I do?" you ask?

Yes, you do.

"How can I be giving back? I'm desperately trying to get what I need here. I need something. I can't be giving stuff away. I don't have the time. I don't have the energy. I don't have the money. I don't have anything."

Whatever you have—it can be meager, it can be a lot—somebody has less and somebody has more. You're no exception. You're neither the worst person in the world nor the best person. You don't have the least, and you don't have the most. There are people who are worse off than you, and there are people who are better off than you.

Whatever you give to others comes back to you manyfold. I can assure you of that.

And, while I did say, "What are you going to give to somebody when you're a Star?" remember, I've already asked you to start acting as if you were already a Star, so in effect I want you to start giving now. Again, if you give away the things you want in your life, they will come back to you manyfold. If you help another actor get a role, you'll get a role. If you help another hairdresser find a job, a better one will come to you. If you help another person prepare for his law school exam, you'll ace yours.

So, I'm not saying you have to go out now, drive down the street, and find people that you can give to; but I do want you to be kind to people. Not just to people who are on your Team. Not just to people who are going to help you. I want you to be kind to everybody. It all will come back to you.

When you make a phone call to some important person you hope is going to help you do A, B, or C, the first person you probably will talk to is their receptionist or secretary. Be kind to that receptionist. Be kind to that secretary. Ask his or her name. Personalize the call. Be nice on the phone. You certainly don't think you're just going to be able to snap at them and bark at them and suddenly turn Mr. Nice Guy when you get Mr. Whoever on the phone, and that when you get off they're not going to say to their boss, "Boy, who was that? What an attitude she (or he) had!" That will tell Mr. Whoever what a Mr. Two-Face you are.

Be kind to everybody you talk to, everybody you deal with, especially receptionists and secretaries, especially people who are hired to be on the frontline and to guard the perimeter of the power that you're trying to impress. This includes being kind to people you might take for granted but shouldn't, such as your sister—younger or older—or your brother, parents, grandparents, and Team members.

You had a Team helping you out long before you even knew how to walk. You had people feeding you. You've had someone taking care of you your whole life. Even if you're an orphan, and my heart goes out to you, there are people who went to work to take care of you. Maybe they didn't do it well, but they were there. You have much to be thankful for. You have much to give. You have much inside you that people need and want.

So, part of acting like a Star, starting today, is to start helping other people. I want you to make a list of those people you're going to help. I want you to identify the people that you already know need your help. Right now, in the same way you've been focused on yourself—and rightly so—I want you focused on others. I've said from the first pages of this book, "You have to be selfish." You do, and I'm not suggesting to you that you're not going to be, but while you're working on yourself, work FOR others too. Know that when you get to a place in your life in which you're fulfilled, and you have even more to give, the world will expect you to give even more. And you will. So, if you're going to act today like you're a Star, start giving like you're a Star. I promise you that even though this is Step 10, it isn't any less important than Step 1, Step 2, Step 3, or the others.

Helping others will make you feel good. And the good you do for others will come back to you.

Helping others will not only make you feel good, but it will also attract good feelings and fortune.

Make a list of things you can do to help others today, tomorrow, and in the days, months, and years to come. You will be blessed for it.

Rise and Shine: Your Personalized Map

You have now filled out 10 steps. You have created your Map to Stardom.

This is your personal Map. Isn't it interesting now when you sit down and hold this piece of paper in your hand and you look at it and you realize how unique you are? If two million people filled out this Map, no one would have filled it out the same way. Every person has different goals. Even if the goals look similar, people's plans will vary, their Teams will have different members, their completion dates will differ, their levels of Rage will range widely, and what they are willing to do may differ too.

This Map to Stardom reflects your uniqueness. It states very clearly who you are, where you're going, and how you're going to get there.

Do you have a sense of satisfaction now that you've gone through all these steps? This book was created to train and motivate you to create and follow this personalized Map. If you had just picked up this form before you read the book and filled it out, you would have had some answers there, but not with the clarity and the depth of what you now have. So look at it; think about it.

When you're a navigator and you're going somewhere and you've got a map, you don't put it in the drawer and forget about it.

Because every time there is a turn in the road or an intersection or a galaxy to turn left from, you have to look at your map. So, I want you to keep your Map to Stardom out. I'm not suggesting that you have to post it on the bulletin board at school. But I want you to look at it every day. More than that, I want you to read it every day. I want you to be reminded every day of what your goal is and who's going to help you.

Even if you've been out in the world for a decade or two, it can be extremely helpful to get the Map out and check where you are in relation to where you started and where you want to end up. If you feel stuck, bogged down, or out of sync, it is probably because you've wandered off course or because your goals need to be readjusted to fit your levels of Talent, knowledge, and experience. I've never met an established Star who wasn't constantly taking stock, reevaluating his or her career, and adjusting themselves according to changes in the market, trends, and the advice of managers, agents, and other counselors.

This Map will nudge you and keep you moving forward. Did you make that phone call to get help? Did you do what you said you were going to do? Are you acting? Are you dressing? What do you have on right now? Have you slipped back?

Listen, you are going to slip. It's easy to do. Trust me. But you've got to get up and go again. You can't quit. You've got to stay with it. And have some fun. Remember, you're already acting like you're a Star. You're already acting like the person you want to be. How bad could it be? Believe me, if acting like who you want to be isn't fun, it's not going to be any more fun when you actually get there. Maybe you need to rethink about where you want to go or who you want to be? Maybe you don't want to be that person you thought? And maybe it feels just fine, thank you.

You know, this shouldn't be just work for you. This is your life. I'm trying to help you enjoy your life. I'm trying to show you how special you are. I'm trying to encourage you to be the best you can be. You've now created your own map. You've made your bed. Now I want you to sleep in it. But I want you to sleep soundly. I want you to sleep with the bliss that a baby sleeps. I want you to sleep knowing that if you truly want to go to the Stars, you've created your own unique, absolutely guaranteed Map. So, Rise and Shine, and meet your destiny.

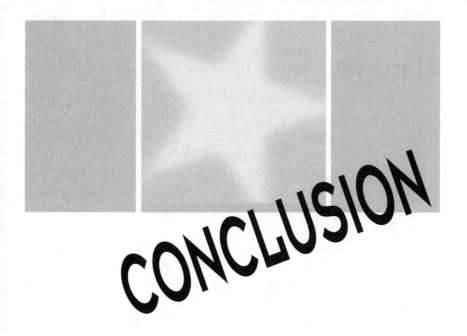

CONCLUSION

Millions of people are obsessed with celebrities and have a deep desire to improve their own lives and become as much like their celebrity role models as possible. While all that is great, never lose sight of your own uniqueness. You don't want to be someone else. You want to be the best YOU.

You no longer need to say, "If only I knew the secrets of the Stars," for their secrets have been revealed to you. And not only their secrets, but how they applied them to their lives—and how you can apply them to your own life to become the Star of it. Not all of you can or even want to become Hollywood Stars. But all of you can become as successful as you choose, and on your own terms, and in your own world. Get involved with your life. Look at what a very big Star had to say about that:

"I guess when all is said and done, if there is one last commentary on me, I would want it to be that I participated in my life. I was a full participant."

—*Julia Roberts*[1]

A Last Word

I know there are a lot of people who think they are not very special. They think they are not pretty, or not smart. They have no money. Their peers snub them, and their self-confidence has been shattered. They feel unimportant, even irrelevant. They don't believe they have a Talent or gift or could ever be liked, let alone become a Star.

Well, I believe there is a beauty and uniqueness in each individual. And I have always wanted to help people find the Stardust in themselves. It is there.

In Frank Capra's 1946 classic *It's A Wonderful Life*, George Bailey, played by James Stewart, despairingly questions his worth in life. Years after the movie was made, James Stewart was quoted as having said:

> *The character I played was an ordinary kind of fella who thinks he's never accomplished anything in life. His dreams of becoming a famous architect, of traveling the world and living adventurously, have not been fulfilled. Instead, he feels trapped in a humdrum job in a small town. And when faced with a crisis in which he feels he has failed everyone, he breaks under the strain and flees to the bridge.*
>
> *"That's when his guardian angel, Clarence, comes down on Christmas Eve to show him what his community would be like without him. The angel takes him back through his life to show how our ordinary everyday efforts are really big achievements. Clarence reveals how George Bailey's loyalty to his job at the building-and-loan office has saved families and homes, how his little kindnesses have changed the lives of others, and how the ripples of his love will spread through the world, helping make it a better place.*
>
> *Today, after some 50 years, I've heard the film called "an American cultural phenomenon." Well, maybe so, but it seems to me there is nothing phenomenal about the movie itself. It's simply about an ordinary man who discovers that living each ordinary day honorably, with faith in God and a selfless concern for others, can make for a truly wonderful life.*[2]

There's a little of George Bailey in all of us. We all, on occasions, have to be shown and reminded how special we are.

I'm no Clarence, but I've tried my best in this book to help you see your own uniqueness and how much you have to offer the world. Hopefully, every time this book is read, a new Star will light up and Shine.

Congratulations, you have now completed the first steps to Stardom. I am already bathed in your brilliance. I hope to meet you on life's Red Carpet.

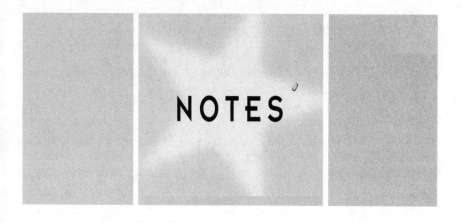

NOTES

CHAPTER 1

1. Thomas, Bob. *Astaire: The Man, The Dancer*. New York: St. Martin's Press, 1984. 78.
2. Smith, Liz. "Cover Story" Julia Roberts. *Good Housekeeping*, August 2001, 102.

CHAPTER 2

1. Twain, Mark. *Mark Twain's Autobiography*. Edited by Albert Bigelow Paine. New York: Harper and Brothers, 1924.
2. Roosevelt, Theodore. *The Strenuous Life: Essays and Addresses*. New York: The Century Co., 1900.

CHAPTER 3

1. White, Barry Eugene. "I've Got So Much To Give." ©1973 (Renewed) UNICHAPPELL MUSIC INC. and SA-VETTE MUSIC CO. All Rights Administered by UNICHAPPELL MUSIC INC. All Rights Reserved. Used by Permission, Warner Bros. Publications U.S. Inc., Miami, Florida 33014.
2. Aristotle (384–322 B.C.), Greek philosopher.
3. Perkins, Ken Parish. "Mr. Clooney Takes on Washington." *Ft. Worth Star Telegram*. September 12, 2003. Friday Final Edition, Section: LIFE & ARTS; p. 1E.
4. Ibid.

CHAPTER 4

1. Origin unknown, possibly an Arab or Persian proverb.

2. Schuller, Robert H. *Prayer: My Soul's Adventure With God—A Spiritual Autobiography*. Nashville-Atlanta-London-Vancouver: Thomas Nelson, Inc., 1995, 55.

CHAPTER 5

1. Perry, George. "How an Actor Can Suffer in the Cause of His Art." *London Sunday Times Magazine*, November 28, 1982.

CHAPTER 6

1. Ebb, Fred, and Kander, John. "Mr. Cellophane." ©1975 (Renewed) UNICHAP-PELL MUSIC INC. and KANDER & EBB, INC. All Rights Administered by UNICHAPPELL MUSIC INC., All Rights Reserved, Used by Permission, Warner Bros. Publications U.S. Inc., Miami, Florida 33014.
2. Silverstein, Shel. "Cover of the Rolling Stone." Copyright ©1972 (Renewed) and 1973 (Renewed) Evil Eye Music, Inc., West Palm Beach, Florida. Used by Permission.

CHAPTER 9

1. Bunnell, Lee. "Tin Man." ©1974 (Renewed) WB MUSIC CORP. All Rights Reserved, Used by Permission, Warner Bros. Publications U.S. Inc., Miami, Florida 33014.

CONCLUSION

1. Coyne, Kate and Landman, Beth. "Cover Story" Julia Roberts. *Good Housekeeping,* September 2000, 102.
2. *"Jimmy Stewart Remembers: It's a Wonderful Life"* by Jimmy Stewart, reprinted with permission from *Guideposts*. Copyright © 1987 by Guideposts, Carmel, New York 10512. All rights reserved.

LARRY A. THOMPSON
FILMOGRAPHY

Movies Made for Television

A DATE WITH DARKNESS:
THE TRIAL AND CAPTURE OF ANDREW LUSTER (2003),
Lifetime/Carlton America
Aired 8/11/2003 (3.1– 3.3 million viewers)
Jason Gedrick, Marla Sokoloff, Lisa Edelstein, Sarah Carter, Stefanie von Pfetten
Directed by Bobby Roth

MURDER IN THE MIRROR (2000), CBS/Carlton America
Aired 1/19/2000 (10.9/17)
Jane Seymour, Robert Desiderio, James Farentino, Alex Mendoza,
Directed by James Keach

AND THE BEAT GOES ON:
THE SONNY AND CHER STORY (1999), ABC/Carlton America
Aired 2/22/1999 (12.5/19)
Jay Underwood, Renee Faia
Directed by David Burton Morris
3 Emmy nominations

REPLACING DAD (1998), CBS/Hallmark Entertainment
Aired 3/14/99 (11.0/17)
Mary McDonnell, Tippi Hedren, William Russ, Eric von Detten, Camilla Belle
Directed by Joyce Chopra

FACE OF EVIL (1996), CBS/Hallmark Entertainment
Aired 4/9/1996 (10.6/17)
Tracey Gold, Perry King, Shawnee Smith
Directed by Mary Lambert

SEPARATED BY MURDER (1994), CBS/Hallmark Entertainment
Aired 4/12/1994 (11.8/19)
Sharon Gless, Steve Railsback
Directed by Donald Wrye

BROKEN PROMISES (1993), CBS/Hallmark Entertainment
Aired 12/26/1993 (12.6/22)
Cheryl Ladd, Polly Draper, Ted Levine, Robert Desiderio
Directed by Donald Wrye

LUCY AND DESI: BEFORE THE LAUGHTER (1991), CBS/Republic
Pictures
Aired 2/10/1991 (16.4/25)
Frances Fisher, Maurice Benard
Directed by Charles Jarrott
2 Emmy nominations

LITTLE WHITE LIES (1989), NBC/New World Entertainment
Aired 11/27/1989 (16.9/26)
Ann Jillian, Tim Matheson
Directed by Anson Williams

CLASS CRUISE (1989), NBC/Republic Pictures
Aired 10/22/1989 (11.4/19)
McLean Stevenson, Richard Moll, Ray Walston, Marc Price, Shelley
Fabares, Billy Warlock, Brooke Theiss, Michael DeLuise
Directed by Oz Scott

ORIGINAL SIN (1989), NBC/New World Entertainment
Aired 2/20/1989 (16.8/26)
Charlton Heston, Ann Jillian, Robert Desiderio
Directed by Ron Satloff

THE WOMAN HE LOVED (1988), CBS/HTV/New World Pictures
Aired 4/3/1988 (14.5/25)
Jane Seymour, Anthony Andrews, Olivia De Havilland, Julie Harris, Tom Wilkinson
Directed by Charles Jarrott
2 Emmy nominations and a Golden Globe nomination

INTIMATE ENCOUNTERS (1986), NBC/Columbia Television
Aired 9/28/1986 (14.4/23)
Donna Mills, James Brolin, Cicely Tyson
Directed by Ivan Nagy

CONVICTED (1986), ABC/Columbia Television
Aired 5/12/1986 (17.4/27)
Lindsay Wagner, John Larroquette, Carroll O'Connor
Directed by David Lowell Rich

THE OTHER LOVER (1985), CBS/Columbia Television
Aired 9/24/1985 (13.8/22)
Lindsay Wagner, Jack Scalia, Max Gail, Shannen Doherty
Directed by Robert Ellis Miller

MICKEY SPILLANE'S MURDER ME, MURDER YOU (1982), CBS/Columbia TV
Aired 4/9/1983 (17.9/31)
Stacy Keach, Don Stroud
Directed by Gary Nelson
Subsequently became the series Mike Hammer

MICKEY SPILLANE'S MARGIN FOR MURDER (1981), CBS/Hamner Ent.
Aired 10/15/1981 (20.1/33)
Kevin Dobson, Cindy Pickett
Directed by Daniel Haller

TELEVISION SERIES

THE JIM NABORS SHOW (1977), nationally syndicated/NTR
Jim Nabors (75 one-hour episodes)
Nominated for an Emmy

BRING 'EM BACK ALIVE (1984) - CBS/Columbia Television
Bruce Boxleitner (22 one-hour episodes)

Television Specials/Pilots

CELEBRITY HOME VIDEO (2003), Sony Pictures TV
Starring: Coolio, Steven Schirripa, William Shatner, Kelly Hu, Tony Danza,
Erik von Detten, Michael York, Orlando Jones, Christopher Titus, Kelly
Rowland, Paul Sorvino, Eric Roberts, Mindy Sterling, Chris McDonald,
Gene Simmons

IRON CHEF USA: SHOWDOWN IN LAS VEGAS (2001), UPN/Lions
Gate
Aired 11/16/2001
William Shatner, Todd English, Jean François Meteigner, Alessandro
Stratta, Roy Yamaguchi, Kerry Simon, Michael Burger, Sissy Biggers,
Anthony Dias Blue, Bruce Vilanch, Elise Neal, Brande Roderick, Mark
Famiglietti

IRON CHEF USA: HOLIDAY SHOWDOWN (2001), UPN/Lions Gate
Aired 12/26/2001
William Shatner, Todd English, Jean Francois Meteigner, Alessandro
Stratta, Roy Yamaguchi, Marcus Samuelsson, Michael Burger, Sissy
Biggers, Anthony Dias Blue, Ron Popeil, Loretta Devine, Kelly Hu, Steven
Schirripa

TONIGHT @ HOUSE OF BLUES (1998), Columbia TriStar
Blues Traveler, Chuck D, Tommy Davidson, Gary Busey, Adam Carolla,
Eric Roberts, Victoria Jackson and Kevin Dillon
Directed by Tony Morina

EAGLE AND THE BEAR (1987), ABC/Columbia Television
Howard Sherman, Jeff Allin

MANN IN THE MIDDLE (1989), ABC/New World Entertainment
Joan Severance
Directed by Lee H. Katzin

Motion Pictures

CRIMES OF PASSION (1984), New World Pictures
Kathleen Turner, Anthony Perkins
Directed by Ken Russell

FRATERNITY VACATION (1985), New World Pictures
Tim Robbins, Sheree J. Wilson, Stephen Geoffreys
Directed by James Frawley

MY DEMON LOVER (1987), New Line Pictures
Scott Valentine, Michelle Little
Directed by Charlie Loventhal

QUIET COOL (1987), New Line Pictures
James Remar, Adam Coleman Howard, Nick Cassavetes
Directed by Clay Borris

BREAKING THE RULES (1992), Miramax
Jason Bateman, C. Thomas Howell, Jonathan Silverman, Annie Potts
Directed by Neal Israel

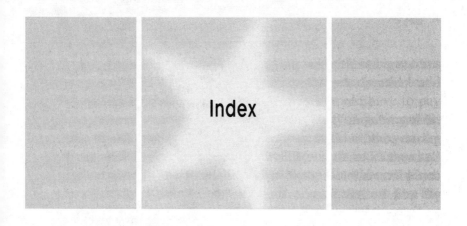

Index

About the Author

Larry A. Thompson is the founder of the Los Angeles-based Larry A. Thompson Organization, an entertainment company devoted to film production and personal management of talent. He and his team have represented over 200 clients, including Drew Barrymore, William Shatner, Cindy Crawford, Mariska Hargitay, Barry White, and Sonny and Cher.

Having produced 17 movies for television, including the highly acclaimed ABC World Premiere Movie *And the Beat Goes On: The Sonny and Cher Story,* 5 motion pictures, 2 television series, 3 television specials, and various series pilots, Thompson was voted "Showman of the Year" in 1998 by the U.S. Television Fan Association. He has received the industry's prestigious Vision Award and his productions have received nominations for 8 Emmy Awards, 2 Prism Awards, and a Golden Globe. He is perennially listed in *Who's Who in America* and *Who's Who in the World.*

Larry lives in Beverly Hills, California, with his wife, Kelly, and their daughter, Taylor.